PASSPORT
TO FOOTBALL

FOLLOWING
AROUND
THE WORLD
FOOTBALL

PASSPORT
TO FOOTBALL

STUART FULLER

SPORTS
BOOKS

Published in Great Britain by
SportsBooks Limited
PO Box 422
Cheltenham
GL50 2YN
Tel: 01242 256755
email: info@sportsbooks.ltd.uk
www.sportsbooks.ltd.uk

Front cover: Alan Hunns

A catalogue record for this book is available from
the British Library.

ISBN 978 1899807 83 3

Printed and bound in England by
Cromwell Press Group

CONTENTS

INTRODUCTION

'There is a corner of a foreign football field that will be for ever England. For that sad lonely git sitting on his own has flown in on Ryanair to visit a new ground.'

Welcome to a snapshot of three years in my life. As those close to me will know all too well, my life is dominated by football. I'm not happy to just sit in front of the TV and watch a game from Spain, Holland or Germany – I want to be there to sample the atmosphere, the stadium and, of course, the game. This book is a reflection of that passion. Each of these trips is planned with almost military precision, but the stories show how unpredictable travel is, even in Europe. All these stories are based on fact, although a few names have been changed to protect the innocent. Flying around Europe is now cheaper in some instances than the cost of a match ticket, and with more and more strange destinations being accessible the opportunity to watch football all year round is more possible than ever.

You will meet a cast of characters. I'm not going to spend time here running through a full biography of each as hopefully the tales themselves will allow you to form a mental image. However, they are all real people and in most cases as passionate about travelling to watch football as me. You can find more of my travels on my blog, http://theballisround.co.uk, including the trips that didn't make it into the book as well as full details on how to get to the stadiums, where to buy your tickets and what to expect when you get there.

I'd like to thank my wonderful girls for giving me the opportunity to indulge in this passion, as well as sometimes coming along to share the pain and the pleasure. I'd also like to thank you, the reader, for picking up this book and (hopefully) buying it. Everyone has a passion for something in life and to be given the opportunity to develop mine is a privilege to which I hope I can do justice. So thank you and please enjoy these trips through the undergrowth of European football.

The Cast of Characters

During the research and travels to compile this book I was lucky enough to be accompanied on a number of trips by some real true friends who I list below. In most instances their names have been changed to protect their modesty, but their background and interests are as true as they are in real life, so be warned if you ever come across them.

Yours truly

Football has been my life for decades and I spend most of the time trying to fit in a quick trip here or a long weekend full of games there. I started writing prior to the 2006 World Cup, having seen a gap in the market for football-related travel information designed specifically for fans. Believe it or not I also have a day job!

CMF

The Current Mrs Fuller. Long-suffering football widow who actually likes nothing better than a game on a hot sunny day. Used to follow Nottingham Forest as a girl, and could be classified as a true football groupie in her teenage years. Now diverts all of her love and attention to supporting my cause. Is incredibly clever and uses her immense talents to help the greater public within the health service.

Littlest Fuller

The youngest member of the Fuller family, who has absolutely no interest in football and simply loves to travel, taking Chocolate the dog (a toy not a real one) on new adventures. Has her own language in which she converses with everyone, much to her own amusement. Bonkers!

Lolly

Our elder daughter, who has always had a love for football and has recently earned her first ever West Ham season ticket. Loves nothing more than travelling abroad and watching 1970s British comedy and is an expert on books by Roger Hargreaves.

Football Jo

She is a real person, trust me. A diehard West Ham season ticket holder who has no knowledge of the club's history prior to 2003. Has strange nocturnal interests and is an expert in absolutely useless information on C and D list celebrities. Would class reading *Heat* magazine as a vocation in life although she is a phone systems salesperson really.

Dagenham Dan

The first, and only, real Dagenham & Redbridge fan I have ever met. Dan likes nothing better than slipping away for a game or three although his boyish looks mean he is often asked for ID when buying cough medicines. Works for a trading company in the City during the day and plans his trips to far-flung football at night.

Big Ben

A Tottenham Hotspur diehard who now lives in Copenhagen. Loves a beer, loves his football and was framed alongside me by the *Daily Express* in 2008 as an English football fan who now gets his kicks watching foreign football as he is a IF Brøndby season ticket holder. One of Europe's domain name experts in his real life.

Rob the Red

An educated Nottingham Forest fan, which is a paradox. Rob has been following England for many years and was once a truly great right back – based on his performances for the England Veterans team that was probably pre-Second World War. He is a big cheese in travel to the Far East.

Dennis

Mr European Ground Hopper. I have never met anyone else who has been to more grounds in Europe than me or is able to travel away as much as me! He is an expert in obscure foreign lower league grounds and can sniff out a stadium at two miles.

Big Man

Sadly now departed from these shores on a round the world adventure, the Big Man knew nothing about football before he was taken to Malmö. Famous as the founder of the legendary Shepherd Seven, he was more at home outside the Market Porter in Borough than anywhere else in life.

passport to football

SEARCHING FOR DENNIS

A weekend of football, culture and queuing in the Russian capital

A weekend in Moscow at first didn't appeal to a sane person like me, but with UEFA deciding to award the 2008 Champions League final to the city, and England due to visit in October 2007 in a European Championship qualifier, it seemed like a good time to arrange to catch a match or two in the name of research. With six top-flight clubs playing in or around the city centre in the 2006 season there was always going to be a couple of games on each weekend during the summer. The weekend that caught my eye saw four games in four days in three stadiums, which would give me a full taste of football in Russia, as well as an opportunity to see some sights in one of Europe's greatest capital cities.

There are a lot of misconceptions about Moscow, and Russia in general. First it is only a three-hour flight from London. Most people assume that it is much more than that because there is a three-hour time zone difference. Second, people think it is impossible to get a visa. Wrong again. If you go through a private company you can get them to do all the leg work and deliver your passport back within forty-eight hours with all the right paperwork. Finally, people assume it is snowing all the time. Well, August in Moscow saw temperatures of more than 35 degrees Celsius, hotter than most of the Mediterranean.

I'd originally planned to meet Dennis, a chap I had got to know through a shared passion for foreign trips, and his happy band of groundhoppers at a hotel in the north of the city, but at the last minute on a random search of a well-known internet site an absolute bargain of a hotel came up. And so for the same price of a three-star with IOL (apparently standing for Instant On Lighting) and hot water between 5 a.m. and 7 a.m., I got a room at the Swissotel – the tallest building in Russia at thirty-three storeys and the newest five-star hotel in the capital. But first I had to get into the city. Because I was flying with British Airways, the landing was at Domodedovo, the newest of Moscow's five airports and supposedly the best in terms of facilities. I thought I had completed the landing card correctly, but at the first security check the forms were thrown back because I had put my name the wrong way round. To the back of the queue I went. Next came the currency exchange. With roubles still almost impossible to get in the UK you have to change money on arrival. And none of those tatty English £5 notes, thank you, only pristine £20s for roubles here, but don't forget to sign the currency release note in triplicate and carry round a copy just in case you are stopped by the police.

Then you are ready to take your chances in the big bad world of Russia's ancient capital. The sliding doors open into the arrivals area and you are met by utter chaos. People everywhere, going nowhere and making a lot of noise about it. The advantage of flying into Domodedovo is that it has its own railway station with trains running direct to the city centre. So with purpose I went along the terminal, using a luggage trolley as a battering ram of which Boudicca would have been proud, to the railway ticket windows and purchased a single ticket for 100 roubles (about £2). I got a receipt, which I screwed up and binned, and tried to enter the platform but found I needed a ticket. So where was my ticket? Well it appears that the tatty bit of paper in the bin was the ticket and so I had to push a tramp out of the way to rummage in the bin, much to his disgust.

The ancient train travelled through the most uninspiring of suburbs on its way to Paveletsky Vokzal station, a trip of around forty-five minutes. The Swissotel was a short walk from the station, so in theory it should take only a few minutes. But surprise number two for the day was the sheer number of people just milling around outside the station at 4 p.m. on a Friday. I soon realised this was common in Moscow.

People obviously classed a day out as standing around in Red Square having a can of beer. So it was another fight through a crowd, past the slot machine arcades full of Asian men desperate for a gambling fix, and towards the Swissotel which was visible from everywhere. A guard on the main road asked to check my passport and reservation before letting me walk up the drive into the lobby. Top of the range BMWs and Mercedes lined the car park and the entrance was staffed with bellboys galore, all clamouring for the next big tip. With check-in completed they told me I was upgraded to a mini-suite. The room was on the twentieth floor with floor to ceiling windows and a view to die for over the Moskva River and one of Stalin's 'seven sisters' buildings, the Kotelnicheskaya.

It was going to be a quick turnround as I was due at the CSKA Moscow v FC Saturn game on the other side of town. Dennis and the rest of the groundhoppers had arrived the previous day and had already got a game under their belts by travelling towards Sheremetyevo Airport to watch second division league leaders FC Khimki. Dennis was going to be at the CSKA game and I thought that he would stand out in the predicted sparse crowd. CSKA had been the team to beat in Russia for so long, vying for top spot on an annual basis with Spartak, their greatest rivals. They were also one of the most hated teams in Russia, having originally been the army club, ans more latterly possessing the cash reserves of Roman Abramovich's Sibneft oil company, although the only funding the club had from him was a lucrative shirt sponsorship.

They had finished the previous season as league champions as well as having the audacity to win the UEFA Cup against all the odds in Sporting Lisbon's backyard. However, despite all the Chelsea owner's money they still lacked their own stadium and had recently moved from the Luzhniki Stadium across town to the Dinamo Stadium to share with Dinamo Moscow, with Spartak going in the opposite direction, their long-term plan of a stadium of their own still not moving off the drawing board.

I ventured onto the metro for the first time. This was one area I had researched, not feeling confident of walking into the heart of Moscow without a clue. I knew a multi-pass ticket was needed so I approached one of the fearsome women behind the counter, slapped down a 150 roubles note and grunted my thanks. What initially struck me about the metro was there was absolutely no security or prevention of fare dodgers. After going down the long escalators I saw one reason why nobody would dare to try and sneak through the barriers. At the bottom of the stairwell was one of the most fearsome-looking women I had seen – ever! These women are known as 'Babushkas' (grandmother or old lady in English) and they frighten everyone into behaving. They take a dim view of anyone talking, using iPods or even reading a newspaper, let alone misbehaving.

Moscow is renowned as having one of the most efficient metro systems in the world, and even with a change of line required, the nine-stop trip took less than fifteen minutes. Leaving the train at Dinamo station

I followed the crowds into the street, passing the impressive statue of legendary goalkeeper, Lev Yashin, and into the car park where temporary bars looking like sheds had been opened to serve beer and sausages. I looked for Dennis, but had no luck. Match tickets are bought for 150 roubles from a small booth outside the metro station where you had to almost bend down to pray before passing money through a tiny window. It gave me a place in the main stand, or at least the stand containing the fewest skinheads.

Dinamo's stadium is a classic Eastern European ground. Completely open to whatever the elements decide to unleash, with massive, dominating floodlights, it was hard for fans to generate an atmosphere, especially as the rain was falling heavily. With a crowd of less than 2,000 on a hot, rainy night, the empty blue and white seats made picking out some of the blue-and-white-shirted fans difficult. CSKA scored two early goals which effectively killed off the game and ensured they would stay top of the league irrespective of other results. I scanned the crowd looking for Dennis but couldn't see a six-foot English bloke anywhere, especially as he has as little hair as most of the CSKA 'fans' who had populated the stand behind the goal.

After a fruitless search around the stadium afterwards it was back to the hotel for the evening. I had arranged dinner in the hotel's thirty-third-floor restaurant, an absolute treat, with the whole of Moscow laid out in front of me. All of a sudden I was joined by a guest. A female guest. A strikingly beautiful female guest. Blonde, with all the right curves in all the right places and squeezed into a little black dress. She had her own drink and immediately tried to pour me a glass of champagne. With the speed of a gazelle I placed a hand over the glass and declined. After a few minutes negotiating, during which she offered her full list of services for $500 for the night, I let her down gently by saying I was here with my wife, who was about to join me for dinner. 'OK, no problem . . . so I join you as well, yes? $700 for both of you.'

Now the Current Mrs Fuller (CMF) has a very wicked side but I am sure even she would have drawn the line at paying such a price, especially as she wasn't here to throw in her demands. I quickly finished dinner, gave her a long last smile and returned to the room to find a note from 'Carolina', available 24/7, giving me her mobile number as well as a long list of services she could perform, although I noted ironing was not among them.

The following day was planned as sightseeing time. The football later on was at the Luzhniki Stadium, a local derby between Torpedo and Dinamo. So it was off to Red Square for a spot of culture. In the course of the next few hours I squeezed in visits to Lenin's tomb, the GUM department store opposite and St Basil's Cathedral. One thing you need to get used to in Moscow is queuing. For instance, to see Lenin's tomb you have to stand silently in line in Red Square. Bags have to be left here and are individually checked for cameras which you are forbidden to take inside. You are then escorted in parties of four along the edge of Red Square (which is neither red nor square) to the red marble tomb, where you wait to enter on the fifteen-minute mark. Then it's an escort into the darkened room, staying for exactly seven minutes to look at an apparently embalmed body, less convincing than Elvis Presley's waxwork in Blackpool, before being escorted through the back door past the monuments to other Russian leaders, which include Stalin and Brezhnev.

GUM was interesting in that it was absolutely deserted. All the stores were open, with the likes of Adidas, Nike, Louis Vuitton and even a Gap displaying their wares but absolutely no customers. I bought a few items and realised what the issue was. None of the shops was interested in customers. They ignored you on entry, ignored you when you needed help and then ignored you when trying to pay. This was the same customer service locals experienced when GUM was the only real shop in town, one in which they would queue for hours to buy basics such as beetroot and bread. Good to see the authentic Russian customer experience hasn't been lost with rampant capitalism.

The last visit of the day was to St Basil's Cathedral, one of the most iconic buildings in Moscow and I reckon the most beautiful in Europe. The story goes that when he saw it for the first time, the czar Ivan the Terrible had the architect who built it blinded so he could not build anything as beautiful again. Try as hard as I could, I simply could not find the main nave in the cathedral. Surely there had to be a main bit somewhere instead of all of these little crypts and chapels. After an hour I gave up, took the shopping back to the concierge at the hotel, declined his offer of his friend Isabella for the rest of the night and then headed onto the metro towards Sportivnaya station and the Moscow derby.

The road was lined by young conscript soldiers who were obviously expecting a different class of supporter than a fat, sweaty Englishman walking past. The ticket office was at the north end of the stadium in a historic-looking building. It was either 120 roubles for a ticket in the end stand or 150 for the VIP section. I went for the latter, taking the opportunity for a spot of luxury (or so I thought) for the same price as a tube ticket in London and carried on looking for Dennis, assuming he would choose to sit there too. The Luzhniki had clearly seen better days. It was the main stadium for the 1980 Olympics and it seemed that since they ended, apart from adding a translucent roof, no one had given it a thought, a lick of paint or even a light dusting. Each entrance had its own metal detector to check for weapons and I was searched twice by burly female (I think) soldiers; obviously as a VIP you got a double helping of search!

The inside was impressive from a distance. The seats were red, orange and yellow and a great backdrop to the game being played out in front of no more than 1,500 fans – for a local derby being played in an 80,000 all-seater stadium! To say it lacked atmosphere was an understatement. Torpedo eventually ran out 3-0 winners and moved above Dinamo at the foot of the table but the standard of play was very poor and I lamented not bringing any boots to Moscow as I was surely better than most of the players on display despite carrying a few extra stone.

Still looking for Dennis, halfway through the second half I moved from the VIP area (plastic seats with armrests) to the normal seats (plastic but no armrests) but I couldn't find him. I started to wonder if it was the wrong weekend and he was not really in Moscow.

Walking around the stadium after the game, I came across one of the few remaining statues of Lenin. Most had been pulled down by Stalin in his purge during the 1950s to rid the public of the memory of a man who had given them hope after the First World War. The poor chap looked as bored as the homebound Dinamo fans.

The stadium was supposed to be the jewel in the Russian sporting empire but since 1980 it had not hosted many sporting events. Torpedo Moscow moved in as primary tenants in 2003 with big plans for domination of the domestic game which failed to materialise, and CSKA and Spartak have had stints there as well. Even the national team prefers the more intimate Lokomotiv Stadium on the other side of the city to the vast empty spaces of the Luzhniki.

Again there were hundreds of soldiers lining the route to the station, the oldest seemingly about twelve. They stood there menacingly, batons at the ready as the few hundred fans walked silently back into the metro. Much has been written about the beauty of the Moscow metro system, and I have to say that stations like Dobryninskaya, Prospekt Mira, Belorusskaya and Krasnopresnenskaya on the central ring line are stunning and are more like museums, putting London's overpriced, cramped and dirty system to shame.

After the previous night's escapade in the hotel's restaurant I decided to go to Red Square, or Okhotny Ryad as I had come to know it, to find out what Moscovians got up to on a Friday night. The square was buzzing with people, although nobody seemed to be walking in a particular direction, or doing anything. I decided to be cultural and headed for the Mc-Donald's in the shopping centre opposite the Kremlin. Now this wasn't just any old McDonald's. During the twenty-five years since it opened as the first branch of the chain in Russia, it has become the busiest in the world, turning over more cash than any other on an average day. I waited in line and was impressed with the speed of the service and that they still had the same type of pickle inside the burgers as in the western world. One day they will run out of these and the world will be a better place.

My aim was to track down the legendary Hungry Duck bar, where women are welcomed free of charge until 8 p.m. and plied with free drink before men are let in at 8.30 p.m. The ensuing tumult is supposed to be jaw-dropping, although in modern Moscow the bar has been taken over by working girls pretending to be drunk and out of control when the men arrive, only to hit them with a big bill at the end of the evening. I couldn't find it, although later I was to learn I had walked past it several times but had mistaken it for the entrance to the Kuznetsky Most metro station. Instead I found Sportland: the biggest sports bar on the planet, apparently. It is on Novy Arbat, close to Smolenskaya station and was rammed full of TVs getting ready to show Ajax v Manchester United from the pre-season Amsterdam tournament.

Next day it was off to the Kremlin, setting off early in an attempt to avoid the coach parties of Japanese and Chinese tourists. I booked a ticket for 11 a.m. and went back to the shopping centre opposite to sit and watch life go by for an hour. It seemed that every Saturday wedding parties queue up to have photos taken at the entrance to Red Square, silhouetted by St Basil's Cathedral. While they waited their turn they all went into McDonald's (now you know why it is the busiest in the world: '143 Big Mac Meals, please') in a form of weird wedding breakfast routine, the burgers washed down with fake champagne and vodka cocktails judging by the antics of the bridesmaids.

11

The Kremlin is not, as many think, one building. It is a huge complex within massive fortified walls. There is simply too much to see and do in one day so I satisfied myself with a visit to the impressive Armory, Assumption Cathedral and the Diamond Exhibition. It was hard work as the explanations for most exhibits were in Russian only, and the number of tourists shoving cameras everywhere was annoying, ignoring the history and just interested in collecting pictures.

I was going back to the Luzhniki to watch Russia's premier team, champions-elect and richest club, Spartak Moscow, play Rostov at 3 p.m. So, not knowing how many would be there – the team got 70,000 for a midweek Champions League game – I set off along the banks of the river at one o'clock. The plan was to walk through Gorky Park, made famous by the novel and film of the same name in the 1980s. It is comparable with London's Greenwich Park and contains a small area of amusements and funfair rides.

The reason for my visit was the Sculpture Park on the opposite side of the road. Basically this is the resting place of all those marvellous ex-Soviet statues, including those of leaders such as Andropov and Brezhnev. It was used in a wonderfully moody scene in the Bond film *Goldeneye*, where 007 came face to face with 006, played by Sean Bean, who had turned traitor. It didn't have the same effect in the boiling hot sunshine although it did have the overwhelming feeling of Big Brother control that marked the country during the cold war.

Spartak Moscow 5 Rostov 2 – The Luzhniki Stadium – 5th August 2006

The crowd at the Luzhniki was certainly more impressive than for the previous day's game, although bizarrely there were noticeably fewer policemen and soldiers. Tickets were more expensive so I declined the 750 roubles VIP seat, opting for one at 500 roubles, simply because the entrance was the closest to the ticket windows. On entering the stadium, with the game just kicking off, the scene was unreal. Behind the west goal, the Spartak hardcore fans filled the end right the way to the top. Opposite them were a handful of Rostov fans who had made the four-hundred-mile trip. But in my section on the halfway line there were only a hundred or so fans (but still no Dennis!) while opposite in the VIP area there were another hundred, giving the stadium a massively imbalanced look.

Spartak dominated, scoring four goals in the first half an hour. It was only at this point, for some strange reason, that I realised the pitch was plastic. Despite watching ninety minutes the previous day and thirty minutes today I had failed to realise that the grass was a very strange dark grey colour and the bounce was untrue.

Spartak eased off in the second half and allowed Rostov to get back into the game, and for a period after they had pulled two goals back it appeared they might get something out of the game. However, a last-minute goal from Spartak's expensive Argentinean import Fernando Cavenaghi restored the three-goal advantage.

With less than twenty-four hours of the trip remaining there were still two of the four grounds which host top-flight football in Moscow to see. FC Moscow, who play at the Brighton-esque Strelstov Stadium, were due to play at home on the Sunday afternoon when I would be en route to the airport. So the plan was to try and sneak a peek inside this stadium as well as Lokomotiv's impressive Cherkizovskaya or Lokomotiv Stadium, widely known as the best in Russia. I went to the latter first as it is just one stop from the end of the red metro line, and on a direct course from the Sportivnaya station outside the Luzhniki.

After a thirty-minute journey there was another chaotic scene at Cherkizovskaya. This time it was because of a local market that was coming to an end. It seemed comparable with a Sunday car boot fair at Flamingo Park in Sidcup; lots of rough-looking people buying and selling junk. After wandering around to the stadium's main entrance I noticed a number of people going through. I followed into the main stand, kept my head down and walked confidently. On the pitch was a presentation, which appeared to have been going on for quite a while judging by the long line of people wearing medals.

There was also a group of veteran footballers (aged fifty and above by the looks of their waistlines) kicking balls around as if in preparation for a game. Does this count, I thought? It was a game in the stadium, granted, even if it was one that would be played at walking pace. The presentations finished and a number of the girls who had been giving out awards came and sat in the stands. As they were dressed in long evening dresses and wearing heavy make-up it wasn't hard to see what their next assignment would be later that evening. I was sure there were one or two from the Swissotel bar the previous evening. One of them struck up a conversation,

13

and on hearing I was a) English, b) staying in the Swissotel and c) on my own immediately offered to be my dinner date for the evening. Although flattered, I do have morals and the thought of an evening with Tatia and having to pay for the honour was not exactly appealing. Anyway, CMF would not have been impressed, even were I to use cultural exchange as a mitigating circumstance.

I stayed for thirty minutes, not really watching the game but admiring the stadium and the girls who were trying their sales pitch on anyone who would listen. The Lokomotiv Stadium had been built less than five years before, and was a very smart two-tier ground, with a canopied roof in each corner. Each stand had different-coloured seats, and the roof and fascia was red to reflect the club colours of Lokomotiv. The favoured home of the Russian national team, it also played host to CSKA's Champions League matches.

Lokomotiv are one of the best-supported teams in Russia with an average attendance of more than 20,000 and since moving to the new stadium in 2002 they had won the title and the Russian cup. The area around the stadium is not exactly plush, as apart from the market, large blocks of flats loom over the ground and a car scrapyard complete with burning tyres tops off the effect.

I had originally planned on diverting towards VDNKh, which as every good Soviet knows is the Vystavka Dostizheny Narodnogo Khozyaystva SSSR. It is an old exhibition centre that showcased everything great about the Soviet Empire. Since the fall of communism it became better known as the massive Central Museum of the Armed Forces, with a display of nearly a million military items, and the Cosmonautics Museum. Unfortunately, due to a rare service interruption on the metro system at Komsomolskaya, where I was due to change trains, the visit had to be put back by twenty-four hours.

Returning to the hotel around 7 p.m. I toyed with the idea of another night out in Sportland. One of the best bits of the hotel room was the fantastic bathroom, which had a separate wet room and a special glassed wall that allowed those in the shower to see out but not those in the room to see in. It also had a wall-mounted remote control for the TV and I started surfing the channels. All of a sudden Jeff Stelling came on the screen, then Tony Cottee and then Chris Kamara with his soul-glow perm in all its glory. It was *Soccer Saturday* on Sky Sports. Excited by finding this I had to call CMF. She was also very excited, especially as she was driving home from Chessington World of Adventures at the time and had to pull across three lanes of the M25 to take the call.

I stayed glued to the opening day of the Football League season, and became engrossed by exclusive (well, they said it) commentary from Birmingham City v Colchester United. Sad but true. Fly a thousand miles from home and such things become very important and unmissable! Eventually it was back to the city centre to find Rosie O'Grady's for a couple of pints of Guinness (a pint at 200 roubles was nearly as expensive as a ticket to watch Torpedo Moscow!) and have a decent chat with the expat West Ham-supporting barman, who like me thought our chances of staying in the Premier League were slim to none with a strike force of Carlton Cole and Dean Ashton.

After an early start on the Sunday it was off to VDNKh to visit the space museum. This is certainly worth a few hours of anyone's time, especially the superb videos of space missions. What does strike you is that the Soviets spent so much time and money trying to get ahead of the Americans only to give up after the first moon landing in 1969.

There were a couple of stops left before needing to head back to the airport. First was to Detsky Mir, the biggest toy shop in the world (I had thought this honour belonged to Hamleys) to pick up things for the Little Fullers. The shop was an Aladdin's cave of all things precious to children, but with typical Russian service I was becoming used to. The shop is at the top of a steep hill running down to Red Square. Off it were a number of 'exclusive' shopping streets that included Porsche showrooms, Hugo Boss stores and Gucci shops, all with armed guards outside. What made this more remarkable was that these streets sat side by side with the 'peasant' shops, which made Aldi seem upmarket. It seemed to be a common sight in Moscow – extreme poverty next door to absolute wealth.

A very entertaining weekend ended with a brief trip to Avtozavodskaya to visit the Strelstov Stadium, home of FC Moscow. Despite being just one stop south of the hotel on the metro, the walk took around twenty minutes along very pleasant, tree-lined residential streets. The stadium sits in a valley, and you enter via a public park. As it was open, I wandered in. Basically there was an athletics track with a couple of temporary stands, although the traditional ceremonial stand dates back to the 1920s. It was like Brighton's Withdean Stadium. The views from the top row of the stand were impressive though, with the city skyline silhouetted in the distance.

At the time of this visit, FC Moscow had existed for only two years, having been created after the Torpedo club had been taken over and moved to the Luzhniki Stadium. While money was tight, and the support base small, they had held their own in the top division, seeing both Torpedo and Dinamo struggle while they gained stability. They reached their first cup final in 2007, although they lost 1-0 to Lokomotiv in the Luzhniki.

So that was it. Just over seventy hours in one of the world's fastest-growing capitals of wealth and consumerism. The airport was as chaotic as it had been three days earlier, although having been pre-checked in by British Airways I passed through the almost non-existent security, exchanged roubles back to pounds (after completing the forms in triplicate of course) and attempted to buy something (anything) from duty-free to use up the final few roubles. However, there was obviously a time warp to the dark days of communism as the only thing on the shelves were potato vodka and Russian dolls.

On to the flight, on with the iPod and into a comforting sleep all the way back to London. It had certainly been an experience, some good, some interesting and some crazy. I'd go back, that is for sure, armed with the knowledge to cheat the system and make some kind of madness from the capitalist revolution. It is a city of real contrasts. I have never been anywhere before where there was such a contrast between rich and poor and the haves and have nots. It was also a city of stunning locals, stunning buildings and stunning bureaucracy. I just wish I knew what happened to Dennis!

SO WHERE THE BLOODY HELL IS MACEDONIA ANYWAY?

England kick off their European Championship qualifying in September 2006

When the draw was made for the UEFA 2008 Championships qualifying, there was a collective sigh from England fans when the name Macedonia was read out. The fear was another return to familiar and problematic places such as Poland or unknown and unloved destinations such as Moldova, Kazakhstan or Turkey. Instead the draw gave England the chance to play Russia, Estonia, Israel, Andorra and Croatia for the first time in a qualifying tournament as well as a return to Macedonia. It was less than three years since the teams had met in Skopje in a game infamous for the FA refusing an allocation of tickets, fearing for the safety of the England fans. This time it was different – in fact, drawn in a qualifying group with Russia (gun crazy), Israel (still at odds with at least half a dozen neighbours), Croatia (always going to be volatile) and Estonia (stag party heaven), Macedonia looked a positive walk in the park for the fans.

This was one trip I had to go on after vowing not to miss an England away game since being unable to be in Belfast in October 2005. Unfortunately no airline flies direct to Skopje from the UK, causing immediate logistical problems. England fans, however, are very resourceful and soon found ways to reach the city; by taxi from Sofia in Bulgaria, train from Saloniki in Greece, rickshaw from Ljubljana in Slovenia or paragliding from Albania – all seemed viable options and preferable to an overpriced day trip from Thomas Cook with its very early start and very late finish. It was questionable how they could call it a day trip when it left in the dark and returned the following day in the dark. However, it was the only option for many fans who had used up precious annual leave following England during the World Cup in Germany.

Ask a hundred people in the street where Macedonia is, and I guarantee you that fewer than five will know. It's one of those unusual landlocked countries, which is not bad considering how close to the Black and Adriatic Seas it is. Very few European countries are surrounded by four countries and Macedonia has Serbia to the north, Bulgaria to the east, Greece to the south and Albania to the west. The country gained its independence in 1991 after ceding from Yugoslavia. It has a population of just over two million, with a quarter living in the capital Skopje, and is famous for being the birthplace of Alexander the Great.

What made this trip even more appealing was the offer of a game of football against the Macedonian fans, or so we thought. Our team was relatively new, and was set up as a positive move to show other countries that there was more to England fans than finding the nearest Irish bar and chanting offensive songs, and basically being a nuisance.

The England Veterans XI had played their first game just before the World Cup in Germany in 2006 and with a number of new trips coming up we had built a squad that on paper at least looked promising – and it was under my control. Now, we were pretty badly organised. I bet Sir Alex doesn't conduct training via email, but we had to. In fact, faced with a team selection issue (i.e. I did not know one single player), I opted for the approach, taken by many a new foreign manager when they arrive in the UK, of simply picking the players whose names sounded like they might be footballers. And so on the plane on the way to Skopje, the team sheet was filled with five Pauls, a Rob, a Bob, a Mark, a Jamie and a Tim. After all, as player-manager, by shouting 'Paul' I would get it right at least half of the time!

It was with some trepidation that we landed in Skopje's tiny airport, not knowing what sort of welcome we would get. The Foreign Office had not sold the trip enthusiastically during a travel forum we arranged, highlighting human trafficking problems and the civil unrest in the city centre. Some fans had been at the game, played three years ago to the day, when England had won 2-1, buying tickets for peanuts from locals. The ever cautious official guide published by the Football Association mentioned that the locals had kept their guns after the Yugoslavian civil wars. Even Lonely Planet said it was one place in the world where gypsies would pester you to death, refusing to take no for an answer in their demands for money. Sounded great!

As we drove towards the city centre in a convoy of coaches, with police outriders no less, we passed through a gypsy shanty town, which was being bulldozed whether or not the inhabitants were at home. 'We are making way for the new American Embassy,' said our guide 'This hill has the best view in the city and they have paid us very well.'

Asked where the gypsies were to be housed, he quipped, 'Albania, although neither the Albanians nor the gypsies know that yet!'

The coaches parked across the river from the smart national stadium known as the Gradski (which roughly translates as Municipal; in February 2009 it was rather grandly renamed as the Philip II National Arena), and the long line of fans headed into the city to enjoy a day avoiding guns and gypsies. What we encountered was an eye-opener. Expecting poverty and war-torn buildings, we found cafes and bars that would not have looked out of place in the smartest resorts of the Med. And the locals certainly did not look as if they were struggling after the war for independence. In fact quite a few looked like they could have walked off the pages of *Vogue* – or at least *Nuts*.

My job was to meet the veterans team in the bar of the Holiday Inn and at this assembly point were Garth Crooks, Glenn Hoddle and Andy Gray, alas none of whom were available for selection (I was even prepared to ignore the fact that Mr Gray had previously played for Scotland). It was then we found that the game's organisers had perhaps misunderstood what the England Veterans XI actually was. It was to be shown live on local TV and posters had been plastered around the city advertising the game, which was to be played at a first division ground in the suburbs with spectators being charged the equivalent of 50 pence to watch our fat, sweaty unfit bodies! A police escort took us to the small stadium (think Welling United, not West Ham United) where a small crowd had already gathered in the beautiful sunshine.

My pre-match team talk took place in a tiny dressing room where the squad of eighteen had to take turns to get changed. I emphasised the need to 'keep it tight early doors', 'support the man with the ball on the counter' and 'get the ball in the box for the big man up front' which was lapped up by the local TV crew standing in the doorway. We took to the pitch, lining up for 'God Save the Queen' and raising hilarity from the locals at our out of tune efforts. The local team, which turned out to be

19

FK Macedonia, had managed to dig out a copy of the anthem, but had the full version with all six verses, which led to more laughter when we simply sang verse one over and over again.

To say we had a footballing lesson is an understatement. At 5-1, I put myself on for the final ten minutes to shore up the defence. By this stage on a sweltering hot day I had been humiliated in the dugout by the local fans, who kept shouting 'Shut up Arsène Wenger' every time I barked instructions to the team. Trying to conjure up the name of a famous Macedonian as a retort I could only think of Alexander the Great!

Our defence had been ripped apart by a player who was at least forty and twenty stone but who nonetheless managed to outpace players half his age and bag four of their five goals. (On my return the following day I looked up the club and found out that FK Makedonija Gjorce Petrov, to give them their full name, had won the Macedonian Cup the previous season and consequently just a few weeks prior to our game on the very pitch we had graced had played Lokomotiv Sofia in the UEFA Cup, losing 3-1 on aggregate. Mr Blobby, who had caused us so much pain, had been one of the top scorers in the Macedonian first division in 1997 when the club finished third.)

And so it was back to the city centre for the main event. We were given a list of things we couldn't take into the stadium, and although it didn't include such things as shin pads, Vaseline and shower gel we doubted we'd be allowed to take these in. But the police, who at least looked strict, waved us through, interested more in smokers, who had their cigarettes taken from them (apparently one explained in broken English that fans could light them and flick them at the home fans who were seated at least fifty yards away). For once the away fans were housed along the side of the stadium, opposite the huge main stand that dominated the whole city – the stadium itself held 15,000, with more than 10,000 in the one curved stand.

Macedonia 0 England 1 – Gradski Stadium – 6th September 2006

England huffed and puffed, going into the half-time break all square at 0-0. In fact the Macedonians had the upper hand in the first half, and many fans were reminded of the amazing 2-2 draw they got the last time they played England, at Southampton's St Mary's Stadium in 2003. A few minutes into the second half, clueless manager McClaren had obviously run out of ideas and stole some from my team talk earlier in the day as his

Plan B of lumping the ball into the box for the 'big man' worked, with Peter Crouch grabbing the only goal despite calls from the home team that the ball had not crossed the line.

The 1-0 win was not convincing against a team expected to fight it out with Andorra for the group's wooden spoon, but it put us joint top at that early stage. After England's 5-0 win against Andorra the previous Saturday we had been expecting more of the same, and having heard about Germany's 13-0 victory away to San Marino there was a feeling that England simply did not have the cutting edge needed to qualify from the tricky group.

We had been instructed to get on the coaches as soon as the game ended – which we managed to achieve within thirty minutes. It was an impressive achievement considering around a thousand fans had to 'police' themselves. But the direct fifteen-minute route back to the airport took thirty-five minutes before we were pulled over at the side of the road by the police. We assumed some kind of problem with one of the coaches or that the police had received notice of a problem ahead. All became clear within a few minutes as a new police escort passed us, sandwiching an FA-emblazoned coach, clearly carrying the team who wanted to have a quiet passage through the airport. After all, what right did the fans have to talk to them, let alone share an airport?

So twelve coaches containing just over a thousand fans arrived en masse at the small airport and we were dumped on the kerb outside the terminal building. Cue a mass free-for-all as the fans tried to fight their way through two passport desks and the usual security checks to try and board one of the six flights leaving for the UK, another great piece of organisation from Thomas Cook, who were absolutely clueless about the logistical requirements for such trips.

Another stamp in the passport, another country under my belt and now I know where Macedonia is, although the chances of returning as a tourist are about the same as the gypsies being invited to tea by the US Ambassador to explain their one-way trip to Albania. I had also made my international debut, and the memory of singing the national anthem while wearing the three lions badge in front of a feisty atmosphere will stay in the memory for a long time, unlike my actual playing performance which will be filed along with the thirty-seconds substitute appearance for Lloyds Bank Ladies XI in 1989.

EXCUSE ME, WHAT TIME DOES THE FOOTBALL START?

A weekend in the Baltics, where football is no more than a distraction from the drinking

The Baltic States had been off my football radar for far too long. Since the budget airlines started on their bid for world domination they have come to realise that the most profitable destinations are those that offer cheap beer, cheap food, cheap nightlife and the chance to indulge in all of those things off limits to us westerners, but a part of normal life in the east of Europe, which includes Riga in Latvia, Kaunas and Vilnius in Lithuania and Tallinn in Estonia. All these places had become very popular with British stag trips, heading for a weekend of strip-joints, firing guns and narrowly avoiding arrest. But visits to football matches had not become part of these wanton weekends. So a day in Tallinn to watch their Premier League football was long overdue, especially as they embraced the summer months within their season.

Tallinn is one of those cities where a number of clubs share a small number of stadiums, so it is always possible to see at least a couple of matches in a weekend. Now, being resourceful, it was time for background reading on Estonian football. There have been low attendances before, such as 180 for a Coppa Italia at the Stadio delle Alpi for a game between the mighty Juventus and Bologna, and 300 for a Simod Cup game between Brighton & Hove Albion and Lincoln City, but Estonian football is in need of a boost from somewhere to match these attendances for its league matches. It is not as if facilities were still stuck in the communist era. In 2003 brewers Le Coq agreed to pay upwards of ten million pounds to build a spanking new national stadium in the south of town.

Estonia's biggest club, Flora Tallinn, were asked to move in and have since called the stadium home. That's the positive part. The negative part is that despite being the best-supported team in Estonia, they regularly play in front of crowds of less than 300, which means more than 9,000 empty seats on a weekly basis.

Hearing that easyJet have more issues with drunkenness on these flights than any other route, and that the worst offenders are Estonians on the daily 6.50 a.m. outbound flight from Stansted, I wondered what I was in for! But armed with a small guidebook, a handful of phrases and stout walking shoes it was off to Tallinn on a windy September Sunday. The first thing that strikes you about landing in Tallinn is that everything looks green – the scenery, the buildings and the people's clothes and their complexions. A short bus ride into town stops outside one of dozens of casino/bars dotted around the city. Gambling is a legacy of living too long under repressive Soviet rule; the locals are now making up for lost time, willing to bet on anything and everything.

The short walk into the old town was a pleasant amble with no British pissed-up parties in sight, although the bars and cafes were in full flow with locals putting back a few Le Coqs even at such an early hour.

The old town is very picturesque but very small. A ten-minute walk is all that is needed to traverse it, and after checking into the immaculate Domina Ilmarine Hotel just outside the city walls, I was back in the town square within half an hour. If anywhere in the world is made for England fans it is the old town main square in Tallinn. Four terrace bars, with outside seating, a massive curry house, a stage area and of course a lap-dancing bar. When England went there in June 2007 I doubt if ninety per cent of the fans ventured further than this spot. In the glorious September sunshine it was too tempting to say 'sod it' to the sightseeing, and 'hello' to a couple of cold beers.

Two turned into four and I was on the verge of breaking a tradition of boycotting the plan to see any football, let alone two games in an afternoon, and instead watch the delights of Bolton v Everton/Wigan/Middlesbrough (delete as applicable from this list of dire games that Sky are forced to show to make up their quotas). However, a conscience call from the CMF asking what the football ground was like stopped me. Football ground. Doh! There was a reason for the trip.

So setting out on foot down Pärnu mnt, the main road out of town to the south, for about fifteen minutes, I followed the railway line towards what looked like an underpass on the map. Estonians must be more responsible than us Brits as they decided that the railway lines don't need fences or barriers. Who would walk across the tracks when there is a bridge or underpass half a mile away? Tempting as it was I followed the railway line until finding an underpass. It was a tunnel for dwarves. At less than five feet high and two feet wide it would be worth seeing the scramble when crowds swell over the four-figure mark. You emerge right in front of the magnificent Le Coq Arena, where for some reason the car park was packed with learner drivers!

Five minutes to kick-off and there was not a soul in sight. I must have got it wrong and put my watch forward too far or even missed the game by twenty-four hours. But then I spotted the ticket office, or actually a ticket table which would not have looked out of place in a school fete. The princely sum of £3 bought a ticket for anywhere in the ground and a full-colour programme. For £2 more there was a bag of sunflower seeds and a scarf, but I didn't want to blend in too much. The ticket number was twenty-nine. Surely I wasn't only the twenty-ninth person to buy a ticket?

The ground was impressive. Shiny new green seats everywhere, excellent views and brilliant acoustics, and how could I tell? Because there were only twenty-eight others watching.

FC Flora Tallinn 5 Ajax Lasnamae 0 – Le Coq Arena – 26th September 2006

FC Flora versus Ajax Lasnamae wasn't a big pull in Estonian football terms, but you could drink beer (a pint of Le Coq turned out to be the same price as a seat in the main stand. I can't somehow see a similar situation ever happening in England) and it was sunny enough to sit back and sunbathe during the breaks in play.

Ten minutes into the game and Flora were 3-0 up, all the goals coming from corners. The hardcore Flora fans (one drummer, one trumpeter and a dog) sat on their own in the stand behind the goal and every time Flora attacked cheered as if they had won the cup final. Apart from the occasional good-looking young lady wandering past, which was obviously off-putting for some Ajax players as well judging by their defending, the game passed in a blur (OK, I went to sleep, thanks to the beer, the sunshine and the early morning flight).

Waking with a start as the ball hit a seat the row in front, all fifty-odd spectators (obviously people had taken advantage of the cheap second-half admission turnstile) laughed at my yelp of surprise. Apparently it was 5-0 at this stage and a chant went up of 'we want six' from the hardcore, who were getting lonely and wanted company. I decided against my normal tactic abroad of leaving a minute or so before the end to avoid the congestion and when the final whistle blew, both teams came over to shake us all by the hand and ask if we needed a lift anywhere. So one game down, one to go.

The second stadium, the Kalevi Keskstaadion, is home to Estonia's number one team, TVMK Tallinn, as well as new arrivals on the scene, Tallinna Kalev. It is also the biggest stadium in Estonia with a capacity of 12,000. I'd discovered that Tallinna had averaged a mighty twenty-four for their past few games and so there was no need to worry about trying to buy a ticket online beforehand. The twenty-minute walk eastwards through the suburbs was made all the more pleasant by passing (four or five times based on my newly designed route) an obvious brothel, where the girls, dressed in full evening clothes, sat outside enjoying the sun while awaiting their next customer.

What a choice. The company of five of Estonia's best-looking girls or a football match with twenty-odd other fans. With the CMF's warnings still ringing in my ears after the adventures in Moscow that all the grounds for this book had to be researched, it was time to find the stadium (turn right at the Renault showroom, then left past the Méganes and you cannot miss it). It was a huge bowl with an athletics track; two steep banks lined with wooden bench seats edging each side. As pre-match entertainment, people were throwing javelins on the pitch, certainly a first for me. At 3.55 p.m., the crowd had reached at least forty when the clapping started and the teams emerged. They were short of numbers, only eight on each team, and they were mixed gender, and looked young. Off came their tracksuits and down they squatted on athletics blocks. Hmm, having seen well over a thousand games in my life I guessed that this wasn't going to be played by the Laws of the game. The second football match was, in fact, an athletics meeting.

The Tallinna v Kalev game had been moved to the Kadrioru Stadium about a mile away because of an expected crowd of more than fifty for the athletics. I could have given up and found a bar (or even gone back to see if the ladies were still outside feeling lonely and wanting a chat) but this was a mission.

It meant a march, across main roads, roundabouts and a motorway, to reach the woods around the Kadrioru Stadium. It was the wonders of modern technology and satellite navigation which got me to the stadium, although having to ring CMF to fire up the TomTom in the car and then input the destination was cheating, but it did the trick. The game had just got under way and a seat was £1 – 'anywhere in the woods' said the gate man.

The Kadrioru Stadium is a single-stand athletics track, similar to that in most UK towns. One issue about walking into an almost empty stadium (even the players stopped and stared when they saw me) is that it is not clear which side is which. Which was the home team? Who am I supposed to support? What happens if one team score and I cheer and it's the away team? Being an athletics ground, the ball spent most of the time a long way from the pitch with ball boys chasing after another John Jensenesque shot from thirty yards.

After half an hour I deduced that I must have been the only paying spectator as everyone else at some point engaged in intimate conversations with at least one of the players. Leaving the ground after a 1-1 draw, I was still unsure who was who and who scored first (both goals were met with polite applause from all fans) but safe in the knowledge that being a professional footballer in Estonia is not much to boast about. The long walk back into town was sustained by the thought of finding a quiet bar to watch football from Spain or Italy. After twenty minutes there was at last a stag party; bare-chested, tattooed and in full voice singing 'If it wasn't for the British you'd be commies'; classic Brits abroad, holed up in a topless Irish bar. It wasn't worth going to the old town so it was a traditional Estonian night – a sauna and a skinful of vodka.

As a postscript, the following morning the flight was delayed by more than an hour after an Estonian woman had got drunk and abusive on the outbound flight from Stansted and the captain had to threaten to divert to Copenhagen to have her arrested. A nice touch and obviously a classy lady. Welcome to the new Europe!

SICILY IN SEPTEMBER.
YOU MUST BE MAD!

West Ham's last ever European adventure – potentially – in my lifetime

West Ham United are one of the most successful teams in the history of European club competitions – fact! Let me pause while you mop up the tea you have just spat out in amusement. It's true. Prior to the end of the last century (the twentieth, not the nineteenth for those who want to mock), they had played in the European Cup Winners' Cup on four occasions. In each campaign they reached at least the quarter-finals. In 1981 they were defeated at that stage by one of the greatest teams ever to play in Europe, Dynamo Tbilisi, although they did inflict a home defeat on the now Georgian club for the first time in more than two years. Prior to that West Ham had reached the final twice, losing to Anderlecht in Brussels in 1976 and, of course, winning the trophy at Wembley against TSV 1860 in 1965. The following year they reached the semi-finals, losing to eventual winners Borussia Dortmund. Not even the likes of the great AC Milan or Ajax can match such consistency.

In 2000 they became the first British winners of the much derided UEFA Intertoto Cup and in the process qualified for the UEFA Cup. They managed to overcome a tricky first-round game in Croatia before being eliminated by Steaua Bucharest, thus sending their UEFA ranking plunging, although they still retain a win ratio of fifty per cent of all European games, higher than such 'lesser' teams as Barcelona, Real Madrid and AC Milan. In 2005–6 the club returned to the Premier League after a two-year loan spell to the Championship. Under the guidance of Mr

Motivator, Alan Pardew, they finished a creditable ninth, having been among the favourites to be relegated, but more importantly reached the FA Cup Final. On a very sunny day in mid-May at Cardiff's Millennium Stadium the Hammers were desperately unlucky not to beat Liverpool in ninety minutes, with only a last-gasp Steven Gerrard piledriver taking the game into extra time. Even then they refused to give up and had Marlon Harewood not been suffering from severe cramp West Ham would have surely won the game at the death. It was not to be and Liverpool won on penalties. But as they had already qualified for the Champions League through their Premier League position, West Ham took the final UEFA Cup spot for the season.

So, for only the second time in twenty-six years, West Ham were going on a European tour. While the travels in the Intertoto Cup in 2000 to Helsinki and Heerenveen were enjoyable, it wasn't the same as a decent UEFA Cup run and going to more established clubs. The way the competition was set up, the draw in August could make or break the campaign. Pull out one of the favourites at this stage and elimination happens before the English summer has started. The incentive is to get through the first round and into the group stages where TV money starts to kick in. West Ham were unseeded, which meant they were put in a pot with four seeded teams.

They could have been paired with Osasuna, from northern Spain; Palermo, the capital of Sicily in Italy; Feyenoord, of Rotterdam in the Netherlands; or Steaua Bucharest, from Romania. On paper all appeared very tough on and off the pitch, considering the reputations of the clubs and the fans, although I suspect the nightmare tie would have been against Feyenoord, who had been warned about their fans' conduct in the previous campaign (and would actually go on to be kicked out of the competition later in the season due to persistent problems). When the draw was eventually made USC Palermo were drawn away to West Ham United. Sighs of relief all round that we had avoided the Romanians and the Dutch were quickly replaced with furious logging onto the internet to get a seat on the only cheap flights from London, offered by Ryanair. In fact the flight prices went from a manageable £14.99 each way to £149.99 each way within five minutes of the draw being made.

Being away enjoying the comforts of the Alton Towers Hotel with the Little Fullers, I was for once slow off the mark at arranging travel. Fully aware of the logistics and options, having been tasked by West Ham to provide a brief supporters' guide for each of the four potential opponents for the next home programme, I thought there would be no problems. There was no point in thinking about arrangements until a ticket for the away leg had been secured. While it was likely West Ham would take a fair few, the casual supporter would surely baulk at travelling so far.

Pick up a guidebook on Italy, flip to the section covering Palermo and the most common question asks simply 'Why . . . ?'Described by one travel website as 'dirty, cramped, crime ridden, morally and financially bankrupt, and they are the plus points', it sounded a wonderful place to visit in late September.

Of course West Ham being West Ham did not miss an opportunity to reward their loyal fans who had travelled on cold, wet nights to Burnley, Gillingham and Stoke City in the Championship. I think not. No match tickets would be sold to West Ham fans for the away leg unless an official club travel package, organised by Thomas Cook Sports, was booked; a two-finger salute to those who had already bought seats on the Ryanair flights. Surely it wouldn't be too much of an issue. Surely a one-night trip would be sensibly priced around £400. Wrong! West Ham had managed to secure some 'exclusive rooms in a five-star central hotel' and a one-night trip would cost the bargain price of £799 per person! Oh, but of course, it included a match ticket and a limited edition club gift (the same silver-plated corkscrew given to all hospitality guests, which, incidentally, the club had to give out on landing back in the UK as they were not allowed to be taken in hand luggage. – brilliant forward thinking). A day or so later they released package number two, a four-star hotel instead of a five-star option at £699 per person! Take-up must have been slow because the day trips were released very quickly at a bargain price of £279 for a 5 a.m. departure, but as it was the only way to get a ticket it was the best option.

Thomas Cook took their revenue for the year from me to more than £1,000 and it was off to Gatwick for a 3 a.m. check in with trusted travelling companion, Football Jo, who you will get to know well if you finish this book. The reason she is called 'Football Jo' is that she is called Joanne, to differentiate her from the other Jos in my life and to make it simple for the children to understand: she is the Jo who goes to football.

We were blissfully unaware of the near riots that had occurred overnight in Palermo's city centre between West Ham fans and the local police. Apparently the locals had been offended by the club's 'funny' idea

29

of producing Mafia-mocking T-shirts at the home leg a couple of weeks before, when we had played with complete naivety despite the presence of our new world-class signings, Tevez and Mascherano, in a 1-0 defeat. Still, it was evident from a number of sources that many so-called 'names' from the past would be coming out of retirement for one last European adventure, free from the restrictions placed on them in the UK.

What was on offer on the 5 a.m. flight for the £279? A 'freshly prepared breakfast' which looked suspiciously like Gate Gourmetto, or did I mistake the chefs for air stewardesses? A limited edition badge, sold on eBay for £1.99, and the added security of a Thomas Cook guide, who was so knowledgeable about our destination that he initially thought we were going to Sardinia as 'Sicily is not part of Italy; it is a country on its own'. The match tickets were personally handed out by a club official on the plane to ensure that we didn't sell them.

Leaving the airport, we were met with the usual suspects whenever English football fans arrive. Riot police in full combat gear, bemused locals assuming we would exit the terminal armed to the teeth and traders who wanted to sell us limited edition 'official' match-day merchandise such as T-shirts, scarves and programmes. The latter were being sold for €5, complete with wrong names being matched against team photos, and the manager was 'Alan Purdew'. They were soon being traded on eBay for more than €20, such was their rarity and humorous value. The journey into Palermo was uneventful, following the coastal highway through uninspiring countryside that could have been anywhere in southern Europe. The coach was buzzing with mobile conversations relaying news and stories from those in the city centre the previous evening.

The centre itself was exactly as described in some of the more 'cutting' guide books – certainly no one there had heard of B&Q, let alone DIY – but it did have a rustic charm in places. All was quiet after the previous night's antics, and a general wander around the city saw nervous riot police and a few groups of Hammers drinking in bars.

Jo and I opted to get an overview of the city with a 'hop on, hop off' open-top bus tour, although quite why anyone would want to hop off at such sights as the bus station, railway station, old flea market or port was lost on me. Apart from the cathedral, the majority of the sights on the ninety-minute trip involved another traffic-clogged street.

Lunch was obviously the focal point of the day's entertainment. Italians take this meal very seriously (as well as every other meal), spending hours working their way through courses accompanied by a variety of wines, and we planned to do something similar. The problem was that most restaurants had either shut after the antics of the previous night, or served just junk food. Eventually we found a quiet side-street spot far from the madding crowd with a few of the more sensible and educated Hammers (yes, there is such a group and some even have GCSEs!), who regaled us with the events of the night before. All handbags by the sounds of things but still enough for the young lads who will dine out on the fact that they 'stood firm with the ICF against the Mafia' in years to come. Lunch was chaotic as the bar ran out of beer and had to go to the local supermarket to get more. Unfortunately the bar owner could not carry much and had to enlist the help of the West Ham fans to carry it. He then charged them a two-hundred per cent mark-up to drink it! After six courses, food fatigue took over and a sleep was definitely required.

With no hotel, and not fancying a lie down in the municipal park, the options were very limited. For once, Football Jo, not known for great ideas, hit the jackpot. Still having our tickets for the open-top tour bus, we settled down for a two-lap trip which took up three hours. There would have been a third lap had it not been for Jo dribbling on the shoulder of a Japanese tourist, after which we were asked to leave to avoid offending anyone else.

The coaches picked us up in the main square at 6 p.m. Despite the stadium being a three-kilometre hike, the police took the coaches on what can only be described as a 'nature ramble', up hills, down mountain paths, in and out of country parks for thirty minutes until we reached the stadium, which, with three hours to go before kick-off, was in complete darkness.

A policeman had to wake the groundsman from his post-lunch snooze to open the gates, and we started the slow process of entering the stadium. Security was tight and there were three separate security checkpoints, plenty of time for the local police to have a good grope of the female fans. We were herded into a cage that ran the length of the main stand, driven onwards by the police, in complete darkness and with water slopping over our feet. At the far end there was a fourth security check before we could get into the stadium.

Facilities were appalling to put it mildly. One toilet for two thousand or so fans and one refreshment kiosk that served only ice creams. It underlined why Italian stadiums still had a long way to go to be compared with those in England or Germany over the way supporters are treated.

31

USC Palermo 3 West Ham United 0 – Stadio Renzo Barbera – 28th September 2006

The West Ham fans had been given a corner, hemmed in by thick glass on two sides and a caged roof on the lower tier. With hours still to go before kick-off we did the only thing we could to pass the time. Sing! After exhausting the traditional West Ham songs we started on Duran Duran's greatest hits, followed by an Elvis and Sinatra medley before descending into the surreal with the *Flintstones* theme. The players came out to warm up and were greeted with great relief; the kick-off was approaching.

At regular intervals West Ham fans, who had bought their tickets from Italian booking agencies, were seen being led from the home end and around the pitch to be deposited in our stand, giving the police plenty of opportunity to practise their golf swings using their batons on any who dared to step out of line.

One-nil down from the first leg, West Ham battered the Italians' goal, but soon fell behind to a flukey, deflected shot on a counter-attack. Our expensive pre-season signing, Carlton Cole, was then carried off and Pardew's tactical substitutions failed to work as the team crumbled. A 3-0 defeat on the night was hard to swallow, but a lesson was learned on how far away from European football West Ham were in terms of technique and approach.

Any seasoned football fan who has travelled abroad will know the local police like to have the last laugh by keeping visiting fans in the stadium 'for safety reasons' after the final whistle. There are small delays and there are Italian delays. Why they thought ninety minutes would be a reasonable time to keep tired fans in the stadium is unknown. But when they eventually opened the gates, we were again herded into the cage and out of the stadium, which was, of course, completely deserted apart from the groundsman waiting to lock up.

The trip back to the airport was conducted in silence, tired from the twenty-three-hour day so far and not looking forward to going to work the next morning. Thomas Cook had issued us with return boarding passes earlier in the day to speed our passage through the airport and ensure the planes took off before it was closed for the night. Unfortunately, with six full planes due to leave at the same time, the Italians got confused with the boarding cards, so they turned away everyone trying to pass through security, sending them back to the check-in desks, where two helpful airport workers tried to dish out new boarding cards for around 1,000 people. Thomas Cook lost the plot. 'Just get on any plane, they all go to the same place!' was the classic final quote of the evening, making a complete mockery of the heightened security measures in place for airline travellers.

So the day came to an end as I entered Chez Fuller at 4.30 a.m. wondering if I had just seen West Ham's last ever European adventure. But at least the grandchildren can be told that I was there on the day we took on the home of the Mafia, and survived! Oh, and the pasta was very pleasant too.

CHAPTER
5
CHAPTER

ADVICE FROM THE FOREIGN OFFICE: 'DON'T GO!'

England's quest to tame the Blue Boys in their homelands

About a month before England's European Championship qualifying game away to Croatia in Zagreb, the Foreign and Commonwealth Office issued updated advice for England fans without tickets – don't go! Blame it on the fact England have one of the best away followings in the world, which meant demand would be high. Out of the Official EnglandFans Group of twenty-five thousand members, more than eight thousand applied for tickets for one of the most anticipated away games in recent years.

Not only was this a new country for England, but Croatia were seen as our biggest rivals in the group and this, coupled with the prospect of cheap beer and some more than average local sights, meant the only official source of away tickets was bound to be stretched by high demand. As soon as Zagreb was confirmed, fans started booking by any route possible. The most popular, direct to Zagreb, via Ljubljana in Slovenia or Graz in Austria, filled up quickly as fans had to commit to flights and hotels and hope they would get a ticket from the ballot. In the end only 3,688 tickets were allocated to England.

Do the maths and you can see that 4,300 would be travelling in the hope of getting one. Of course, anyone who travels without a ticket is someone looking for a fight – right? Well, yes according to our unbiased media and government. The authorities don't factor in that in most cases fans can't get refunds on flights and hotels, and faced with a slim chance of getting a ticket against no chance by not travelling, they go. How many of the media travel with the fans instead of ligging on their expense accounts? (Tip for tabloid press reporters who want to stay undercover: approaching a group of England fans drinking in a bar and saying 'All right lads, anyone been fighting?' rather gives the game away.)

I was lucky enough to be one of the 3,688, but had no luck with finding a reasonably-priced flight or hotel, so it was the day trip option again. The usual security warnings were handed out before travelling with the Football Association. No guns, no throwing objects onto the pitch (so what should be done when a ball goes into the crowd? Throw it back and break the law or keep it and get accused of theft?), no drugs and of course no singing songs likely to incite hatred. They also took the unusual step of announcing that English police officers would be present at the stadium, working with their Croatian counterparts in an advisory capacity.

The good thing about the day trips is that they are normally well organised in terms of transport: they escort you from A to B, giving confidence that if fans are stuck in the stadium, the plane is not going to leave without them. The downside is crappy flight times, meaning the 'day' trip is normally more than twenty-four hours. And the local aviation authorities find it amusing to schedule all return flights at the same time, meaning absolute disorder as thousands of fans try to pass through security together, an experience I had already undergone in Macedonia and Palermo in the previous few weeks.

Zagreb was also going to be my second game in charge of the EnglandFans Veterans. After the humiliating defeat in Macedonia I received the dreaded vote of confidence and was invited to pick a team to play in a six-way tournament, featuring three English teams and three from Croatia, to be played at the training centre of Dinamo Zagreb, Croatia's biggest club side, and again in front of TV cameras, plus the Croatian deputy prime minister no less. With little time for sightseeing after a mammoth walk from the coach park in Zagreb to the meeting point in the historic Ban Josip Jelačić Square, we trudged to the ground, turning down an opportunity to enjoy a beer or two with some very nice-looking locals.

The tournament was an absolute disaster for us. Five games, five defeats, ten goals conceded and none scored. In the play-off for fifth and sixth place against the England Seniors XI we failed to score in the penalty shoot-out! Secure in the knowledge that the next game was six months away I managed to avoid awkward questions about my immediate future.

With the energetic part of the day out of the way, the time had come to leave for the stadium. As luck would have it we had been playing just a five-minute stroll from the stadium in the Maksimir Park area to the east of Zagreb city centre. So, decked out in red England shirts, a small advance party of Dagenham Dan, Rob the Red, Shents and I decided to head for the ground. We passed a number of groups of Croatian fans who stared at us in bewilderment. We simply waved and carried on, unaware of the precarious position into which we were walking. We could hear the noise of the crowd increasing, just through the trees and then we were suddenly in front of the stadium . . . four of us . . . standing on the edge of the road opposite the turnstiles for the fiercely loyal home fans . . . in our England shirts . . . looking lost.

In such situations you can do three things:

1. Be French or Italian and turn around and run away quickly.

2. Be German and take the attack to them.

3. Be British and carry on regardless, talking about tea and the weather and ignoring the life-threatening circumstance.

So we walked against the tide of fans, chatting about team selections and the like – and the most astonishing thing happened. As we walked down the street, the Croatian fans started moving out of the way, allowing safe passage around the stadium to the away end – the curved south section on Budakova Street. Here there was a checkpoint set up to check for tickets. Excellent idea, but one person trying to check thousands of tickets, with only a waist-high temporary fence separating those who had tickets and those who didn't, was a recipe for disaster. At the turnstiles they checked bags, trying to understand why us 'crazy' fans would want to take shinpads into the ground. No sign of the promised English policemen.

Our entry passed without incident – although ten minutes later the riot police decided to lock the gates to stop the ticketless fans who had managed to pass the first checkpoint. When those at the gates (with tickets) started being pushed forward by ticketless people behind them, the riot police could have:

a) told everyone to stop pushing.

b) told the guy on checkpoint one not to let fans through or even do his job in checking tickets.

c) randomly batoned people around the head who were being pushed forward and offering no defence.

No surprise that they chose option 'c'. Sod the fact there were women and children: innocent England fans were again subject to the kind of brutality recently seen in Madrid and Bratislava. Fans covered in blood started wandering into the stand, underlining the brutality of the police in dealing with a completely avoidable issue.

Croatia 2 England 0 – The Maksimir Stadium – 17th October 2006

The less said about the game, the better. We lost, McClaren got it all wrong, the pitch was rubbish, blah blah blah. The game was summed up by Paul Robinson's horrendous mistake which gifted Croatia a second goal after Gary Neville's back pass went over his foot as he tried to clear (looking at it later it was clear the goalkeeper suffered a horrendous bobble, and what was Neville doing directing a back pass towards the middle of the goal?).

Come the end we were kept in for the customary hour while they made sure all the proper Croatian hooligans outside the ground had a chance to collect enough rocks to throw at the coaches parked behind the stand. The simple fifteen-minute journey back to the airport took on a new dimension, most of us sitting nervously in fear of being attacked. The logical route would have taken us direct to the airport, but with the Croatian police involved nothing was so simple. In a repeat of the journey back to the airport in Macedonia it was a magical mystery tour of the Croatian suburbs and airport car parks, all seventeen coaches in a convoy!

Eventually there was a parking spot at the airport, only for the police to refuse initially to allow anyone off the coach for a pee. It transpired we were being held there while, you guessed it, the England team was being rushed through the airport.

Finally, we were driven to the terminal where we had to queue to pass through security and passport control, all the while with 'last call' announcements being made for the flights. Thanks, England. Because of the FA I had to endure another three hours without sleep after a spineless performance, a nervous tick every time there is a back pass to a goalkeeper and a hatred of red and white checks!

Zagreb was very pleasant, and the Croatians welcoming. Although I did not see at first hand any of the issues outside the ground it's clear these were not caused by the opposing fans, whose bark was certainly worse than their bite. Even the ones who threw stones got them nowhere near us.

FOOTBALL, MICKEY MOUSE STYLE

An Englishman's journey to watch the beautiful game in a land that doesn't understand football

Every couple of years the Fuller family flies to Florida for a few weeks' sunshine and empty Gulf Coast beaches. By going in late October we risk the wrath of the local education authority by taking the Little Fullers out of school but it is worth it. They get to spend quality time with their dad, as he is unable to escape to watch a game or two. However, he is not averse to taking in American sports, whether it be watching the hopeless Orlando Magic in the NBA (basketball), the equally appalling Tampa Bay Rays in the MLB (baseball) or the relatively newly formed Orlando Predators in Arena Football (indoor American Football).

Normally it's about a week before I try to catch a game on TV in Mick's Irish Bar on International Drive. This time around West Ham were being featured on US television twice in the first week of the break.

A negotiated family breakfast in the Sports Bar on International Drive resulted in me catching West Ham against Arsenal early in the holiday as the kick-off was at 8 a.m. US time and it still left the whole day to spend being Disneyfied. A few days later the Hammers were away to Chesterfield in the Carling Cup. This time the game kicked off at 2.45 p.m. so substantial promises were needed about breakfast with Minnie Mouse (a bargain $25 per head) in order to take the kids back to the hotel so I could get to the bar. A 2-1 extra-time defeat was not a pleasant way to spend two hours of the holiday and I vowed there would be no more football for the duration.

However, sometimes you cannot plan for events. We had tickets for Orlando Magic the following evening. Orlando, as mentioned earlier, had not been a real success since the franchise was awarded in 1989. However, a number of excellent signings in the draft meant big things were expected for the 2006–7 season and thus the few home friendlies they played were in high demand.

I have never really understood why the holiday companies such as Virgin do not try and package trips to American sporting events. With huge venues and world-class players, the opportunity is perfect for sports-mad Brits. And as we want to be spoonfed, they could make a fortune.

While we were waiting at the 'ticketing center' at the T.D. Waterhouse Arena in downtown Orlando, a small poster in the corner of the box office window caught my eye. Columbia v Mexico, Tuesday night, 8 p.m. at the Citrus Bowl. A chance to see an international in one of the biggest stadiums in North America seemed too good an opportunity to miss. I didn't mention anything to CMF for fear of reprisal attacks but instead made a mental note to try and find out more information. The FIFA website, the de facto source on all international football fixtures, did not list any such game. Nor did the Citrus Bowl's own website. They didn't even list an event for the Tuesday evening, and there was nothing in the TV schedules.

Florida was hosting the National Hispanic Heritage week starting on the Monday, so I reasoned that it must be something else. Perhaps a display of bands from Mexico and Columbia instead of a football match. But on the Monday morning the *USA Today* sports section, in small print on page 17, stated that a game was to be played. It kicked off at 8 p.m. the following day. That was it.

Based on the fact it was an evening kick-off and we had planned to travel down to the coast on Wednesday morning, I argued that the children could do with an early night, and after reading them a story I could be away by 7 p.m.

For those who don't know central Florida I should say that the Citrus Bowl is in a part of Orlando not mentioned in guidebooks because the local police do not want the hassle of rising crime figures that would result if tourists wandered around. To put it into movie terms, the nearest main road is Orange Blossom Trail, which resembles a scene from *Mean Streets* or *On the Waterfront*. Rows of liquor stores, pawnbrokers and dive bars interspersed with parking lots full of undesirables. Anyway, I followed the advice of the satnav, locked the doors of the Grand Dodge Caravan hoping that the Texas license plates gave the impression I might be packing a weapon, and walked toward the stadium.

Lesson Number 1 – When going to sport in the US, no one does 'street parking'. It's parking lots or nothing.

I was confused. Columbia traditionally play in yellow and blue, Mexico in green and white but I was seeing a mass of yellow and red shirts, and a few green and blue ones, none of which appeared to be the shirts worn by the international sides. Quite a few people were waving flags, again looking nothing like those of either country. But crowds there were, especially at the ticket booths where the concept of queuing was completely alien. After finally reaching the booth I realised that this was not an 'international' but a friendly between two club sides who didn't have a game that weekend, the equivalent of a game pitched as England v Scotland being between Reading and Albion Rovers. To this day I couldn't tell you who they were, and confusingly the Columbians played in green, and the Mexicans in yellow.

Most American stadiums are huge concrete monuments to their owners. Anyone who has been to Tampa and seen the Ray James Stadium, where the Glazer family spent millions on one of the biggest-supported teams in the National Football League, will testify it is palatial. Likewise, the Giants Stadium is built with spectators in mind. Not so the Citrus Bowl in Orlando, although it holds fond memories for many people. In June 1994 it hosted the classic games between Ireland and Mexico and Ireland and Holland in the World Cup finals; fans who recall the tournament will never forget the argument between John Aldridge and the fourth official in the game against Mexico when he was trying to enter the field as a substitute.

Twelve years later and it looked as if the stadium hadn't hosted a game since. Outside of the 'bowl' there were few facilities, and queues were huge at the few refreshment stands. They love their sport in the US and they love their food. Nobody was in the least bit worried about missing the start as long as they had their Jumbo Texan Chili Dog with a gallon of Coke. Five minutes went by and the queue didn't move. After ten minutes I gave up – it was kick-off time, allegedly.

Lesson Number 2 – In the US, a kick-off time just means the time all players will be on the pitch, not when the game will start.

Strange Columbian Team 0 Strange Mexican Team 2 – The Citrus Bowl – 30th October 2006

It was as if someone had sent a message to the referee to say 'Hang on a minute mate, Scottie hasn't got his Dr Pepper and his Florida Corn Dog on a stick, so don't kick off just yet.' At 8.12 p.m. the game started, albeit with one team in white and the other in yellow, with me still none the wiser about who they were, or which country they represented until I saw that the yellow team's fans were wearing green Mexican shirts. Both teams certainly seemed fired up for the occasion, and there was none of the pedestrian play that characterises friendlies in the UK.

The crowd behind the goal was colourful to say the least and it took all of ninety seconds before the first firework was launched. Note *firework*, not a flare. This was a fully-fledged-repeated-bangs-and-bright-lights-in-the-air variety of firework. They were set off at regular intervals and I waited with anticipation to see who was going to hold up a Catherine wheel, but nobody seemed that keen. On the pitch the Columbian goalkeeper was doing a fantastic impression of a fish out of water, flapping at everything as soon as the ball was delivered into the penalty area.

It took only fifteen minutes for the Mexicans to take the lead as a corner was bundled into the net by two Columbians who seemed to be trying to outdo each other in the politeness stakes about who was going to clear the ball. Instead, they simply let the ball hit both of them as it passed. Five minutes before half-time and it was 2-0 as a free kick from twenty yards passed under the Columbian wall as they all jumped to try and block the ball.

It took a while but I realised eventually why the stadium had an odd look. A whole end was missing. It was as if a huge crane had removed a two-tier structure, and replaced it with a puny scoreboard that barely hid the view from the side of the road. The match was obviously so enthralling that locals simply walked on by, completely oblivious.

I couldn't tell who won it in the end. With the game entering the last quarter (sorry, slipped into American speak already!) and the Mexicans still holding a 2-0 lead, the fans behind the goal ran out of fireworks. They did try to start a bonfire, but this was a step too far for the stewards, who waded in and took away their matches. This was a good excuse to depart and avoid the pending pandemonium when leaving the parking lots.

Lesson Number 3 – When you park in the parking lots at major events/theme parks in the US, make a note of the parking lot number and the car number plate. Sneaking out early to avoid the traffic then spending forty minutes looking for the car is not the best use of time.

OK, it would have been a good idea had I written down details of the car but I didn't. At night, with little in the way of lighting, I could not find it. I could not even remember the colour! There were hundreds of Dodge Caravans parked there and I attracted the attention of security staff by bending down to view the number plates. Then I had the idea of walking up and down and trying the remote locking key fob, hoping to hear a welcoming beep. That didn't work either, and with the game finishing and fans returning to their vehicles, my only hope was to wait for the majority to leave.

Thirty minutes later the parking lot was almost empty and there was no sign of the car. Then I realised it was the wrong parking lot. The car was sitting alone across the street on a patch of waste ground and just about to be locked in by the security guard. I ran towards him, shouting for him to stop and, of course, he didn't understand English. My Spanish is poor but fortunately he eventually got the message.

Trying to find the way back to the freeway was hard enough, especially after stopping by what I thought was a convenience store to reprogramme the satnav. There was a tap on the window. A police officer had seen me driving slowly, pulling over to the kerb without signalling and then fiddling in my lap (with my satnav I hasten to add). He thought such behaviour was erratic and consistent with a driver who might be enjoying the pleasures of a working girl, as this was the 'strip alley' of Orlando. Apologising profusely, I explained my predicament and he offered an escort back to the freeway. He even wished me a good holiday and told me to look up his cousin's bar in St Pete's Beach where we were heading the following morning.

When I arrived at the lodge just before midnight, the Fuller family were still awake and watching a Champions League game on the TV, surrounded by takeaway pizza. Looks like I again chose the wrong option. On the next visit to Uncle Sam I will stick to those simple sports like American Football that have no complicated rules or regulations a visitor needs to get his head around.

SEX, DRUGS AND PETER CROUCH – ENGLAND INVADE AMSTERDAM

A night out in the capital of sin watching McClaren's clowns

Rumours circulate all the time in football. For the members of the EnglandFans group, the team's official away following, there are constant stories about who we will be playing in the future. Some destinations are mentioned more than others, based on a fans' 'wish list'. Stories first started appearing around Christmas time that it would be Holland in Amsterdam and so when this game was announced by the FA in the spring of 2006, the level of interest was huge. England had played only once in the city in living memory. The lure of a game that would potentially yield up to seven thousand away tickets, the ease with which the city could be reached and the legal delights on offer were going to be too good to miss.

Of course, there were always going to be problems associated with such a game, the first of which was the FA announcement that England fans would get only four thousand official tickets. England fans are known for their investigative powers and so it was no surprise when stories started to appear of how to book tickets in the home end via agencies in the Netherlands. Travel was easy to arrange. Amsterdam Schiphol is used by more than a dozen airlines on a daily basis from all over the United Kingdom, and supplemented by flights to Rotterdam and Eindhoven, not to mention the city being only a few hours' drive from the channel ports.

So surely a couple of days in the home of sin to watch my beloved England was high on the list of priorities? Well, no actually. Having spent a year working in Amsterdam, enduring the constant delays in and out of Schiphol, the poor hotels, dodgy drug dealers (are there any normal drug dealers?) and groups of tourists vainly trying to barter with the girls in the windows of the red-light district I decided to spend the minimum possible time there while still taking in at least a little pre-match atmosphere. Fortunately British Airways catered for this. There was a flight arriving at 5 p.m. and leaving at 7 a.m. the following morning. A cheap hotel just outside the city centre completed the trip.

The expected number of England fans travelling was more than ten thousand and the scene outside Amsterdam's Central Station was reminiscent of the 2006 World Cup in Germany. On the short walk to the hotel, bar upon bar was full of fans watching Sky Sports and enjoying a leisurely liquid build-up to the game. It was almost like back-street English northern towns had been transported across the North Sea to the Netherlands, although there was a shortage of whippets.

The main issue facing the local authorities was getting the fans to the stadium with five minutes to spare. These efforts were compounded by a local transport strike which meant no tube trains or trams until 7 p.m. local time.

After meeting Rob the Red in a relatively quiet small bar near the station – it did not have British TV programmes – we set off for the ArenA (as the locals pronounce it while us Johnny Foreigners simply say 'the Arena') to sign in, the process fans have to go through to prove to the FA we were there and get the all-important caps. The route took us through the red-light district and left us concerned that so many people were looking for this bloke called Charlie. We also saw the bargaining skills of the England fans at their best as a group of five chaps tried to negotiate a group discount with one particular lady which, unfortunately, at the rate of €60, did not push any of her buttons.

The nearest metro station to the RLD (as people familiar with the area now call it) is Nieuwmarkt, which would allow us to get a train straight to the ground. The one thing the Dutch sometimes don't do very well is signage at stations or public transport stops. So here is the guide to how to buy a train ticket in Amsterdam:

1. Work out which button is for a daily travel card
2. Try to pay by Visa card, then realise you can't
3. Try to pay by MasterCard, then realise you can't

4. Scrape together enough cash to pay
5. Start putting cash in
6. Get approached by a station attendant who tells you it's cheaper to buy a Strippenkart ticket
7. Work out what button is a Strippenkart ticket
8. Realise that you don't have enough cash
9. Go and find a cashpoint machine
10. Come back and find out that the same station attendant who told you to buy the Strippenkart is now saying that because of the strike all transport is actually free

The rail network is fast and efficient at moving people to and from the stadium but the process of buying the ticket took ten minutes longer than the journey. The Dutch authorities built public transport with the stadium in mind, unlike what we have done with Wembley.

There are a number of great things about the ArenA. The first is that it has a number of excellent bars around the ground, including the Soccer World bar owned by former Dutch internationals Danny Blind and Frank Rijkaard. Secondly it has three railway stations within a five-minute walk and thirdly it has one of the loudest acoustic systems in the world. Let's deal with them in order. The bars were very welcoming, although at €5 a pint we had moved from back-street northern town to poncy Soho club. However, the evening was balmy and the England fans were in good voice so time passed quickly. A strange-looking Dutch couple dressed from head to toe in orange and followed five paces behind by a Kevin-esque stroppy teenager with a trolley – upon which was a huge ghetto-blaster blaring out a song about Marco van Basten – kept walking through the crowds.

The ArenA at night looks like a UFO floating in the sky with green lights radiating from its roof. Some say this is the result of radiation left over from the Bijlmer plane which crashed close by in 1992 and was rumoured to have been carrying a radioactive cargo!

The pitch is three levels above ground with car parks underneath, and so after going through the turnstiles you climb and climb and climb before even reaching the lower tier. The concourse levels are spacious but you have to remember before rushing to buy frites with mayo and ketchup that Euros are useless here. You have to buy an ArenA card. These are an ingenious way of making you spend money. The concourse is full of vending outlets supplying these cards, and, yes, you can cash back any unused money from your card at the end of the game. Of course, for every ten places to buy a card there is one to refund it. The number of fans who spent ages queuing for food only to be turned away waving their €20 notes was in the dozens so early in the evening.

Netherlands 1 England 1 – Amsterdam ArenA – 15th November 2006

England came into the match on the back of two poor results after a draw at home with Macedonia and the Zagreb defeat, while the Dutch had recorded two victories, going to the top of their qualifying group. Many England fans had started expressing concern about Steve McClaren after only a few games as his promised revolution in team selection had thus far extended only to dropping David Beckham, who was playing superbly for Real Madrid. He insisted that the midfield partnership of Lampard and Gerrard would work and again for this match he chose them to start.

International friendlies have been devalued for years, especially those featuring England. They used to be the perfect opportunity to blood the more impressive youngsters but instead they had become experiments in trying to fit existing players into new positions. For this game, McClaren did give a debut to one such youngster as Micah Richards started at full back but he also put Andy Johnson, an out-and-out centre forward, on the right wing.

Despite England ranking higher in world football than the Dutch (going into the game), the structure of the teams showed a different picture. With an average age of just twenty-four the Dutch were expected to win.

The game started as badly for England as you would expect. Huff and puff and Andy Johnson sending in wasted cross after cross for Wayne Rooney, when the perfect replacement – Peter Crouch – sat on the bench. Crouch was rumoured to have said that he would have rather been out on the town than sitting on the bench for a friendly. Rooney wasted a couple of good chances in the first half before latching on to a Steven Gerrard through ball and putting England 1-0 ahead. The atmosphere in the stadium was excellent – no sign of any animosity, a genuine noisy environment and half-time entertainment bar none! Not many people realise that Holland's second most popular sport is darts, so what better way to entertain the fans than with an England v Holland darts match on

47

the pitch at half-time and beamed live on to the big screens. In a tense game of 701, England just pipped the Dutch to checkout. You can keep your Hammerettes, penalty shoot-outs and Bonnie Tyler (West Ham take note!) – just give us darts any day.

The second half was poor, with both teams making frequent substitutions and thus disrupting the game's balance and flow. With time ticking away the Dutch equalised after an Arjen Robben throw-in was not dealt with and Rafael van der Vaart headed in from close range. Long throw-ins had caused England major issues in previous games and this was the third goal we had conceded in this way in less than six months.

The remainder of the night continued predictably in the city centre. Lots of people still looking for their mate Charlie, lots of business for those lovely, friendly ladies and many fans failing to find their hotels in the maze of almost identical side streets. As for me, after a quick drink with Rob the Red it was back to the hotel for a few hours' sleep. Then a short hop to Gatwick, and I was at my desk before 9 a.m. without the chief executive realising that I'd been in Amsterdam, rather than the server room downstairs for the past eighteen hours as I said the previous day when he saw me dressed in civvies.

Nothing though could change my dislike for the city. Even an England win would have put a false shine on the trip.

NEVER ON THE SABBATH

England's woes continue in the Middle East

Israel was always a trip to worry about. The horror stories seemed to become more prevalent the closer the match got. CMF certainly wasn't keen on me going and selective use of carnal pleasures was used as a tactic for only the second time in our married life (the first was when I threatened to buy a Spearmint Rhino Gold membership). In fact, at one point when the troubles on the border with Lebanon kicked off again, it was odds on that we would be heading to Cyprus to see this one – surely the overpaid, pampered English players wouldn't be allowed to set foot on the hallowed soil for fear of swarms of Middle Eastern terrorists trying to get at them? But the fans seemed to think it was a goer, and so flights via almost every European capital were hastily snapped up as soon as it was officially confirmed that Tel Aviv would indeed host the game. Some more adventurous fans planned routes to take in as many Middle Eastern countries as possible, whereas others who had been in Barcelona a few days before flew directly from Spain.

Being short on annual leave just three months into the new year it was with a heavy heart that I booked a day trip with our friends from up north, Thomas Cook, as opposed to spending a few days on the beaches of Tel Aviv. Spending ten hours on a plane is not the best idea, but to spend it in economy, squashed in with two hundred and fifty other England fans, is even less appealing. But we must suffer for our art, and so I pitched up at Gatwick at 2 a.m. on Saturday 24th March with an iPod and a book, having deprived myself of sleep in preparation. At least there was a good travelling crew, with Rob the Red and Dagenham Dan also making the trip.

Everything went smoothly for the 4 a.m. departure, until captain Paddy Doyle came on and told us we had a problem with the windscreen heater. 'Only a small problem, ladies and gents, and we will be on our way in a moment.' This was a first, as every captain I had ever heard make an announcement on a plane had been either very posh, or foreign. Captain Doyle sounded as if he was from Hornchurch. Twenty minutes later and a decision was made to vacate the plane for a spare one across the runway as at that early hour they could not find someone to fix the heater. Swapping planes is not as simple as borrowing the wife's car when yours has no petrol. Not only do you have to move two hundred and fifty passengers and re-issue the boarding cards, you have to move the crew, the bags and the all-important catering.

It took an hour before we were fuelled, loaded with bags and warmed up. But wait! The food for the return flight was missing. 'It's OK, ladies and gents, we have asked the ground staff to go and fetch it from the other plane.' Thirty minutes later we were told that the ground staff in question had actually clocked off for the rest of the day. A further twenty minutes passed before the captain made an executive decision: 'We've decided not to wait for the food, but to get going.'

What he should have said was: 'After waiting on the tarmac for two hours, dear ripped-off, tired and squashed customers, I have decided that I could actually get a sandwich in Tel Aviv to stop me getting hungry on the way home, and actually now I should really fly this bugger to Tel Aviv so that you actually get to see some of the city before the game, or even the game itself.'

We were told the two-hour delay was not the fault of Monarch (the chartered airline and crew) or Thomas Cook (the charter company), but BAA who run the airport. The word here is accountability, boys, and is fundamental in the process of customer service.

Four hours and fifty-one minutes later we touched down in a sunny Tel Aviv, expecting guns, troops, a basic little airport and hostility. What did we get? A clean, modern airport, plenty of smiling locals and a T-shirt and hat that said 'Israel loves you'. Immigration was a formality and twenty minutes after landing we were on coaches in the beautiful sunshine. The plan was to drop us in the old port area for a few hours before taking us to the stadium 'for security reasons' at 6.15 p.m. The coach driver proceeded to give a rundown of the city, and then how scared the locals were of the English drunken fans! How ironic that in a country which has experienced almost daily attacks on its people and infrastructure they should be scared of red-faced, sweaty men brandishing cans of Carlsberg. He also pointed out that as the Sabbath wasn't due to end until 'the third star appeared above the belt of horizon' or something, everywhere would be quiet, and few bars would open until later in the evening. Put a bunch of English fans in a war zone and they will happily carry on with life as long as they have access to alcohol. Take away this pleasure and panic sets in.

The Israeli bar owners had obviously chosen to ignore the religious beliefs of thousands of years for the once-in-a-lifetime opportunity to double their annual profits and open early. The seafront was more akin to San Antonio or Malia. Bars were overflowing and offering the most hospitable surroundings. After all, when was the last time England fans got to drink on the beach before a game (let's exclude the beach bars set up in Germany in the World Cup). We decided on a traditional meal, in traditional surroundings. Plate after plate of hummus with onion, with garlic, with chilli and so on appeared before the main course of meat, all washed down with the local beer.

What a perfect way to spend an afternoon, and the locals seemed impressed too. 'Look,' you could hear them say, 'England fans eating hummus. Perhaps they will pillage our city later.' It was far too relaxing to even think about that. Instead we ate merrily, then got the bill, only to have been charged an arm and a leg for those hummus dips that no one asked for or ate! The twelve per cent mandatory tip was not forthcoming and it was made it quite clear we would not be returning there again, which would really serve the owners right. Instead we went to look for the celebrity hangouts on the beach. Word had reached us that Glenn Hoddle had been spotted and the Wolves fans among us wanted to have a word after he had single-handedly ruined a promotion-chasing team the previous season.

The rest of the afternoon was spent playing the usual English game of 'woodya' while sitting in the beachfront bars watching the townspeople promenading up and down the sand and occasionally taking part in team-specific beach football games, where a West Ham team consisting of me and, er, me lost 3-0 to a Notts County team consisting of five players in a thirty-second game. The coaches arrived dead on 6.15 p.m. for the transfer and as the sun fell, the England fans rolled into the Ramat Gan Stadium full of hope of a win against a tough-looking Israeli team who had a very impressive home record. The stadium was surrounded by security checkpoints and despite thorough searches we were soon inside thanks to the sheer numbers of military personnel, who chatted away and then thanked us after finishing their frisking. Word got round that my team (or is it my ex-team) of England Veterans Fans had won their second consecutive game earlier in the day, also the second game in a row I had missed, which almost certainly meant an enforced removal. The team had been awarded a trophy that was so big it had to be left at the ground.

Israel 0 England 0 – Ramat Gan Stadium – 24th March 2007

The stadium was completely open-air, and with the running track it seemed as if there might be a lack of atmosphere, but the Israelis had gone out of their way to make this a special night. Jugglers, fire eaters, marching bands and local pop stars entertained the crowd for ninety minutes before the kick-off, building it into a frenzy, and the national anthems were certainly stirring, albeit with the sound being pumped out of huge speakers in front of the England section. Or was it the England section? Every so often a local-looking face would appear among the England fans. A whole family of Israelis appeared and immediately showed their grasp of English language – 'McClaren is a twat' seemed a very popular saying in Tel Aviv.

The game was the low point of the day. Witless, clueless, spineless, passionless and gutless should be used to describe England's performance for the second time in less than a week. Too many players just couldn't be bothered and a 0-0 draw was unfair on Israel. But McClaren did not see it that way. He saw it as almost the perfect performance. 'All we were missing was a goal,' claimed the ginger clown. I cannot recall one decent chance England created, apart from Defoe's disallowed goal near the end, while some of the team looked scared to be out there. Rooney showed his petulant side by getting needlessly involved with Ben Haim and going into the referee's notebook. With a fourth blank in the past five games, many fans began to doubt that we could actually beat Andorra in a few days' time. Surely we would.

The immediate concern at the final whistle was whether we would get back through the airport before the 2 a.m. curfew. Due to security regulations, no flights are allowed to leave Tel Aviv after that hour and no exceptions are made to this rule even for royalty. But as the only other option was to leave fans hanging around the airport the security forces did everything in their power to ensure we got a clear passage from the stadium. No repeats of waiting in lay-bys for the pampered ones tonight. Straight to the airport, straight into the anticipated questions at security to check if we were true England fans, such as 'Why were you here?'; 'What football match have you been to?'; 'Is McClaren ever going to drop Lampard?' (I made the last one up) and other tough questions, but we made it and at 1 a.m. were ready to board the flight, apart from the crew who, of course, had not yet had their twelve hours' rest (and why is that, Paddy Doyle?). They eventually agreed to drag themselves from the Hilton next to the airport so that the fans could actually get home. We departed with minutes to spare before the curfew.

Of course you would expect to breeze through the airport if you landed at 5.35 a.m. on a Sunday at London Gatwick. Wrong. However, I was in bed by 7 a.m. as I had promised. CMF stirred as I slipped under the quilt, asking the killer question: 'So was it worth a ten-hour flight and a huge increase in the chances of suffering from DVT?' Er no, but at least I had a new stamp in my passport, memories of the warmth of the locals and a limited-edition 'Israel Loves Me' T-shirt, which in the words of a famous credit card was 'priceless'.

ENGLAND VERSUS THE SHEPHERDS

How one man can ruin English football within nine months

Andorra versus England was always destined to be a disaster. It shouldn't have been. We had beaten them comprehensively at Old Trafford a few months before and in recent years we had a good record of putting the smaller nations to the sword, including a 13-1 aggregate against San Marino in the build-up to the 1994 World Cup and a similar score versus Luxembourg a few years later. Managers always toe the line about 'there are no easy games in international football' but that is a lie. In the past couple of years Germany and Spain had both scored 13 in a single game against such countries as Malta and San Marino, and we should have scored more than double figures in our 2006 World Cup warm-up game against Jamaica. From the moment that England and Andorra were drawn in the same qualifying group 99.9 per cent of the population of the tiny principality sandwiched in the mountains between Spain and France wanted nothing to do with the game, and couldn't wait to see the match moved elsewhere. The other 0.1 per cent, the Andorran FA, saw only cash. Cash the travelling English fans would bring to the country by spending a fortune on duty-free alcohol and staying in the municipally owned hotels. Sod the fact their national stadium was in worse shape than Welling United's (no disrespect to Welling) but with a capacity of less than two thousand, including the temporary stands, it was never going to be played there. The precedent had been set in previous years when Andorra played both the Netherlands and the Irish in Barcelona.

The debates started about where the game would be played. Barcelona was the favourite, with the mini-Nou Camp the venue of choice. The thirty-thousand all-seater venue across the road from the main Nou Camp was home to Barça reserves and would be a perfect venue for the match. Perpignan was suggested as well (despite the fact that all they have is a rugby ground) and even San Sebastian in northern Spain got a mention. The decision was to be taken by UEFA in late November 2006. In the meantime every England fan seemed to have already booked flights and hotels to the Catalan capital. This was one trip where it would be easy to get a reasonably priced flight and hotel and almost everyone would be guaranteed a ticket. Seeing an opportunity to use up some airmiles earned through the family Nectar card, I booked flights with British Airways and secured a very nice suite at the Hotel Gran Marina, one of the city's newest five-star hotels.

And UEFA did not disappoint, deciding the game should be played in Barcelona; the surprise was that it would be staged at the Olympic Stadium, home of Espanyol. This meant everyone would be assured a ticket as the capacity was much bigger, although the Andorrans soon announced that the crowd would be restricted to thirty thousand, still more than enough to meet demand, but 26,000 under capacity. With the resultant huge sections lying empty the atmosphere would really suffer, although the fans could at least sit in the early evening spring sunshine to watch the game . . . or so we believed.

By the time the official ticket sale had ended, the twelve thousand EnglandFans who had expressed an interest had dwindled to just over nine thousand. Add to this a couple of thousand sold via the Andorran FA to non-EnglandFan members and it was starting to look like the game would be played in a venue that was far too big. The greedy Andorran Football Association were starting to lick their wounds. Perhaps they had a premonition as to how bad the game would actually be!

Barcelona is not one of my favourite places. It is a real dive. It's the only place I have been threatened, pickpocketed and ripped off on three separate occasions. The internet is full of horror stories of people being mugged, especially those who venture drunk down the dark alleys close to Las Ramblas, yet the likes of Lonely Planet and *Time Out* play down the problem, insisting it is limited to isolated areas in the city centre. It was always likely to be a petty crime bonanza, and the locals did not disappoint. From evidence I collected, one in every three fans who travelled had something nicked, were robbed or were simply attacked for the sake of it.

55

Arriving on the Tuesday afternoon, I immediately made my first mistake by getting a taxi from the airport instead of the train. Forty minutes later we ground to a halt in the post-siesta traffic with the taximeter the only thing moving. The driver gave a rundown on what the local press were saying about the England team, and how based on recent results they were becoming a bit of a laughing stock. Eventually we arrived at the beautiful hotel on the harbour's edge and it was straight to the bar, not bothering to risk a night out on my own. Most of my companions would not be arriving until the morning, and it was especially pleasing to be welcoming CMF off the early-morning flight to Girona thanks to a last-minute arrangement of some Little Fuller cover. The bar was full of the usual media darlings, including Terry Venables, Jamie Redknapp and Alan Shearer as well as a large delegation of UEFA officials; easy to spot as they were drinking Cristal campagne, obviously on expenses.

Barcelona conjures up an image of all-year-round sunshine. What joy it was to see on the day of the game weather more common to Blackpool with wind, rain and plummeting temperatures greeting fans arriving from the UK in just T-shirts and shorts.

Barcelona is served by three airports and on the day of the game they were full to bursting with UK flights. The main airport, El Prat, is about eight miles west of the city and is normally served by the flag carriers and Easyjet. Ryanair, of course, doesn't actually fly to the city despite its claims that it has two destinations for Barcelona. Barcelona Reus is the main airport on the Costa Brava, the original package tour destination, and serving classic resorts such as Tossa del Mar and Torremolinos. It is forty-five miles from the centre of Barcelona. Girona on the other hand is fifty miles to the north and actually closer to France than Barcelona. Ryanair put on extra flights to Girona; after all, if five hundred SLCs (Self Loading Cargos, as they are known) were willing to pay up to £400 for a return why would the company turn down £200,000?

Oh, how the fans must have laughed at Ryanair's decision to cancel two out of three of its Girona-bound flights, with fog the excuse for the first one, couldn't be arsed to carry a planeload of English fans the second. 'Never mind,' they said at Stansted. 'Fly to Perpignan (in France), Valencia (two hundred miles away) or Carcassonne (on the other side of the Pyrenees) instead as they are all nearby . . . or of course we will refund you your ticket, but not any match ticket or hotel.' Good old Ryanair. They have done so much for the spirits of England's travellers. The good news was that CMF's flight arrived on time despite the fog and to her surprise we were soon dodging the showers in the city centre.

The rain continued all day and this scuppered our plans to get the cable car from outside the hotel direct to the top of Montjuïc, the huge hill that dominates the city. It is one of the city's cultural centres and the location of the stadium used for the 1992 Olympic Games, as well as the National Museum and the Joan Miró Gallery.

Andorra 0 England 3 – Olímpic Lluís Companys – 28th March 2007

The rain continued to fall heavily and most fans who were located in the upper tiers of the open stand got soaking wet. To keep up pre-match spirits a couple of fans worked out how to access the flagpoles sitting on the concourse area, and so within minutes the UEFA and Andorran flags were replaced by St George crosses from Oldham and Hornchurch. And that was the highlight of the first half. It was the worst forty-five minutes of English football. Ever. To go in at half-time at 0-0 was an insult and should have led to immediate expulsion from the competition.

How any commentator could criticise the fans for booing that performance I will never know. Not one single player came out of the first half with any credit. Premier League players earning fifty times as much as their Andorran counterparts could not work out how to break down an organised yet unfit side.

It took nearly seventy minutes for England to break the deadlock, with the only player who could actually be bothered, Steven Gerrard, firing home. While history shows a 3-0 win, anyone who braved the cold, wet weather, the free-wheeling batons of the Spanish police (again, thanks FA officials for standing by and watching) and the annoying performance of the band will say that this was the most embarrassing performance in England's history. How the clown McClaren could walk away from that without apologising to the fans was a travesty, yet he criticised the people who paid to watch. The players were also critical of the fans, ignoring the fact that in the build-up the same players had called us 'the best fans in the world' – quote Gerrard, Lampard, Terry, etc. If you really feel so strongly, put your hands in those huge pockets and buy each fan who saw this embarrassing game a beer: eight thousand fans at £3 equals £32,000, which is half a week's wages for the likes of Rio Ferdinand.

The journey back to town saw everybody soaking wet and fed up at having wasted money on another spineless performance. The sensible option was to head for the Funicular to go down to Parallel – the reverse of the way we had reached the stadium – but being Spain this had closed at 10 p.m. and so a group of a hundred or so fans decided to find their own way down the hill, via the posh Miramar restaurant, through a villa and then across what can only be described as an allotment.

Barcelona – firmly established as one of the worst places I have visited. At least there would be no return for a few years, I thought, only for England to be drawn to play Andorra again in Barcelona in the qualifying for the 2010 World Cup in September 2009.

IT'S NOT ALL ABOUT THE CHOCOLATE

A weekend of cleanliness, efficiency and not a cuckoo clock in sight

A weekend in Switzerland is not everybody's idea of fun, but in June 2008, more than half a million fans descended on its four major cities to watch the European Championships. With typical Swiss efficiency, they had completed their preparations way in advance, with two new stadiums being built under budget in Zurich and Geneva and major redevelopments in Basle and Berne. It was time to take in a domestic game in those two cities to see how their plans were progressing.

Switzerland is full of anomalies. Landlocked in the heart of Europe, the country won sailing's America's Cup for the second consecutive time in 2007. They are fiercely proud of their heritage, yet do not have their own language. They are one of the financial powerhouses in Europe, yet have flatly refused to join the European Economic Union and they still use their own currency. And for a country that has been neutral in the past two world wars it is remarkable to think that their famous Swiss Guards have fiercely defended the honour of the Pope and the Vatican City for well over a century.

The plan was to fly into Basle Mulhouse Airport, which sits in a customs-free zone which is almost a country in its own right. Turn right as you exit the baggage hall and you will be in Switzerland. Turn left and you are in France with no way of turning back. One false move and you will end up like a real-life Terminal Man.

The airport is well served by a bus to the town centre, although why so many people would want to visit Basle is a mystery to me. It is clean and efficient, as you would expect, but there is very little to see or do. A couple of hours wandering around the centre taking in the Münster Cathedral and the bridge over the River Rhine and that is really about it. Wondering what to do with the next few hours before the football started I stumbled into the wonderful street of Steinentorstrasse, which has six Irish bars. I wondered if I had missed any sights to recommend. My guidebook was going to look very thin on the ground in terms of sightseeing, but there wasn't anything else.

My research would be done in the dry confines of Mr Pickwick's Pub. With a Carling in one hand, a bacon sandwich in the other and the Manchester derby just kicking off on the large-screen TVs, any thoughts of cultural highlights went out the window as I watched Michael Ball try and put his boot through Cristiano Ronaldo's chest. Sometimes life is good and this was one of those moments that could only have got better if Martine McCutcheon was to bring me another pint wearing her bottom-drawer finest.

Straight after this game the channel was changed and coverage switched to Upton Park, where West Ham had to beat Bolton Wanderers in their seemingly impossible quest to avoid relegation. I managed to watch the first half, leaving for the St Jakob stadium with the Hammers well in control of a must-win game. The transport network was really efficient as you expect from the Swiss. Ticket machines had English instructions, there were clear signs to show when the tram was coming and even 'football specials' that meant within fifteen minutes of leaving the pub I was at the stadium. The match ticket had been booked via the internet and I soon had it. It is worth putting a word of caution in here. Do not end up confusing the credit-card-style ticket with an airport car park ticket in your wallet. They look identical, but only one will work in the turnstiles at St Jakob. Insert the other and alarm bells start flashing and stewards appear within seconds and escort you away for interrogation. The good news, according to the prohibited items list, is that you are not allowed to take handguns into the stadium as it is 'expressly forbidden'. Presumably this does not apply to AK-47s or Uzis.

With building work still going on, and heavy rain falling, trying to avoid the puddles in the construction site outside the stadium was causing a major mess with fans trying to reach the entrances being forced to walk along walls to avoid a soaking. Inside the atmosphere was boisterous, and the concourses were packed. Trying to get a beer was impossible, so it was time to get to the upper tier for the kick-off.

FC Basle 2 FC Aarau 0 – St Jakob Stadium – 5th May 2007

The St Jakob Stadium is weird. From the outside it is hard to spot, as it is hidden behind a huge office block and supermarket, but inside it is unique. The stands are joined together, but are at different heights. The biggest was a three-tier structure similar in design to the main stand at Everton's Goodison Park, with supporting pillars causing some obstructed views. At either end the stands were two-tier, with the upper tier being quite small. The 'main stand' with its double-decker executive boxes was certainly unique. Think of that crap stand at Luton Town's Kenilworth Road that runs along the side of the pitch opposite the main stand and then imagine it sitting on top of a stand at Derby's Pride Park and you get the picture. The interesting aspect of this is that none of the boxes had balconies, meaning that the 'Corporate Bung' customers have their atmosphere in a vacuum, a great way to spend €1,000 a head listening to the game via a TV set.

The 'hardcore' Basle fans located in the east stand tried to make a noise, and did unfurl a couple of banners describing how they would like to get their hands on the away fans from the powerhouse that is FC Aarau. Their following must have its own Smart Car in which to drive to games! Were I an Aarau player I would be ashamed to clap when Laurel and Hardy (well one looked fat and the other was thin) greeted the entrance of the teams.

Going into the match, Basle were second in the league, six points behind leaders and reigning champions FC Zurich. With only a handful of games remaining victory over Aarau, who sat near to the bottom, was essential. With their blue and red seated stadium, blue and red 'halved' shirts and FCB logos everywhere, imitation was obviously the finest form of flattery although I can't see Barcelona being too bothered by their branding. Clearly inspired by one of the most clueless coaches ever to appear in England – step forward travelcard-holding ex-Spurs manager Christian Gross – the team started with a bang and soon had Aarau on the ropes. After six minutes a free kick was expertly curled around the wall and into the top corner to put Basle into the lead.

But despite pressing and pressing, and the news filtering through that FC Zurich were scoring goals for fun away from home, Basle couldn't score again. The referee (a spitting image of Tim Henman) tried to help, awarding a staggering thirty-seven free kicks to Basle in the second half, but the home team's own version of Clueless and Witless up front could not score. With ninety minutes on the clock Basle threw everyone forward, the winger fell over and with a sigh of relief Tim awarded the home team a penalty. Two-nil was a win after all but it was not convincing and would hardly send shivers down the necks of the team from Zurich.

Trams were lined up outside, and departing when full (take note please, Wembley: it is called crowd-flow management) I found myself in the suburb of Muttzer where my hotel, 'only a five-minute walk from the stadium' according to their website, was located. It might have been that quick to walk but it took fifteen minutes by tram! The hotel certainly wasn't central as described on the web. I like peace and quiet, especially away from home, but this was taking it to the extreme. Imagine Amersham High Street, with antique shops and small cafes, at 7 a.m. on a Sunday morning and you will get the picture of life in Muttzer on a Saturday night. However a bed is a bed and it was clean and who needs the adult channel when the bedtime viewing is the Masters Snooker on Eurosport on a tiny portable TV with German commentary?

Skip forward eleven hours and, refreshed and rested, I was on my way to Berne on a fine example of how train travel should be managed. The great thing about Swiss trains is that they are clean, run on time and link the major cities, but the downside is that they are not cheap. They took £40 off me for a return.

Good things are said about Berne, the capital of Switzerland, although there was a worry that it would be on the quiet side. Arriving at 10 a.m. on a Sunday in the capital of a country that is hardly known as lively was a concern.

There were four hours to kill before kick-off so I reckoned it was possible to see everything the city had to offer and enjoy a big Sunday lunch. A detour was made into the Tourist Information Centre at the railway station, more for a better look at someone, best described as Michelle Marsh's twin sister, who worked there and seemed happy that queues of men were asking for the same information, thus requiring her to bend down to get a map from the bottom drawer and then lean across the counter to show the route.

I left with a smile and the infamous 'Berne Tourist Guide', basically a do-it-yourself walking map that takes in all the main sites in less than two hours. And I saw them all. Historic buildings lined with colonnades, nineteenth-century churches, soft porn photo shoots and bear pits. Yes the latter two are correct. Obviously this must be a common thing in Berne as the locals passed by oblivious to two semi-naked girls being photographed posing in a fountain in the old town. The visitors to the city were obvious to spot – they were the ones watching the shoot's progress, and giving handy advice, such as 'get 'em off'. As for the bear pit, follow the old town main street, Kampgasse, down over the absurdly pretty old town bridge and there it is, outside the tourist information centre. A bear pit with two fully grown brown bears wandering around and ignoring tourists taking pictures. Apparently they are the symbols of the city, and there have been bears within the city boundaries for more than two hundred years.

The old town was fantastic, though. A Friday night out there must be memorable as almost every cellar space has been converted into a bar, meaning that there would be little down time when wandering from bar to bar. Unfortunately Sunday lunchtime drinking isn't that popular in Switzerland and the doors remained firmly shut. Nevertheless, I did stumble on the Rosti restaurant, which was quoted in the guidebook as serving the finest example of this national dish of flaked potato, onions and cheese in Switzerland. The restaurant served more than thirty different varieties including sweet and savoury versions, and on this Sunday lunchtime it was packed with tourists.

Fully refreshed, it was time to head north to the best-named stadium in Europe, the Wankdorf. Obviously slightly embarrassed by the attention the stadium would get in 2008 for the European Championships, the authorities had officially renamed it the 'Stade de Suisse'. Although much smaller than the Basle ground, it is the national stadium, and the preferred home for the Swiss team. Glittering in the early summer sunshine, it looked more like a fancy exhibition hall or shopping centre from the outside. Oh hang on, this is Switzerland: of course, it was a shopping centre!

Young Boys Berne 1 St Gallen 1 – Stade de Suisse – 6th May 2007

Now clearly, with an average attendance fewer than fourteen thousand, the club needed to come up with ideas to boost attendances. Whoever thought of Ladies' Day should get some credit for imagination. However, having the stewards dressed in black tie did not endear them to the ladies who bothered to turn up. An ugly man dressed like James Bond is still an ugly man, and would only improve if each female was given a free bottle of Lambrini. The official stadium presenter, looking as comfortable as Jodie Marsh at a Mensa meeting in his cheap suit, had to present the show from the middle of the pitch.

The stadium was very smart on the inside, if a bit sterile. It was more pristine than FC Basle's newer redeveloped ground and certainly more uniform with a simple two-tier square construction. From a seat in the lower tier the views were good and facilities on the concourses were plentiful, meaning fans could queue up to get their beer and food without missing the action.

The game promised to be good, too, with Young Boys Berne sitting in third place, one above the visitors, St Gallen, There was no time to visit the club shop beforehand to check if they had T-shirts proclaiming support for the team (somehow I cannot see the 'I love Young Boys' shirts taking off here!).

The stadium also boasts one of the new generation of artificial pitches, used as an ice rink during the winter when they flood the 'grass'. You would have expected the home team to have mastered the bounce of the ball, but it was the visitors who took advantage of mistake after mistake as the Young Boys defenders misread the bounce, although none of the chances were converted.

Switzerland's most famous international is Hakan Yakin, a striker of Turkish descent, recognisable by his Valentinoesque pencil moustache and lanky hair. He was picked out by the St Gallen defenders for special treatment and fouled time and time again. The first really bad challenge resulted in Yakin retaliating, first kicking a St Gallen player, then pushing him in the face. The referee decided he deserved a mild talking to. Two minutes later an appeal for a penalty from a St Gallen player was met with a straight red card for dissent, much to the disgust of the away team bench.

In the end a 1-1 was a fair result, with the St Gallen fans happy to set off a flare or two, actions which, of course, it being Switzerland and a Sunday, were met with shhh's from the home end. It was time to reverse the route back to Basle Mulhouse airport, completed in less than ninety minutes, which left enough time for a pit stop at the Sports Bar which was showing highlights from the rest of the Premier League weekend matches.

So what did I learn about Switzerland that I didn't already know? Transport good, stadiums good (certainly functional – nothing eye-catching like some of Portugal's stadiums in Euro 2004 or Germany's in World Cup 2006), food good, beer good, access to soft porn for free good and not a single sign of a cuckoo clock, which can't be bad.

Berne certainly won my vote as one of the best-preserved cities in Europe, and a perfect Valentine's Day idea, especially if the photo shoot was a regular Sunday morning event. Next time I might be brave and try the Apple and Potato Rosti with chocolate sauce – how very Swiss.

CHAPTER
11
CHAPTER

RUBBER STANDS AND DANISH BACON

Not all the best stuff is exported you know

In January 2007 my company acquired another business in Copenhagen. The merger was complicated in that a number of key IT systems, as well as staff, would have to be integrated as quickly as possible. As the responsibility for the new division was mine it meant spending a couple of days a week in the capital of cool. While the snow was falling on my first trip to Denmark it was a pleasure to see we had inherited a workforce full of passion for the beautiful game. And they didn't only know about their domestic game. They knew more about the Premier League than me!

Now, any city where the three main exports are beer, bacon and tall blondes can't be a bad place, as long as they keep some of the trio back for themselves. In my regular trips I experienced plenty of the first two, and a little bit of the third, but obviously only from a distance and no touching of course!

As winter turned into spring and the evenings started getting warmer, the talk turned to going to a game with the boys from the office. The Danish Superliga was not due to start until late March but as soon as the fixtures were announced I was invited to attend games with the blue half of the office (the Brøndby fans) and the white half of the office (the FC Copenhagen fans).

When May arrived it was obvious the title was going down to the final few weeks of the season, with one fixture standing out more than others: the final Copenhagen derby to be played at the Brøndby Stadium in late May.

Traditionally, Brøndby are seen as a middle-class team, where as FCK (as Copenhagen are more commonly known) are from the lower-class northern suburbs. In reality they are both clubs created for the city's convenience. Brøndby were formed in 1964 and financed by the city council for years in an attempt to foster a team with a chance in Europe, but despite moderate domestic success, they failed to make an impact. So the council decided to take a number of smaller suburban clubs and turn them into a 'super-club', basing them at the underused Parken national stadium. That is how FC Kopenhavn or FCK were formed.

In the fifteen years since their formation, the championship has been won by either Brøndby or FCK on all but one occasion. Who says money doesn't buy success? However, European rewards have been elusive, and the closest either has come has been occasional appearance in the Champions League group stages.

The 2006–7 season was a nightmare for the blue half of the city. They started losing early on and going into the final months they were sixth, with no hope of European football. Brøndby's season was best remembered for them having three coaches by the start of April. FCK, on the other hand, had led the way since day one, and coming into the final derby needed just three points to secure another championship. Everyone in the city was up for this as you might imagine. Well, not quite. Most people seemed more interested in the Chelsea versus Manchester United game that would decide the Premier League title.

The local media talked up the local game, though, and reported that Brøndby fans were going to unfurl banners and T-shirts saying 'The blood of the reds would flow on the pitch'. But in practice it turned out to be as tame as a West Ham/Fulham derby.

Quite a crowd from the office had arranged to go but only Big Ben and I were brave enough to get a ticket in the Faxe Tribune, home of the most fanatical supporters. Since the merger Ben has headed up one of our operational divisions in Denmark, and being an avid Spurs fan he was used to supporting lost causes and a team constantly in disarray. Not surprising then that he had adopted Brøndby, although it seemed more to do with a young woman in the office he was trying to impress. Especially as he lived no more than a five minute walk from FCK's stadium.

IF Brøndby 0 FC Copenhagen 1 – Brøndby Stadium – 9th May 2007

As we arrived at the stadium at 6 p.m., there were bored policemen with riot vans everywhere although there were also many families with yellow-and-blue-decked children. Hardly the volatile and hostile atmosphere that was promised. The stadium looked very neat. The phrase 'English stadium' is used a lot, but in this case it is true. A completely enclosed, two-tiered arena with a terrace behind one goal made it look similar to Pride Park or The Riverside.

On the far side is a new supporters' cafe bar, '1964', a good place to start the evening. Inside, booths had been fashioned as mock-ups of the bench, and a decent selection of Carlsberg and bacon sandwiches kept the interest, all the while watching Swedish women's football on TV.

Now let's clear up the beer and bacon mystery. Copenhagen has been the home of Carlsberg for something like two hundred years. Not only are five versions of the beer available almost anywhere in the city, you can also get the strong Elephant beer in most bars, and it does taste better than in England. But bacon is a different story. Apparently they export all the good stuff and eat the crap at home, and because it is so bad they burn it to a crisp. So asking for a bacon sandwich in a cafe will leave you very disappointed and not even a lake of tomato ketchup will save the day.

After toying with the idea of getting a good place by leaving the bar and going in early, we did the usual English thing of staying for one more pint, thinking there would be no more beer for a couple of hours while the game was on. But, of course, this was Denmark and not the English nanny state. Beer had been on sale inside the stadium since 6 p.m. and there were no restrictions on being able to take drinks onto the terrace.

With a sausage in one hand and a Carlsberg in the other, we reached the terrace, which was literally bouncing with an atmosphere I had not experienced for years at an English football match. It was not the first time I had been to Brøndby. In 2000 CMF and I had spent a night in Copenhagen when Lolly was just a few weeks old. The trip coincided with one of Brøndby's rare Champions League campaigns and they were playing IF Reykjavik in the qualifying rounds. They were two-thirds of the way through the stadium redevelopment at the time and it looked as if they were about to kick on in terms of domestic domination, only to make a succession of poor investments off the pitch that almost drove the club to the wall.

The Brøndby fans were well up for the game, leading chants which seemed very English both in terms of words and tunes, meaning we were able to join in and look the part with scarves wrapped around our faces and hooded tops pulled up.

Not that the plan was to look like hooligans (as the *Daily Express* tried to make out in an article in June 2008 about English fans travelling abroad to get their kicks) but because it was freezing. Of course Scandinavia is cold but it was May, a season that normally sees the more hardened Danes strip off to swim in the harbour. The crowd tried to get the team going but they seemed to have already conceded defeat to their deadly rivals and it was no surprise when FCK took the lead halfway through the first half thanks to former Aston Villa striker, Marcus Allbäck.

The game petered out, and once the final flare had been extinguished the lights went out on any challenge Brøndby might have had. No blood was spilt on the final whistle although the FCK celebrations of another title were muted. Indeed it all seemed a bit cordial on the pitch, with not one card being brandished in the ninety minutes.

Back to the sports bar for another couple of beers while awaiting the taxi to take us home. It had certainly been an interesting evening, and one of the most atmospheric derbies I had been to. The locals were passionate but I was left with the impression that despite the noise feeding down from the terraces the players were just going through the motions. On the way back to the airport the following day, chatting with the driver, a big FCK fan, I was berated for choosing 'those bastards' as my team. 'They are just jealous of our success and our stadium,' he told me. So that would be the stadium that was built for the national team, and the success where you were able to buy any Danish player in the league without objection. He must have been jealous because we've nicked all his bacon.

THREE COUNTRIES IN ONE DAY FOR €1

A day in central Europe dodging the addicts and ticket inspectors

Sometimes, despite all the careful planning, things go wrong on these trips. Not spectacularly wrong, more off course. I am quite anal when it comes to the preparations. With a bookcase full of maps and guides, I make sure before travelling to a new destination that I am armed with the information needed to get from A to B, via C if necessary. I also try to sort out the Plan A route from the airport to the final destination, as well as a back-up so there is no need to get out a map and look a) like a tourist and b) prime for the taking by some of Europe's lowlife.

But it seems no matter how complex the planning, sometimes a few basics can be overlooked which can cause pain. For instance, once I planned a night in Madrid to watch Atletico only to arrive late on a major saint's day, meaning public transport had shut for the night, as had, it seemed, every restaurant and bar in the city. Not ideal when you haven't eaten for nearly twenty-four hours.

But even I had an inkling that this trip to Vienna had the capacity for cock-up. The concept was simple. A trip to watch Austria against Paraguay in order to research the Ernst Happel Stadium, which would host the final of the European Championships just over a year later. However, the route was not exactly straightforward. Due to the ridiculous prices being charged by the flag carriers to go direct I decided to take advantage of Ryanair's 'Stupendous Summer Sizzler' fare of €1 (plus the appropriate taxes and extras of course) and fly to Bratislava, the capital of Slovakia.

At least Ryanair had not taken to calling this airport 'Vienna–Bratislava' like another budget airline, although it is nearer Vienna than some of their other locations are to their supposed destinations, such as Frankfurt Hahn, Stockholm Vasteras and Paris Beauvais.

Never having been to Slovakia, and as the Austria game was not kicking off until 5 p.m., I was looking forward to a few hours in Bratislava.

Ryanair's daily flight to Bratislava is one of the first of the morning to depart London Stansted airport. But how wrong it would be to think that nobody would be at the airport at 4.30 a.m. In fact it's worth a bet that the two hours from 4.30 a.m. are the busiest of the day in terms of numbers of people. Gone, as well, are the days when you would be one of a handful of people on a flight, as with flights to exotic destinations like Brno, Kaunas and Lodz (Czech Republic, Lithuania and Poland to the uninitiated) the flight was more than eighty per cent full.

The passengers were split into three categories:

Firstly the Stags and Hens. Off to one of the new breed of weekend 'party' destinations where they would be met at the airport by stretch limos with strippers, go on pub crawls to such unusual pubs as the Golden Lion, Molly Malone's and Chasers, all accompanied by strippers, of course, before ending up in a private club where the stag/hen would be tied to a chair on a stage with strippers pretending to go into a sexual frenzy, lusting over Sharon/Dave/Wayne or whatever the name of the twenty-stone bride/groom might be. You can spot them on the flight as they order alcohol as soon as the trolley arrives and start taking photos of each other ('Here's one of me trying to get the stewardess into the toilet while she poured hot water down my shorts'). They will be dressed in matching shirts with humorous titles on the back such as 'fat slag', 'sex machine' and 'big boobs'.

The second group are those who are flying home. They tend to be badly dressed, in a foul mood and will also start drinking as soon as they can get their hands on those 'Bullseye Baggies' that are subliminally marketed as soon as you board any Ryanair flight.

The final group has taken advantage of a bargain €1 flight, and is now counting the cost of those 'additional' fees and taxes such as Passenger Tax, Airport Tax, Fuel Duty and Ryanair Christmas Party Fund, car parking at Stansted, which starts from a bargain £17.80 for ten hours, plus breakfast at this ridiculous hour and realising it would have been cheaper to have spent the day at Alton Towers.

Fast forward two hours and we were touching down in, for me, another new country, making it forty-three by my reckoning. Then came the first problem. While many smaller airports have tried as much as possible to 'integrate' the arrival of planes full of Brits with bulging wallets, Bratislava gave the impression it couldn't care less. In fact I don't think I saw a smiling person all day in Slovakia. After passing through passport control and collecting a bag from the unmanned luggage area you arrive into what it best described as a small atrium. There are no English signs, nor is there anywhere to get local currency apart from a dodgy-looking cashpoint.

Through a process of deduction I found a bus stop, from where the thrice-hourly bus ran into the city centre. Tickets could be purchased only by feeding coins into an adjacent ticket machine. But, of course, I had no local currency. There was no way I was going to take a taxi and be ripped off so early in the trip. I needed Slovakian change.

The man in the small kiosk beside the bus stop wouldn't change or even accept Euros and as the currency exchange inside the terminal was shut I was stuck. Obviously sensing my predicament, a local offered to exchange 30 Slovakian Koruny for €10, which, based on quick mental calculations, seemed about right. He also gave me some coins to buy a bus ticket. What a nice man.

The bus set off for the city centre. After about one hundred yards an American guy asked if I changed money from the 'bloke with the funny eyes'. I replied in the affirmative and told him the rate – 3SKR to the Euro. Oh how I laughed when he revealed that the official rate was ten times that and for the €10 I had got the equivalent of 80p worth of local currency instead of £8 worth. I thanked my lucky stars it was €10 and not €50.

The bus went around the airport commercial centre, a place that would do the likes of Bluewater and Lakeside proud with an IKEA, Marks & Spencer, Nike, Next and a host of other big-name shops, contrasted by huge industrial manufacturing chimneys in the background. Then I noticed something odd. While the place was busy with Saturday morning shoppers, no one appeared to be carrying bags. Was it that people came to window shop before trudging back to their gloomy industrial tower blocks content with a free day out as we would go to a museum, or do they save for a power spending spree later in the day?

Bratislava has three main stadiums and the first stop on the mission to photograph them was the Pasienky Stadium, home to Inter Bratislava.

The area around it is very pleasant, or so I thought. Lots of parkland, which on this sunny early summer's day was filling with scantily-clad young women, all on their own and wandering around aimlessly. They also seemed very friendly, smiling and waving as if I was some long-lost love. I stopped for a couple of pictures of classic eastern European architecture and stood on some plastic, which cracked underfoot. I was standing on a pile of syringes.

Then I saw one lovely young lady, sitting on the grass no more than a hundred yards away, sticking a syringe into her peachy buttocks. It was time for the Lonely Planet guide, which stated that the Pasienky Park close to the railway station of the same name was the home of 'thieves, crackheads and drug-riddled prostitutes and is best avoided at all times of the day'. What a great place to start the sightseeing. So much for checking beforehand.

Huge floodlights dominated the skyline and after reaching them I was able just to wander into the stadium, as is possible with most European grounds at weekends. It was neat, bedecked in yellow and black with an athletics track, but you could not get away from the massive floodlights that seemed far too large for the ground.

After being one of the strongest teams from Czechoslovakia in the 1950s and 1960s, Inter had gone through a rough patch. They had won the Slovakian league in 2000 and 2001 but since then suffered a couple of relegations and when I visited were in the second level of Slovakian football.

Just across the road is the Tehelné Pole Stadium, home to Slovan Bratislava, FC Artmedia's European matches and the national team. It was here in 2003 that the England fans and players alike were racially abused, an incident swept under the table by UEFA. The stadium is similar in design to Dinamo Moscow's with one large two-tier stand towering over the three remaining stands, only one of which offers cover from the cruel Slovakian weather. It can hardly be called atmospheric.

Two thirds of the mission achieved after being in the city for just an hour. All that was needed now was to find the Petržalka Stadium, home of the new Slovakian champions, ArtMedia. A tram, full of scowling locals showing their displeasure because they thought I did not have a ticket, went to the old town. It was such a shame as the locals are stunning. If

73

there was that quality of women on trains from New Eltham to London Bridge in the morning no one would complain about standing. But here they just didn't want to smile. The sun was shining, it was the weekend and they were stunning, but a pair of sunglasses and a frown is not a good look.

Escaping from the tram as soon as possible for fear of being lynched, I crossed the Danube to find ArtMedia's home. The club came to prominence after dazzling performances in Europe. In 2005 they almost reached the knockout stages of the Champions League, after putting out holders Porto to earn a place in the UEFA Cup. The stadium isn't fit to hold European games as it has no floodlights, which is strange. They had redeveloped the stands, making it a smart little venue holding just over eight thousand. Again, it was open for all to wander in and the team were having a training session before an end of season tournament. With a cold beer in hand it was the perfect place for a thirty-minute break.

From here it was a walk to the south station to get a train to Vienna. The walk was through an area of the city named after the stadium, Petržalka. Hindsight is a wonderful thing, and with it I would have known that Petržalka actually means 'the biggest council estate in Europe'. Not the best place to be walking around wearing an England tracksuit top and carrying a map.

But, not one to miss a shortcut, I ploughed straight through the middle. While it doesn't compete with some places in Madrid or Barcelona for poverty (believe me there is real poverty there if you look for it), it is rough. The gangs of youths hanging around obviously couldn't believe someone was walking brazenly through their 'hood' and it must be assumed that I survived because they thought I was some kind of bait from a rival bigger gang. The weirdest thing was that on the edge of the ghetto, developers had built a brand new residential complex complete with upmarket shops and cafes to match flats that would not look out of place in London's Canary Wharf. You know the type of buildings: smart flats with balconies, wide 'boulevards' with trees and pavement restaurants. Surprisingly no one was eating outside despite it being 1 p.m. and twenty-five degrees.

Finally reaching the station in one piece, I booked an €8 ticket to Vienna, a journey which would take around an hour. In order to board the trains you have to pass through passport control and customs as technically you are leaving for another country; the concept of free travel within EU states must have been missed by the authorities in Slovakia. Although, as this happens for the Eurostar at St Pancras, I couldn't really complain. My camera case was viewed with suspicion in case I might be exporting exotic animals or the like.

The great thing about the train is that in the space of ten minutes it passes from Slovakia into Hungary before crossing into Austria, and as there were stops in all three I reckoned that for less than €1 you could pass between the three countries.

The plan on arriving in Vienna was similar to that for Bratislava. Check out a couple of the bigger club stadiums before heading over to the Ernst Happel in the Prater Park for the game against Paraguay. I had concocted a fiendishly simple itinerary that would mean visiting five stadiums in three hours, having lunch, then going to the game, for which I had managed to secure media accreditation from the very helpful Austrian Football Association. Unfortunately the closure for maintenance of the main S-Bahn line around the city meant Plan A went out of the window. Time for Plan B and within twenty minutes I was trying to find an open gate at the stadium of FK Austria Wien, the 2007 Austrian cup holders and Vienna's second biggest team, which is located on the main ring road around the city. Unfortunately, my luck ran out for the first time on the trip. There was no way in. When this happens it is always deflating, as if you've been cheated in travelling so far without success, although it isn't really a big deal. However, surely the next stop, the Gerhard Hanappi Stadium, home of Rapid Vienna, would yield reward.

A bus and a U-Bahn ride later and I walked into the sunshine outside the railway station to find fans. Not one or two, but hundreds. It was 3.30 p.m., a full ninety minutes before the Paraguay game was due to start on the other side of the city. Undeterred I marched down the road towards the stadium.

As each step hit the ground I realised with increasing embarrassment that I had screwed up and that this small stadium with a capacity of less than twenty thousand was in fact the venue for the game I had come to see and not, as the whole trip had been planned around, the Ernst Happel Stadium. It wasn't a disaster. There was a worry I would not have enough time to enjoy the media accreditation and facilities that go with it, but I had meticulously planned the trip to visit the national stadium, and so to tick off another Euro 2008 venue. Still, having picked up the pass and grabbed a free beer, a free burger and a free Rapid Vienna fans' pack I settled into the padded seat to watch the Austrians try to beat Paraguay.

Austria 0 Paraguay 0 – Gerhard Hanappi Stadium – 2nd June 2007

Despite this being an international, the media area was sparsely populated. It was very evident from recent friendly results and the lack of confidence within the media present that if it wasn't for hosting the 2008 event, there would be no chance of this team competing in a major tournament any time soon. They had lost to a young and inexperienced Scottish team a few days previously, and their squad was very low on confidence. With fixtures lined up against stronger opposition in the coming months it was important for the sanity of the fans, and the Austrian football authorities, that they end the season with a win against a team ranked lower than them in the FIFA world rankings.

The tunnel doubled as the mixed zone (also known as 'the gauntlet of hate' by players and managers alike), where the press are allowed to question players as they return to the dressing room from the pitch, was without doubt the shortest I have experienced. It was twenty-three steps from entering the stadium to leaving the tunnel. This was a stadium that had hosted Champions League football in the past when Rapid Vienna were the most successful club in Austrian football, winning the Austrian title on a record thirty-two occasions.

The stadium is quite unusual for central Europe and a real departure from those visited earlier in the day. It had four separate stands, each of which was single-tier and covered with seats which looked as if they had been installed in the 1920s. They were among the most uncomfortable I had ever experienced. A number of the press had obviously been here before as they had brought huge cushions, concealed within their laptop cases.

What was strange was that in order to leave the press box it was necessary to walk in front of the away dugout and down the tunnel, which was fine in the hour leading up to kick-off, but what was the etiquette during play? Would a journalist be allowed to walk across the technical area? After an overindulgence on the free drink in the media area I was now in desperate need of the gents, which, of course, was back down the tunnel. After holding out as long as possible, I saw another member of the press leave his seat, and decided that following him would be the best course of action.

A great plan, except that this particular member of the media was not really a member of the media. He was part of the Paraguayan coaching team who had been watching the game from the stand and now wanted to relay a message to the bench. This left me standing in front of their bench while the coach took his seat. Faced with the stares of a dozen South Americans I mumbled an apology in German and ran off down the tunnel.

There wasn't much worth seeing in the few minutes I was away. In fact there was no need to have bothered being there at all for the first half. I could have written a load of made-up rubbish about the Austrian defensive performance, and the lack of firepower from the Paraguayans, as a number of the local media had been doing by the looks of the empty beer glasses around them in the media area.

However, the second half did liven up a bit. Austria's goalkeeper, the fantastically named Jürgen Macho, who had a couple of successful seasons with Sunderland, was the busier of the two keepers, having to make a number of good saves. But the whole game was played at a really pedestrian pace.

Paraguay were in between tournaments, a year on from their disappointing performance in Germany in the 2006 World Cup Finals, and with the Copa America just around the corner, while Austria appeared to be content that they were going to be playing in Euro 2008, not really caring if they won a single point. They had no attacking threat and you got the feeling that they could have played all night against West Ham's back four and still not scored!

I stayed behind for a while to see if it was possible a) to think up a decent question to ask a player, and then b) to try and translate the question into German. Fortunately when I grabbed non-playing Alex Manninger he saw from my accreditation I was from London and immediately reverted to English. After some pleasantries, I asked him about his time at Arsenal and what he thought of their chances in Europe that season. He took a deep breath before simply saying 'shit', and then wandered off. Hardly the scoop of the year. *World Soccer* wouldn't be paying much for that exclusive.

So it was time to reverse the route back through Hungary to Slovakia. On reaching the Südbahnhof I worked out from a rough translation that the trains back to Bratislava were delayed, although according to my O-level German it was due to a clown on the line. The train was eventually held up by an hour, meaning I was pushing it to make the return flight to Stansted.

I had managed to change €50 into 1600 Slovakian Koruny in Bratislava earlier in the day and so far it had paid for lunch, three beers, a book on Slovakian football, a one-day transport pass and a return train trip to Vienna. But after clearing immigration back into Slovakia was there enough for a taxi to the airport?

I really had no choice as public transport would have not got there on time, and I did not fancy my chances of trying to find a bed for the night near the airport.

The negotiations with the one and only taxi driver outside Bratislava's railway station went like this:

'Airport – how much?'

'Airport – yes we have airport'

'I know but how much to get there?'

'No bus there only taxi.'

'Yes I know – how much?'

'Five Hundred.'

'Three hundred – is that right?'

'No, four hundred . . .'

And so off we went at breakneck speed, reaching the airport in less than fifteen minutes and with just 200 Koruny on the clock. Of course, he didn't charge this lower rate but at least he became the first Slovakian to give me a smile all day.

It had been a long and tiring day – five football stadiums, three countries, two transgressions of the law through not buying a tram ticket and one near lynching in one of the roughest areas in Europe. It was all topped off by Ryanair's fantastic punctuality record which saw the inbound flight land only thirty-four minutes late. Was it worth it? Yes – after all, how many people can say they have spent a Saturday like that? And how many had spent €1 so economically?

FOOTBALL, ONLY MORE POLITE

No stereotypes, just football played to the tune of Abba

In my quest to see a game in every European country I left Sweden off the agenda for far too long. My love of everything Swedish is well known within the Fuller family. Any visitor to the Fuller Estate in south London would be forgiven for thinking they had stumbled into the pages of a well-known out-of-town flatpack furniture catalogue. There are at least two items I have toiled to put together in each room. Add to this an iTunes library with such classics as Abba, Roxette and, of course, Ace of Base and you can see that I should have been called Sven rather than Stuart.

In July 2000 a great fanfare surrounded the opening of the Øresund bridge/tunnel, which linked Copenhagen to Malmö in one swish structure, thus joining two arch-enemies. Technically it is the longest border crossing in the world, and one of the most impressive feats of construction Europe has ever seen.

Denmark and Sweden are similar in many ways, but they will never admit it. The people are mostly blonde and blue-eyed; they have the same currency (although a different flavour of Kroner/Kronor); they love a beer and they are both prohibitively expensive to visit. Working in Copenhagen for nearly six months, I had been negligent in arranging a trip across the bridge. The journey across the bridge from Copenhagen city centre takes less than twenty minutes, and although it's not cheap it could be done in a few hours after work and before flying home. Of course, the real reason for not making the trip was that the Swedish football season had not yet started. After all, there is no point visiting somewhere new unless you go to a game, right? Or is that just me? So, in early June, with the sun shining late into the evening, we arranged to take in a game in Malmö.

You can almost see Malmö from Copenhagen. It is a hazy silhouette in the distance, past the nuclear power station. Sleepy little Malmö. Once in Malmö it is immediately apparent how neat and tidy everything is. That's not to say Copenhagen is messy, but the city's huge amount of redevelopment means cranes and building sites tend to obscure the image of 'Wonderful Copenhagen'. Malmö has well-manicured lawns, an absence of graffiti, and with pedestrians and cyclists alike waiting for red lights to change it was certainly an eye-opener.

Relations between Sweden and Denmark have never been completely cordial. Four hundred years ago, Denmark ruled most of the area that is now south-eastern Sweden, and it wasn't until the Battle of Helsingborg in 1710 that the Danes were pushed across the Øresund for the last time. Today, the Danes visit on a daily basis to stock up on food, which is much cheaper in Sweden; indeed, due to land taxes, many Danes actually relocate across the water and commute back to their homeland to work.

Events took a turn for the worse between the two countries in June 2007 when a European Championship qualifying game in Copenhagen had to be abandoned after a Danish fan ran on to the pitch and attacked the referee. To make matters worse, the Swedes went on to qualify from the group, while the Danes had to play their next few games outside Copenhagen.

Interest in the trip from the Copenhagen office was high, especially from the English contingent. Big Ben was up for another game, having survived the Copenhagen derby a few weeks previously. We were to be joined by Alex, also known as the Big Man (well, he has a beard, speaks in tongues and is very tall). He was over from London on a marketing mercy mission, and had never been to a football game. He wasn't sure initially but as he would have no one to drink with after work, and we promised him that alcohol would be served in the stadium, he agreed to come with us.

We managed to hitch a lift across the bridge with one of the said Danish refugees and even managed to convince our driver to take us to a bar close to the stadium. A drive past the iconic Malmö stadium, voted one of Sweden's finest architectural structures, ninety minutes before kick-off didn't fill us with confidence. It didn't look like a hotbed of football. In fact the presence of a team coach was the only visible sign that a game was going to start soon. Even the bars close to the ground were empty. While food is cheaper in Sweden, alcohol certainly isn't. The Swedes are one of the most heavily taxed nations in this area although some antics I have seen suggest that government policy isn't quite working. We scoffed at people in Denmark when they told us the beer in Sweden was 'expensive'. The Danes had warned us we would pay more than 500 Danish Kroner for a beer (about £4.50) but armed with Swedish Kronor and another currency rate to understand we couldn't work out if we had paid 50 pence, £5 or £50 for our first beer.

However, a couple of pints in the sunshine watching the world go by was enough to make us ignore the third world debt that was being run up, especially as the waitress kept the beer flowing with a smile and a wink. However, with the game fast approaching we opted for one more and found our supposed five-minute walk to the stadium was more like a twenty-minute hike.

The stadium is in the south of the city centre in a pleasant park. The local council had just allocated funding for a brand new stadium to be built behind the current ground. However, with little noise coming from inside the stadium we assumed that they must be waiting for us to double the attendance.

A bargain 110 Swedish Kronor (£8 or £80 – still not sure) got us through the turnstiles and we were met with a crowd that filled at least half its thirty thousand capacity.

FC Malmö 0 Kalmar FF 2 – Malmö Stadium – 14th June 2007

There were no fans where we were drinking in the city centre, and ninety minutes previously the stadium had been deserted, so where had everyone come from? And where was the crowd noise? Down one side the Malmö fans stood shoulder to shoulder underneath their flags with slogans like 'Malmö Massive' and 'No One Likes Us'. This being Sweden, where everyone is so polite, you almost expected a sign underneath saying 'and that is really upsetting'. The only noise was polite clapping when something exciting happened such as a throw-in.

The stadium is certainly unique in design. Built for the 1958 World Cup finals, it has lots of curves and corners. From a distance the main stand looks like a huge white wave, with its upper tier curving down to a point at each end. It is also one of the only stands I have seen which has a single row of seats at each corner. Behind each goal there was a bank of terracing, set back from the pitch by an athletics track. While the stadium was busy, the ends were empty and we delighted in the fact that beer was being served from an open bar.

This being a football match with 'hardcore' fans you would have expected queues around the block. Not in Malmö. Everyone seemed happy to sit and watch the game, so we took the opportunity to have a beer and a burger. Great plan – except the burgers were organic reindeer and the beer was non-alcoholic. The Big Man was inconsolable.

Not only was it his first match but we had promised him real beer. He saw through the ruse in a flash and started remonstrating with anyone and everyone when we handed him a pint of evil. When he started having a go at Europe's 'The Final Countdown' as another reason why Sweden was crap it was time to bring out the emergency vodka that we had in a coat pocket for such occasions.

The football was pedestrian to say the least. The visitors, Kalmar FF, came to Malmö sitting on top of the table and they looked like league leaders. Malmö were content to play the ball around the midfield without any idea how to break down the visitors' defence. Malmö are the only Swedish club to have reached a European Cup Final, when in 1979 they lost to Nottingham Forest in Munich's Olympic Stadium. The club were given the Svenska Dagbladet, the gold medal named after a top Swedish newspaper which goes to the country's outstanding sporting achievement in the year, and they are the only football club to have been awarded this honour. They have won the Swedish Allsvenskan on eighteen occasions, although the last time was in 2004.

With fifteen minutes on the clock, the visitors took the lead with a well-worked free kick from the edge of the penalty area that seemed to baffle all eleven Malmö players. Surely Malmö would build a defensive wall? But no, so it was no surprise that Kalmar scored.

Five minutes after the break it was 2-0 as Kalmar beat a non-existent offside trap and made light work of a three-versus-two overlap to reinforce why they were on top of the league.

Kalmar have never been a major force in Swedish football. In fact their highest league finish was second in 1985, and apart from a couple of Swedish Cup wins in the 1980s, they made little impact on the domestic game until 2007 when they had built a solid defence and started scoring goals for fun.

After the second goal went in the Big Man went back to the bar, only to return looking shocked a few minutes later. 'They've run out of beer,' he lamented. Although it wasn't real beer he could at least pretend, but now that avenue of pleasure had been closed down and this latest blow reduced him to tears.

There was only one thing left, as by now the noise he was making, like a smackhead being told that the methadone had run out, was waking up the locals on the terrace. It was back to the central station and a final beer in Finnigans Sports Bar before it closed (at 9 p.m.!) and then over the bridge into the safety of the Danes.

We arrived back in Copenhagen just before 10 p.m. and found a bar in Tivoli that was still open. I never thought contentment would come in paying 'only' £4 for a beer but after trying it Swedish fashion it was a pleasure! 'Next time,' the Big Man vowed, 'we do things my way. None of this nice polite stuff. We want hardcore. Let's go to ice hockey!'

A WEEKEND OF FOOTBALL TOO FAR

How a trip to the lowlands of Europe ended as an uphill struggle

In a quest to fill the void left by the end of the English football season, and with no major tournaments ahead, I had months in advance planned a number of trips to countries, such as Sweden and Estonia, which play during the summer. Then something strange happened, something that hadn't happened in the past five years. The England Under-21 team qualified for a major tournament. The 'youngsters' used to be legends under the guidance of Peter Taylor in the late 1990s, with one of the most feared teams of their generation. Players such as Rio Ferdinand, Paul Robinson, Frank Lampard and Jamie Carragher came through the 'juniors' under Taylor's guidance to make their mark on the world scene. It all went wrong when the suits in Soho Square decided to replace the knowledgeable Taylor with the clueless David Platt. Under Mr Potato Head a system of squad rotation was introduced that seemed to mean any and every English player in the Premier League was capped at Under-21 level and consistency in team selection went out of the window.

After a couple of failed attempts at qualifying for the European Championships, held every two years, Platt was on his way to destroy Nottingham Forest, and Stuart Pearce was put in charge. Psycho, as he was affectionately known during his playing days, relished the task and instilled a sense of pride in playing for the shirt again. A new crop of players started to come through their clubs' youth teams, they were thrust on to the England stage and all of a sudden the team started to win.

England finished top of a qualifying group with Switzerland and Moldova and then showed their class by beating the Germans in a two-legged play-off to qualify for the eight-team European Championships to be played in Holland.

The Under-21 tournament is usually well organised. The games are often played in smaller stadiums close together, in countries that take real pride in hosting them. The 2007 version in the Netherlands promised to be no different and was to feature Portugal, Belgium, Israel, Italy, the Czech Republic and Serbia as well as the host nation and England. The games were to be played in four venues: two in the north, Groningen and Heerenveen, and two in the south-east, Arnhem and Nijmegen. England were drawn in a group featuring Italy, Serbia and the Czech Republic, which would be based in Arnhem and Nijmegen.

The opening games were being played in the north and I was planning to take in both games on the first day. The itinerary was comprehensive. It featured a game at each of the four stadiums over two days, and would still see me back in the office for 9 a.m. on Tuesday morning.

Amsterdam's Schiphol airport was sunny on the Sunday morning, quite unusual as it always seems to be dull and wet when I make the short hop over the North Sea. For nearly a year I commuted to Amsterdam once a week, looking after a sales office no more than five hundred yards from the terminal building, which meant that the only red lights I got to see on a Tuesday night were those flashing from the airport's control tower. I travelled to the airport so frequently in 2007 that it seemed likely the authorities had me marked down as a potential drug trafficker.

The plan for this weekend feast of football was to pick up a car, drive up to Heerenveen for the first game featuring the Dutch, leave a few minutes early and continue north to Groningen for Belgium v Portugal, stay the night in a small village outside Groningen and then go south on Monday to watch England's opener in Arnhem and the game ten miles away at Nijmegen.

There was to be an overnight stop in Arnhem, then a drive to Amsterdam airport for the 7 a.m. flight back to work on the Tuesday. What could possibly go wrong? Just about everything as it turned out.

Hiring a car is not what it is used to be. In the olden days they would take a credit card imprint and tear it up in front of you when the vehicle was returned. These days they 'block' a deposit from your credit/debit card, which basically means that for the period of the rental (and actually for as long as they want) the amount they have blocked cannot be used. Fine if you have a credit card, but I didn't. My cash was in an account accessible only by Maestro card. And, of course, the Netherlands is one of the few places in Europe where Maestro is not commonly accepted. There were only a few hundred pounds on my debit card and this was not enough to cover the deposit of €800 they wanted.

As it was a Sunday there was no opportunity to arrange a CHAPS transfer from one account to the other; nor would they take a cash deposit. So I was stuck. The plan was in tatters because of technology. Having made such a fuss at the counter there was no point in trying my luck with another hire company so I threw myself on the mercy of the Dutch railways.

Unlike its German counterpart, the Dutch network is in dire need of modernisation. Its rolling stock is old-fashioned, and travelling long distances (which means more than two hours in the Netherlands) is uncomfortable. But, like its German counterpart, it is very efficient and trains run regularly from the airport to all parts of the country.

The station is under the arrivals area at Schiphol and, of course, the opening day of the biggest sporting tournament the country had held for seven years (since the European Championships of 2000) coincided with the start of a major rail network improvement programme – meaning no trains to Heerenveen.

A great start to Plan B, so Plan C was formed while waiting for a connection at an unremarkable railway station in the middle of nowhere: go to Groningen, pick up media accreditation, go to hotel, check in and get bus to Heerenveen in time for the first game. Brilliant, except that I hadn't bargained that the term 'replacement rail bus service' would rear its head, not once on the journey to Groningen but twice. So the ninety-minute journey from Schiphol took more than three hours.

I arrived in Groningen an hour before the tournament kick-off, and Heerenveen was some thirty miles to the south-west. Jumping in the nearest taxi, I negotiated for the driver to chauffeur me for the next few hours at the bargain cost of €150. As he drove a brand new Chrysler I was getting part of my money's worth by being driven around in a 'pimpmobile'.

The first stop was the media accreditation centre at Groningen's Europort stadium, also known as 'the Big Green Cathedral'. FC Groningen are one of the most progressive teams in Dutch football and many scoffed when they demolished their old stadium and built a brand new twenty-thousand-seater arena, complete with leisure facilities which include a casino, a number of restaurants and a cinema, on the outskirts of the small town. In their first season they averaged more than nineteen thousand and vindicated the investment as the team qualified for the UEFA Cup by beating Feyenoord in a play-off at the end of their first season in the new stadium.

Picking up the pass from the deserted office – most of the officials were getting ready to watch the Dutch play in Heerenveen – I asked how long it would take to get there. The officials scoffed and said 'no chance'. I pointed out the taxi with a smile. 'Yes, but even if it was the Batmobile you would still not make the kick-off. It is Sunday and there are roadworks everywhere.'

The Dutch have a sense of humour and I was sure they were laughing with me and not at me when I set off. Unfortunately Plan C started to unravel soon after. An accident on the motorway out of town meant there was a long detour through the village of Eelde, the location of my hotel, and as the taxi had already run up nearly €70 the idea of getting to the Netherlands game was abandoned, replaced by a few hours' relaxation in an exquisite hotel which looked like a Swiss chalet in an Alpine retreat.

On far too many occasions I try to cram in too much and return exhausted. This time I sat back with a beer and started watching the opening game from a very orange and full Abe Lenstra Stadium in Heerenveen, where single goal was enough to win the game for the hosts. But, of course, things took another wrong turn! So relaxed was I that I'd fallen asleep, not only missing eighty-five minutes of the game but also the hourly bus back to the centre of Groningen. Another €20 for a taxi now meant the alternative travel arrangements had cost more than €200 in a single day, but at least I made it to the stadium.

The crowds weren't exactly flocking to the Euroborg, and those that made the effort and paid a bargain €10 for a ticket were in the colours of the Dutch and not those of Portugal or Belgium. Inside the immediate thing that hit you was that it was very green. Every seat, surface, wall and roof was in the same green. Not even the toilets were exempt from the green paint as the cubicle doors, toilet roll holders and even the toilet seats were the same colour! Not exactly pleasing to the eye. Guess why it was dubbed 'the Green Cathedral'?

Belgium 0 Portugal 0 – Euroborg Stadium, Groningen – 10th June 2007

According to the record books more than seven thousand saw a drab draw, livened up only by a huge fight in the second half when Manchester United-bound Nani pushed his histrionics too far and the Belgians took him down a peg or two. However, it is doubtful there were more than two thousand there for the kick-off. As the teams tried to outdo each other in terms of negative approach play in the second half, this number soon thinned to an extent that by the time the Polish referee blew for full-time I was the only person left in the press area. As I went to the press conference an awful thought occurred. What if I was the only member of the press there? I don't speak Portuguese and my French is a bit rusty. A request for 'Un baguette s'il vous plait' would not cut much mustard with the coaches. Fortunately most of my colleagues had taken their seats early and I pretended to follow what was going on, making the odd random note on my laptop. Two games into the tournament and only one goal. So much for a festival of free-flowing football.

Groningen is not exactly a party town. It does have a large student population, but as it was mid-June they had left for the summer, leaving a few odd bods and loads of cows. The north of Netherlands is basically cow central and is famous for being the home of the black-and-white-patterned Friesian variety. However, the extent that the locals take this whole cow thing to takes some getting used to. A few statues are fine. A couple of cow-themed restaurants is acceptable, but for groups of locals to be wearing outfits resembling the black and white bovines were not the most fashionable glad rags for a Saturday night.

After spending a half an hour looking for a decent restaurant that wasn't empty – I refuse to eat abroad in a place with no customers irrespective of the time of day – I had to give up and return to the hotel (another €14 in a taxi) for dinner. Day One complete, nothing had gone to plan, and I was more than €200 out of pocket.

The sun was shining again when Monday morning broke. Families cycled up and down past the hotel as I waited for the hourly bus to the station. Of course, I had failed to read the timetable correctly and had missed the only bus of the day to the town centre. It had left at 7.30 a.m. Another taxi, another €10, and it was off to a livelier place, the historic town of Arnhem. Only three changes of train were required in the three-hour journey to the town made famous in the Second World War for the heroics that led to the film *A Bridge Too Far* about the failed operation ('Market Garden') to secure a number of key bridges over the River Rhine.

England were in town and wherever England are the supporters will be too, in serious numbers. Although this was 'only' an Under-21 tournament, thousands of fans had taken the opportunity for a weekend in the Netherlands and a chance to support our boys. Our first game was against the unfancied Czech Republic. The team was captained by Nigel Reo-Coker, in the process of making himself thirty-five thousand enemies for life by publicly badmouthing his club, West Ham United, in an attempt to broker a move to Aston Villa.

Our threat came from the free-scoring striking duo of Preston North End's scoring machine David Nugent and Reading striker Leroy Lita. One notable absentee was David Bentley, who had pulled out of the squad the day after being on the bench for the full international with Brazil in late May, stating that he was 'too tired' to play for the Under-21s. This one decision shows all that is wrong with young footballers today. Happy to act like Billy Big Balls when they want to but when given the opportunity they shirk their responsibilities.

Czech Republic 0 England 0 – The Gelredome, Arnhem – 11th June 2007

The Gelredome was one of the world's most futuristic stadiums when it opened in late 1999. An ambitious project, the building was undertaken by the president of Vitesse Arnhem, Karel Aalbers, making his team one of the most progressive in Dutch football. It was the first to be cashless (similar to Amsterdam ArenA and Schalke's Veltins stadium) and the first to have a pitch that was rolled out, meaning it could be quickly converted into an indoor arena when the roof was closed.

England had been given the north end and came close to filling it. In keeping with the games the previous day, excitement had obviously gone on holiday, although a missed penalty by Lita in the final few minutes would have sealed three points if his aim had been true. I had left by this point, heading ten miles south to watch Serbia v Italy in the tiny town of Nijmegen.

For once the journey was incident-free and took only twenty minutes by train. The thirteen-thousand all-seater stadium is in a pleasant park in the town centre and the locals had come out in force for a game which would have otherwise attracted little attention.

To complete the miserable weekend it was another dull match, with Serbia scoring the only goal halfway through the second half. With the eight teams having played their opening matches I can honestly say it had been one of the most disappointing tournaments I had seen. It was back to the Arnhem hotel, annoyed at spending more than £400 on a weekend of depressing, uninspiring football, tedious travelling and a jobsworth car hire company. I could have blown the whole lot in Amsterdam and had a silly grin for weeks plus more interesting stories to tell. To cap it all, the following morning at 5 a.m. fog delayed the British Airways flight and left me remembering why I hated this journey so much.

The tournament did liven up slightly over the next few days. The Netherlands qualified for the semi-finals with a win in their second game in a sold-out Groningen, with rising star Ryan Babel proving to be the man of the tournament and earning a move to Liverpool in the process. They were joined by Portugal, Serbia and England, after Pearce's team had beaten Italy and Serbia. The game against the Serbians had descended into the dark old days of football when some of the opposition had racially abused Ferdinand and Lita at the end.

In their semi-final Netherlands and England could not be separated over two hours and so it went to the longest penalty shoot-out in the history of European football. A total of thirty-two penalties were taken in front of a sell-out twenty-three-thousand crowd. It took a miss by Anton Ferdinand thirty-four minutes after the shoot-out started to settle the game and send the Dutch into the final, in which they eventually beat Serbia 4-1. A cracking end to a disappointing tournament and one I would never forget for the wrong reasons. When travel goes wrong it really does go wrong and it wasn't even possible to blame the hated city of Amsterdam for the events that occurred!

SUPER CUP IN SUPER RICH MONACO

Jumping on the UEFA gravy train for one night only

One must-see place in Europe has to be Monte Carlo, or Monaco to give it its proper name. Essentially Monte Carlo is an administrative area within the principality of Monaco, but as the place is so small there isn't really room for anything else and the names tend to be interchangeable. It still ranks as one of the places to be seen. While other high-class spots such as Marbella, Cannes and Portofino are definitely where the rich come to play, Monaco is were many people work and live. Go a few yards behind the harbour, the Hotel du Paris or the Hermitage and you will find normal people living in normal flats doing normal jobs. But that is not the Monaco people come to see. They want to eat a slice of fame, fortune and high-class living. And that is why once a year all the big cheeses in European football decamp to the principality for a few days. Of course there is work on the agenda. There is the annual Gala of European Football where various stars are honoured, the group stage draws for the Champions League, the UEFA Cup draw and, of course, the UEFA Super Cup, the annual game between the winners of the Champions League and the UEFA Cup winners.

Nobody can give a decent reason why the game is played in Monaco's small stadium apart from it perpetuating a jolly for the men in suits, another night at someone else's expense. It is not as if the clubs who win the Champions League are small, unpopular teams (OK – maybe Porto in 2005) but in recent seasons AC Milan, Real Madrid and Barcelona have played in this curtain raiser, which of course leads to a huge influx of ticketless fans. And if there is one thing Monaco cannot handle it is large crowds, as can be seen with the chaos before the annual Formula One Grand Prix which brings the city to a standstill for days.

Monaco is also not particularly easy to reach via public transport unless you are willing to pay for the luxury of a helicopter. The nearest airport is some twenty miles away: Nice Cote d'Azur International, one of the busiest on the Mediterranean, which handles hundreds of flights a day during the summer when even budget airlines feel justified in selling seats for hundreds of pounds with no sign of a €1 bargain. Arriving at Nice is only half the battle. Most visitors finish the journey to Monaco by coach or train, which adds another hour, always assuming that the French are not on strike, which during peak months is quite often. However, it is possible to book ahead and the helicopter transfer is a bargain at little more than £50 each way. It is a spectacular journey and takes less than ten minutes.

The trip to the Côte d'Azur was ostensibly to visit another of my regional offices. I had secured media accreditation, not only for the Super Cup between Champions League winners AC Milan and UEFA Cup winners Sevilla, but also to the Champions League draw on the Thursday afternoon in the International Congress Centre. After spending a couple of very pleasant days in Sophia Antipolis, the French equivalent of Milton Keynes, but with killer views of the Mediterranean rather than concrete cows, it was off to the rich man's playground.

As the trip coincided with pay day, I decided to indulge in the treat of the helicopter there and the train back to Nice. Arrivals at Nice airport are whisked in a plush Range Rover to the far side of the runway next to the sea where the choppers come in and out. As luck would have it there were only two other passengers for my flight, meaning the views on the short journey would be spectacular. As I was getting ready to board, the other passengers arrived in a limo with blacked-out windows. The wealth that dripped off this middle-aged couple was obscene. Their luggage tags were worth more than my whole wardrobe, and the look the pair gave my brand new Adidas trainers suggested they had stepped in dog crap.

As the helicopter comes in to land, the stadium is visible between high-rise apartments. From the air it appears as if Monaco is no different to Seoul or Bratislava in terms of the amount of apartments squeezed into a small space, except these are worth a thousand times more. Turning down the offer of a free lift in the courtesy limo on the assumption the ground was a few minutes away I set off on foot.

But although the stadium looked close to the harbour from the air, I couldn't find it. There were a few fans milling around, but nobody could see an entrance. There was a petrol station where an end behind one of the goals should have been, a supermarket where the main stand had appeared to be from the air, and where the pitch should have been there was a park. With so few fans it wasn't even possible to follow the crowd. I was about to ask directions from a petrol pump attendant when I saw Gérard Houllier walking down the road. So I followed him.

Ten minutes later Monsieur Houllier went into a posh restaurant close to the station, leaving me looking like a sad stalker. Fortunately, the walk was far enough up the hill for me to see the error of my ways and spot the stadium. Back down the hill, through the small gap between the petrol station and the supermarket and there was the Stade Louis II.

Expecting great things, I was very disappointed. No red carpet, no canapés and champagne on offer, just endless concrete. Armed with the latest media lanyard, it was off across town to the International Congress Centre for the Champions League draw, and a chance to rub shoulders with Mourinho, Ferguson and Wenger. Well, not quite. The media went in via a press entrance (through the kitchen) and were in a separate part of the hall to the main dignitaries. It was good to see some of the reaction to the draw, as well as the surprise on some faces, even during the 'practice' draw when Manchester United were paired with Barcelona and Fenerbahce.

Formalities over, it was time to sample some high life, in this case a drink in the Hotel de Paris. Well, if it was good enough for Sepp Blatter, who entered the hotel with his entourage a few steps in front, it was bound to serve my modest tastes. Herr Blatter and I go back a few years, having shared the same hotel for a few nights in Coimbra during the European Championships in 2004 in Portugal. We often shot the breeze around the pool on those non-game summer days and his misplaced comments about women wearing tighter shorts came after a night in the bar on the sambucas with me. Actually, there is a small element of truth in that. Mr Blatter and his entourage were indeed at the same palatial hotel and at the time I was writing a thesis on Corporate Governance for an MBA. The focus of it was the collapse of the Parmalat empire, which had serious ramifications for AC Parma in Serie A, and I managed to speak to a member of Blatter's staff concerning the issue, even getting a quote from FIFA that earned a couple of credit marks in the final appraisal. Sepp had obviously forgotten me as he was driven in his Chrysler Grand Voyager from the ICC, all of two hundred yards away, while I had to walk. Located opposite the Casino, and on the Grand Prix route, the hotel has long been the principality's most opulent. It has featured in a number of films. Interestingly, my mother claims that the character Charles Wells, the man from the legendary story, song and film *The Man who Broke the Bank at Monte Carlo*, filmed at the Hotel de Paris, is somewhere up in the branches of our family tree.

I passed the second Monte Carlo test (the first was arriving by helicopter) by wearing a shirt, which led me to be ushered inside by an immaculately dressed doorman.

There are not a lot of 'touristy' things to do in Monaco. Casino: check, Hotel de Paris: check, but what everyone wants to do is to drive the Grand Prix route. Fortunately help was at hand. Outside the Casino was a special motorbike taxi that for €20 would go anywhere in the principality. I asked to be taken to the railway station, but via the race route. We took the corners on the infamous downhill stretch with ease and raced through the long tunnel under the International Conference Centre.

After a relatively cheap night out in Nice, where the price of dinner at the hotel didn't quite reach three figures, I finished work the following morning and returned to the heliport. Twice in two days must have singled me out as a regular. I was acknowledged by name by the check-in staff, and given a priority boarding pass, much to the annoyance of the waiting crowd. With a couple of hours to kick-off it was back to the stadium to find the media restaurant. Like the entrance area this was a dump; the food was bland and there was no free drink.

The best part was looking out of the windows and watching VIPs and dignitaries arriving, in the knowledge that if there was someone you disliked it was possible to 'accidentally' drop a dumpling from the inedible stew on them from a great height. I saw Michel Platini, my friend Sepp, Eusebio, Enrique Iglesias and Michael Schumacher in the space of thirty minutes. They, too, were clearly very keen on getting inside for their beef stew and flat Coke!

Another strange fact about the stadium is the tiny media area. For such a high-profile game, when most of Europe's football writers and journalists descend on Monte Carlo, you would think they might provide extra facilities. Not a chance. The seat was cramped, and like ninety per cent of the media I was unable to take notes. I really couldn't move my arms because of a large, sweaty journalist from Spain's *MARCA* newspaper crammed in beside me.

AC Milan 3 Sevilla 1 – Stade Louis II, Monaco – 31st August 2007

Thirty minutes before kick-off, the familiar figure of Silvio Berlusconi, plus his huge minders, walked around the pitch, fresh from having a word with the referee (perhaps!) in the dressing room. He is a tiny man, and you have to wonder if it's a good idea to surround himself with such big men as it just makes him look even smaller. Imagine Ronnie Corbett surrounded by the likes of Hulk Hogan and Lawrence Dallaglio.

The game was going to be very emotional for Sevilla and their fans. Two days before, their young midfielder Antonio Puerta had died of complications after a heart attack following a collapse in the previous weekend's game against Getafe.

The Super Cup was in doubt for a while, but the Spanish wanted to honour his memory by playing. A very moving minute's silence was held, with the Sevilla team wearing shirts with Puerta's name and number on the back. The Milan fans also showed their respect by unfurling a huge banner emblazoned with Puerta's name, which they carried around the pitch to the Sevilla fans.

The celebrations released a lot of emotion, and for once the lighting of flares was seen as a mark of respect rather than a sign of trouble, although again you have to wonder how they got into the stadium when the media had their bags examined in such minute detail.

The game was always going to be tense and emotional, but credit must be given to both teams for attacking from the first whistle and it was not long before from a free kick Renato gave Sevilla an early lead.

After the break Milan were a different team; it was as if they had allowed Sevilla to win the first half. Filippo Inzaghi, a man with no concept of the offside rule, always plays the percentages in that if he is given off ten times then the officials will get it wrong at least once. That was the case here when a blatant offside was missed and he was allowed to head home from a cross by Gattuso to equalise. Gattuso is a strange player. I don't think I have seen him play, whether for Glasgow Rangers, AC Milan or even the Italian national team, without being booked at least. Tonight was no exception as he was yellow-carded for a silly foul on Daniel Alves. Assuming that players are fined for these indiscretions, his monthly bill must be more than most Championship players earn in a month.

Marek Jankulvoski put Milan into the lead seven minutes later with a fantastic left-foot strike and after this goal the Spanish faded. Even the presence of ex-West Ham and Tottenham striker, Frédéric Kanouté in the Spanish team could not inspire an equaliser. After finishing last season as the top scorer in La Liga, Kanouté had been the subject of a number of transfer stories in the run-up to the game and many reporters told me a deal had already been struck to take him back to White Hart Lane. A last-minute penalty from Kaka was saved by the Sevilla goalkeeper but the World Player of the Year managed to head in the rebound to seal the game for Milan. As a final mark of respect the deeply religious star lifted his shirt to show a picture of Puerta.

So AC Milan took the Super Cup for the second time in four years, and while the celebrations were enjoyable the last train from Monaco to Nice was due to leave in less than twenty minutes. Monaco station is as ramshackle as most in Europe, with poor signage, no announcements, rude staff, overpriced tickets and the obligatory dodgy people milling around. The journey back took nearly an hour, and would have been spectacular as the train line hugged the coast around the headlands if it hadn't been pitch black outside. So back to the real world of a Holiday Inn after a taste of luxury in the Café de Paris.

After a hike across the railway line, motorway and beach from the station at the airport, there was just time for a beer in the hotel. I don't know why being charged a bargain €10 for a pint of beer was so surprising having just come from the most expensive town on earth. Thank God for an expense account, although work would have to be done on the receipts for the helicopter trips.

RED BULL SHIT

Take one football club, add a caffeine shot and mix. Stand back and watch it all go flat.

With only two months to go before England's summer fate would be decided by the superpowers of Russia and Croatia, my research for the 2008 European Championships was still on course to be completed by Christmas and hopefully the visit to Salzburg would not be the last time I would see the city for football purposes. I had been looking forward to this trip for months. Salzburg is one of the most historic cities in Europe. Home to Mozart, *The Sound of Music* and centuries of history, as well as one of the most depressing stories of corporate greed in football today.

The aim of the trip was to take in Red Bull Salzburg's Austrian Bundesliga game against Austria Kärnten in a match being billed as the meeting of two teams with no history. Red Bull Salzburg had won the 2006–7 season at a canter mainly because they had more money than sense, and a management team of former Italian national manager Giovanni Trapattoni and German Lothar Matthäus, enabling them not only to dominate the league but also sway the media in their favour. The 2007–8 season looked like it would go the same way, but after speaking out about some of the decisions made at board level, Matthäus was relieved of his coaching duties in June 2007.

Many people may remember Salzburg for their run to the UEFA Cup final a few years ago. At the time they were known as Casino Salzburg, primarily because the Casino was located across the road from the ground, and the club, desperate for cash, did a cheap naming rights deal. They beat the likes of Antwerp, Eintracht Frankfurt and Sporting Lisbon in overcoming all the odds to reach the final, before losing 1-0 home and away to a strong Inter Milan. The club then started on a period of domestic dominance, winning the Austrian Bundesliga in 1994, 1995 and 1997 under their traditional name of Austria Salzburg. Just six years later, on the brink of bankruptcy, they were up for sale. Sometimes coincidence plays a big part in life and the club was just about to be changed for ever. UEFA had awarded the 2008 European Championships to Austria and Switzerland in late 2002, and a decision on the final list of four venues was due to be made in the summer of 2003. Salzburg won one of the regional 'franchises' to build a stadium, but without the necessary investment from the club it would not be able to fulfil its obligations.

In stepped energy drink company Red Bull with ideas from their millionaire owner, Dietrich Mateschitz, who had recently launched the Red Bull racing team out of a hangar at Salzburg Airport. Red Bull took over the club lock, stock, barrel, history, club culture – everything. The deal was finally done in April 2005. They started as they meant to go on, announcing to the fans: 'This is a new club with no history', changing the club colours to red and white and, of course, dropping the name Casino in favour of Red Bull. Quite a way to endear yourself to the fans in the first week of new ownership.

The company tried to work with the hardcore Salzburg fans but talks broke down in September 2005 and they were left to pick up the pieces of the Austria Salzburg team, who re-entered the Austrian leagues at the lowest level the following season.

The new owners were as good as their word in terms of investment and soon started bringing in new faces. They raided the squads of most of the rest of the league, buying all the best Austrian young players as well as a few foreign imports. It took only eighteen months for the club to deliver silverware as they won the Bundesliga with ease. After Matthäus's departure, the club started slowly and could not catch Rapid Vienna, finishing second. All the while work progressed on increasing the stadium's capacity from a humble eighteen thousand-seat limit to more than thirty thousand by raising the existing roof and simply slotting in a whole new tier of seats.

Clearly as this is one of Europe's most visited tourist destinations a quiet few days could not be expected, and with dull drizzle taking hold as soon as the Ryanair flight landed, the original idea of finding a pavement cafe for a few Stiegls was ruled out quickly. The city is compact, with the airport being no more than three miles from the centre, and less than a mile from the stadium. A short bus ride brought me to the gates of one of the most famous houses in Austria, the Mirabell Palace. After fighting a way through the Japanese tourists, all armed with Nikons and umbrellas, a deadly combination in anyone's book, I glimpsed the famous steps where Julie Andrews did her 'Do Re Mi' stuff in *The Sound of Music*. The view from here through the gardens and up to the Hohensalzburg fortress which dominates the city is impressive on a cloudy day, let alone a sunny one. The Far Eastern visitors retraced Ms Andrews' steps, time and time again, laughing out loud on each occasion. Oh how those long winter nights must fly by in Tokyo if that's what they find funny.

Tourist things occupied the day, that and keeping in contact with the London office over a potential HR issue brewing ominously in my absence. Spending time immersed in history is one thing, but having to try and listen to a HR meeting from seven hundred miles away while wandering around Mozart's house is a bit off-putting.

Not that this was the first time such tasks had to be combined. A few years before there was a final interview with a new candidate while wandering around Juliet's house in Verona, which at least gave inspiration for some unusual questions, such as 'If you were ostracised by your family, what would you do to win back favour?' and 'Wherefore art thou experienced?'

I also visited the wonderful Neue Residenz, the Salzburg Museum. While Salzburg is synonymous with Wolfgang Amadeus Mozart, it boasts a number of other famous residents as well, such as Josef Mohr, the composer of 'Silent Night', Herbert von Karajan and Maria von Trapp. I also climbed to the Hohensalzburg, the castle that sits above the city, to enjoy a decent meal in the restaurant before a huge party of Japanese tourists arrived and were served spaghetti bolognese, a classic Austrian meal if ever I saw one! All around the city centre were tourist shops which sold everything branded with Mozart. Underwear, pasta and umbrellas were all adorned with his face but the biggest sellers were Mozart's chocolate salty balls. Basically take a ball of marzipan, cover it in salty, dark chocolate and stamp a face of the dead composer on the front, wrap it in shiny paper and sell them in boxes of a dozen for about £10.

With an early flight the following morning, a few hours' sleep before the football was useful, and it also enabled me to escape the hordes pounding past the hotel window. I woke up starving, and with ninety minutes to kick-off needed to eat. However, during the hour-long power nap darkness had fallen and the city had gone through some kind of time shift. The tourists had been replaced by stylish locals enjoying reclaiming their city.

An unfortunate side to Salzburg is that almost all the restaurants are Mozart-themed. Mozart Soup was (apparently) his favourite – a meat broth with dumplings; Mozart Schnitzel was cooked (apparently) by his mother and was a normal schnitzel in sauce; and of course Mozart Ice Cream was (apparently) his dessert of choice. It was vanilla ice cream with a strange sauce that had the texture of tar. I gave that a miss and had a much less musical (but more delicious) apple strudel.

It had taken more than a dozen emails to secure a media ticket. It is often hard to explain to foreign clubs what it is I do and why a media ticket is needed. Some clubs (and even national associations) issue a media pass with access to almost everywhere without any questions. Sometimes they make me jump through hoops, but eventually give in. And, finally, there are those organisations that, unless you own a national newspaper, or have played one hundred times for your country, will not even return an email. What makes it hard to fathom is that UEFA and FIFA, two of the most bureaucratic organisations in the world, are in the first category, yet clubs like Bury, Rochdale and Wrexham are most definitely in the last.

After sharing the press box at the Rugby World Cup final in Paris with the world's most famous rugby journalists, and having been one of the chosen few for England's away games in Estonia, I tried to get a pass for a game at Accrington Stanley. Emails, phone calls, faxes and letters – perhaps I should have tried a carrier pigeon – to Lancashire brought no luck. Eventually I got a Post-it note letter from the club saying to apply direct to the Football League. After finding the correct person to talk to, he said a media pass would not be a problem, as long as I faxed a copy of some of my newspaper articles (what articles?), a letter from my employers (I own the company) and finally a copy of my public liability insurance document (what?). Fortunately, Salzburg sort of sat in the middle in that it only took a few emails and proof of work before they agreed to the request.

The stadium is outside the city centre but is served by both bus and train, the latter going to a new station opened for the shopping centre at Taxham Europark. This is one of the biggest in western Austria and with a large IKEA has changed the pre-match behaviour of fans who now meet for a quick Loganberry and Meatball sandwich instead of the traditional beer. The stadium is a five-minute walk from the centre, although you have to negotiate the slip road of the A1 Autobahn. From the outside the stadium looked as if it wasn't quite finished. It's on a small man-made hill, like a medieval fort. Around the outside are scaffolding staircases allowing access to the upper tiers. It opened in July 2007 with a friendly against Arsenal in front of a decent crowd. However, as with most other stadiums being used for the 2008 tournament, there is very little chance of it ever being full for a domestic club match. And this game was going to be no exception.

Red Bull Salzburg 3 Austria Kärnten 0 – Red Bull Arena – 29th September 2007

My seat was next to the dugout, three rows from the front. I got there an hour before kick-off to soak up the atmosphere. There was certainly quite a party, with pumping breakdown-type music and disco lights blazing from the roof. But someone had forgotten to invite the guests. Fifteen minutes before kick-off there were no more than three thousand crammed in at one end.

A couple of local celebrities (this assumption is based on the number of people who kept asking for autographs) came into the media area. I'm sure one of them was in a couple of films CMF hides under the bed, although it was worrying that a number of these adoring fans were teenage boys. The celebrities tried to engage me, using the common language, football. They laughed when I admitted to being a West Ham fan, but with the Hammers playing Plymouth Argyle in the Carling Cup back home they understood my anguish as I waited for the phone to ring and bring news of an expected avalanche of goals.

The history of Austria Kärnten is even shorter than that of Red Bull. They were formed in June 2007 after the regional government of Klagenfurt, having built a thirty-thousand-seater stadium for the European Championships, realised they needed a team to play there on a regular basis. They simply bought ASKÖ Pasching, who had been relegated from the Austrian Bundesliga the previous month. The club was moved from north Austria to the lakeside town of Klagenfurt on the borders of Slovenia. In English terms it would be the equivalent of a local council building a brand new stadium in a town such as Milton Keynes that had never experienced top-level football, then buying a team (such as one from south London), and moving them without any care for history or the fans. I can't see that happening in England, can you?

The game was sterile. It was if a large corporate had come along and taken the soul out of the club and replaced it with tins of energy drinks. What was funny was that for a team sponsored by Red Bull, the team was very lethargic and it took a stroke of fortune in the first half for them not to go a goal behind. What became obvious in the second half was that the sparse crowd did not like a) Trapattoni and especially his negative tactics, and b) most of the team. The abuse that started raining down on the play-maker (and ex-Crystal Palace midfielder) Saša Ilić was a case in point. Even when he set up the first goal in the eightieth minute he was booed by the home crowd.

The hardcore fans began to unfurl a banner in the purple and white of their old club, but with the speed of a Red Bull pilot the stewards descended on them and removed not only the banner, but also the fans who held it. The team scored two more goals, which gave the match a lopsided look, but all that mattered for Trapattoni and the Red Bull management was that the team returned to the top of the table, comfort for the Italian who was under increasing pressure after failing to reach the Champions League group stages which had been part of the financial plan for this season. (However, it was lucky I hadn't been at a freezing Upton Park where West Ham had toiled for ninety-three minutes before a lucky Dean Ashton goal sent them through.)

After the game, with everyone making their way from the stadium, all the media guests (and that included me!) got a Red Bull goodie bag, including a postcard of a Red Bull plane, a Red Bull girls' (OK – skinny fit) T-shirt and, of course, a can of Red Bull which was just what I wanted, having been up since 5 a.m. that morning!

The good thing was that the bus back to town was almost empty, most people having driven to the game and parked in the shopping centre opposite. With drizzle again falling in the old cobbled streets of the city centre, you could be mistaken for thinking you had been transported back to Victorian London, with dark, lurking shadows in the mist of the narrow alleys. With the tourists safely back in Munich, Prague and Vienna I wandered around for twenty minutes trying to find a bar. Surely the locals went out for a drink when all the visitors went home? Surely that is what Mozart or Julie Andrews would have done? Obviously not!

THE OLDEST
SWINGERS IN TOWN

A weekend away with some of Europe's oldest talent

Nuremberg is one of my favourite places in Europe. It has so much history, so many fantastic buildings and such a lot of decent bars that it makes a perfect weekend break destination, especially during the run-up to Christmas when it hosts the king of all Christmas markets. In terms of football it has a passionately supported team playing in one of Germany's most unusual stadiums. They had enjoyed success against the big boys, a situation with which it is easy to relate being a West Ham fan. The stadium also has some fond memories, including the World Cup match in June 2006 when England struggled to overcome a very weak Trinidad and Tobago. On that very hot day my travelling companion was Football Jo (who had picked up George the Greek and two unnamed England fans in the hotel in Munich and invited them into the Mercedes for the two-hour drive north), and while enjoying the atmosphere in the main town square we planned to come back at a later point to see the culture without the vomit, sunburnt beer bellies and 'No Surrender' chants.

So fifteen months later we were back, with CMF to keep us (well me) company. There was a rough plan, in which football initially did not play a part. It was to be a weekend of culture, fine food, lots of German beer, and an opportunity for Football Jo to add to her collection of 'alternative' DVDs featuring German men with moustaches who enjoy body cavity searches using whisks. The two things which changed our plans were 1) The wonderful weather, and 2) The prospect of a new stadium within a ten-minute train ride of the city centre.

103

We arrived early on the Saturday morning after depositing the Little Fullers at their grandparents up north. A two-day trip is not quite long enough for them to start forgetting what electric lights are, how to use knives and forks and inside toilets but it is a close thing and the three-hour journey home every time has to be spent retraining them on saying words like 'Bath, Bus and Roll' instead of 'Baath, Bous and Cob'.

As the sun was shining we decided to go direct to the market square for an early morning tipple. Jo had two things on her shopping list, namely clothes-peg porn (as it reads) and bed socks.

The former wasn't on offer in the market square and a futile thirty minutes was wasted looking for the latter, as she toured the stalls in amazement.

'Ohh look, they sell dishcloths.'

'Wow, look at this stall selling batteries. I wonder if they would work in our electrical appliances?'

As I have said before, she doesn't get out much these days.

The next stop was one of Europe's best museums – in my opinion – and also the one with the longest name. The Dokuzentrum Reichsparteitagsgelände: Fazination und Gewalt, to give it its full name, is worth a few hours of anyone's time. If you have ever wondered how the Nazi party went from being basically a trade union with no power to the world's most destructive force in little more than ten years then this is the place to come. It is spread over two floors of a new building within the biggest remaining Nazi structure, a construction that was to be twice the size of the Coliseum in Rome.

The museum traces the roots of the Nazi party from 1933, through the war and to its collapse in 1945, using film, photographs and a self-guided audio trail. It is in the old parade grounds area to the south of the city centre, and is a great base for exploring other remnants of the Nazi empire, including the platforms from which Hitler and Co. used to preach their messages of hate to more than one hundred thousand soldiers, the monument to the dead and the foundations of the Nazi Stadium, a structure that was to hold four hundred thousand when complete. The whole area on a peaceful sunny Saturday was surreal.

On a late summer's day with blue sky above, and families enjoying picnics, boating on the lake and rollerblading it was hard to believe that some of the worst acts of human barbarity had been planned on this very ground. The original plan of making Nuremberg the most famous city in the whole world came within a few years of reality.

The weekend was also slap bang in the middle of some key games of the Rugby World Cup, so with West Ham's early-season defeat to Arsenal already secured it was off to the sanctuary of the nearest Irish bar for some oval-ball action. Having seen Scotland narrowly fail to lose to Italy as we expected, the Guinness was lined up for an hour of so of Welsh humiliation at the hands of the Fijians. They did not disappoint, as they took every opportunity to throw away the game 38-34.

The night was drawing in, and the shops were closing. As most shops are closed in Germany on Sundays, Jo was very disheartened she had not managed to find socks or her new late-night entertainment.

We were walking back towards the hotel when one of Germany's most well-known brands appeared on the horizon. Beate Uhse is as famous in Germany as Primark and Burtons are in the UK, except their wares are a little more adult in nature. Ann Summers is positively conservative in comparison, so it was with glee that Football Jo ran into the shop like a child entering Willy Wonka's Chocolate Factory for the first time. She walked from shelf to shelf trying to find a couple of new titles. Thirty minutes later, after turning up her nose at ninety-five per cent of the films (and trust me she picked up every single DVD), her weekend was made almost complete with two new additions to her library.

Nuremberg is surrounded by old walls with wooden fortifications, giving it the appearance of a medieval citadel. After waking along the walls for a while we came to the road behind the hotel. We had stumbled on the city's red light district. That in itself was not the surprise as most towns and cities in Germany have a 'dedicated area of adult fun'. The issue was the 'quality' of the goods on display. Hanging out of the windows (imagine the red-light district in Amsterdam but al fresco) were some of the oldest and roughest looking women you would ever want to meet.

It is true that most men's taste is drastically reduced over the course of an evening, and we have been known in jest to judge ladies on a scale of pints: for instance Keeley Hazell would be a half-pinter, Charlotte Church a two-pinter, Sian Lloyd a six-pinter and so on until you reach double figures. These women would definitely be over the fifteen-pint mark. It also appeared that the towels they draped outside their windows were significant. We developed a system – a red towel meant false teeth; blue false teeth and wig; and yellow false teeth, wig and new hip joint.

Even more shocking was that it appeared there were lots of customers, if closed windows with the lights and music on inside could be taken as a guide. This was 7 p.m. on a Saturday night, so unless the customers had been on the sauce all day, they obviously had little confidence in scoring on a night out or simply had strange tastes in women. It takes all sorts obviously, but to have such a concentration of 'nifty Fifties' talent all in one place must mean the city is either known for such entertainment or is the equivalent of a rest home for old prostitutes put out to pasture in the German sunshine for one last shift.

A Gasthaus around the corner from the hotel was rammed full at 8 p.m., and with a menu offering home-cooked food and decent German wines, we shared a table with a German family. Now, everyone knows that all Germans can understand English, yet only one per cent of English can understand German. Poor Jo had difficulty getting her head around this and launched into a graphic description of her new DVDs. And, having sampled some before dinner on her laptop, she told us how favourably the storyline and acting compared to those she had bought in Amsterdam a few weeks previously (including the wonderfully named *Dickie Dogg*). As she said, the poorer quality the better. Obviously Mr and Mrs Ballack, and the little Michaels, understood every single word, judging by the red faces across the table, and I have never seen a family eat three courses so quickly.

After a couple of nightcaps, Jo wanted another wander around the houses so to speak, to see who was buying and selling. No real change there, as knitting had replaced whoring as the favourite Saturday night activity for the Darby and Joan club. There was a distinct lack of punters so the 'young' ladies had got out their needles and were busily making Christmas sweaters for the grandchildren.

Sunday brought more stunning blue sky and sunshine, perfect for a quiet stroll. Jo wanted to see what windows were open at 10 a.m. on a Sunday and sure enough the old ladies, who had probably been up since 4 a.m., been to the shops, cleaned the house and cooked Sunday lunch, were open for business.

The old town, painstakingly rebuilt after the Second World War to match its medieval glory, was our next port of call. Old-fashioned mill houses hug the river, and little pubs, restaurants and cafes make a wonderful setting for a lazy Sunday morning armed with English newspapers.

The day we arrived I had announced that, as if by magic, I had found that Greuther Fürth, of Bundesliga 2 (the German equivalent of the Championship), were at home at 2 p.m. I knew this before travelling to Germany, but felt it would be better to drop it into the conversation after plying the girls with food, drink and porn the previous day. Fürth is a suburb of Nuremberg and, being only a ten-minute S-Bahn trip down the road, it would have been rude to have come so far and not gone to the match.

Explaining to the girls that there was a very good chance the team would be promoted to the Bundesliga, I said there was a moral duty to the thousands of subscribers to the website to visit the stadium. Of course they bought this absolutely and agreed to go along, especially after I told them that the team had 'the fittest player in the league' (a ploy that works every time).

It was carnival time in the region and when we reached Fürth the centre was in a real party mood. German football fans love their beer and the Fürth fans were tucking into some proper pre-match hospitality and fantastic Nuremberg sausages (five in a bun with mustard).

Fürth has a reputation as a friendly club. Certainly, based on the fans who willingly came over and started chatting, the reputation was deserved. Seats were less than €20 for what I thought was the main stand and thus in the shade. Here my understanding of German let us down – we were right in the sun. A cooling beer was needed, and, having sensible rules, fans in Germany are able to drink as much as they like in seats in full view of the game, as long as they pay a €1 deposit for plastic cups and promise not to throw them at the assistant referee.

Greuther Fürth's opponents, Carl Zeiss Jena, are one of the most famous ex-East German clubs, having often played in the UEFA Cup in the dark, communist days of the 70s and 80s. They are named after the famous scientist, Carl Zeiss, who developed optical lenses which are heavily used by the military as well as in some top-of-the-range SLR cameras. Carl Zeiss Jena were struggling at the foot of the table early in the season but still brought a fair away following and they were in fine voice. The stadium was not dissimilar to some in lower-league England, with one main stand set apart from three temporary stands. The club had sold the naming rights to the ground some years previously to the children's toy manufacturer, Playmobil, located in Fürth, although they did draw the line at constructing the new stand from plastic.

Greuther Fürth 2 Carl Zeiss Jena 2 – The Playmobil Stadium – 30th September 2007

The teams emerged to a generous welcome, with no one more enthusiastic than a massive fat bloke, who had obviously taken his share

107

of beer and sausages, and was waving one of the biggest flags you are likely to see.

The heat was clearly a factor as the teams struggled to put any decent moves together. It wasn't until the twentieth minute that there was a real shot on goal, and Jonny Wilkinson would have been proud of it. After a goalless first half, the second started with Fürth stepping up a gear. Eventually they found a way through with a corner kick that eluded everyone at the near post, including the Jena goalkeeper, and went directly in.

Despite Carl Zeiss Jena equalising within ten minutes, it always looked as if it was to be the home team's game, especially when they scored in the seventy-fifth minute through the impressive Fürth centre forward. His goal celebrations were worthy of his yellow card as he ripped off his shirt, threw it to the home fans and then tried to follow it by jumping up on the advertising hoardings and screaming at the top of his voice. If you are going to get booked why not go the whole hog and make it worthwhile? But as the game was petering out Jena equalised in time added on. We missed that because the girls were happy to leave with a few minutes to go, on the promise that we would be able to spend longer at the make-up counter in duty-free at the airport (they are so easily bought).

Picking up the bags from the lockers at Nuremberg Hauptbahnhof it was off to the airport and back to reality, CMF and I happy to have spent some quality time together in a beautiful city in the sunshine and Football Jo happy in the fact she had got some more deviant porn. She was disappointed, though, that she didn't get her bed socks.

CAN ENGLAND GET ANY WORSE? OF COURSE THEY CAN!

Vienna – the game that meant nothing to me

In September 2007 the Football Association realised England might not qualify for the 2008 European Championships. The form of Croatia, Russia and Israel had been consistently impressive in 2007, and, coupled with England's failure to win in Tel Aviv and Croatia, they would almost certainly have to take maximum points from the final four games, including the tricky one in Moscow plus the final group game against Croatia at Wembley. The Football Association, concerned at the team's form and the idiotic ramblings of a more and more deluded Steve McClaren, decided it would be in the best interests of the national team to arrange a friendly on the free weekend before the Croatia match.

As time went on, our home form continued to be impressive, with 3-0 victories against Estonia, Israel and Russia. However, a disastrous defeat in Moscow put the heat back on – but if we avoided defeat at home to Croatia we would still qualify.

The friendly was against Austria in Vienna on the Friday prior to the Croatia game. Has there ever been a more pointless game in the history of international football? Well, until the FA decided to try and gain support for their FIFA 2018 World Cup bid by sending a fourth-string team to Trinidad in June 2008, certainly not. Quite why it was decided to play a meaningless friendly just days before the most important game in England's recent history has never been explained, although I am sure money was one reason. Certainly there was nothing in it for travelling fans.

While England fans love travelling in numbers, many had been in Vienna less than four years ago when a David James-inspired collapse saw us throw away a 2-0 lead to draw a World Cup qualifier. However, England still had a chance of qualifying for the 2008 tournament and that meant there would be a mad scramble for official tickets, which would be allocated to those fans who had the most caps. With two caps at stake for this game, it was not surprising that the four thousand tickets quickly sold out.

With opportunities to test the biggest stadium in the forthcoming European Championships running out, the Austrians quite rightly wanted to try crowd control measures against a passionate away following. Normally England would have been a good bet but not this time. I don't think I have ever been to a game where so many fans left the stadium by half-time.

The reasons were twofold. First, it was cold. Not just northern brass monkey cold, but freezing cold with snow piled deep all around the city. Secondly, it was one of the dullest games you can imagine and many fans who had left warm, welcoming bars less than an hour beforehand headed back to them. Despite sitting in the warm press area, I can remember no more than ten minutes of the match. It wasn't that it was completely forgettable but it was also that I had a lovely snooze. The day had been long, with a 4 a.m. start, and I had overindulged at the pre-match banquet. In fact it was a shame to leave the comfy seat for the coach back to Bratislava.

The reason for this trip was that another weekend away from the mini-Fullers was not on, and so I had to sign up for the Thomas Cook day trip. My normal travelling companions, Rob the Red, Knightie and Dagenham Dan, decided not to waste their time on such a pointless game, but as I still wanted to visit the Ernst Happel Stadium after missing it in June, there was no option other than the day trip.

Unfortunately, due to strange regulations imposed by the Austrian authorities we had to fly to and from Bratislava in Slovakia, some forty-five minutes to the east. As it transpired this was a good move. By the time we reached Vienna news was filtering through that the city's airport was closed because of bad weather, which obviously affected the hundreds of fans due to arrive on the day.

It meant another early start from Gatwick Airport and most fans were wondering why they'd bothered when they knew the performance would be dull and uninspiring because McClown would try once again to wedge Gerrard, Lampard and Beckham into two central midfield spaces. But, as I said, every cap counted. I had declined the invitation to play for the EnglandFans Veterans, having realised it was time to hang up my boots. However, my reputation as a tactical genius had been restored after home victories over Germany and Israel in the past few months and so I was once again travelling abroad to manage my country. But this time there was no need for a bag full of shin pads, Vaseline and shower gel, all of which are usually confiscated by overeager police at a foreign stadium.

For once the scheduled flight landed on time at a very icy Bratislava airport, and within seconds it was joined on the tarmac by three other planes, all branded with British Charter logos (XL, Monarch and TUI) as if part of a modern-day convoy. With the kind of efficiency that suggested the authorities couldn't wait to see the back of us, we were on coaches less than fifteen minutes after landing.

As we drove through featureless farmland, the snow became heavier and heavier. Of course there was excited talk that the game could be off and the spectacle of the squad avoiding physical contact just in case they got hurt before the Croatia game could be avoided. But alas, news came through that, despite the snow, the stadium and, more importantly, the pitch, were in perfect condition thanks to a brand new thermal blanket bought from IKEA the day before along with some emergency chairs and a bag of tea lights.

Freshly fallen snow has a beautiful effect on even the harshest of places, and the cold-war style housing blocks which litter the outskirts of Vienna took on a beautiful sheen. The city centre, one of the most stunning in Europe and full of picture-book buildings, gardens and monuments, was covered in a white blanket. The coaches dropped us on the ring road outside the national museum, presumably assuming we were there for culture and not the bars. As my managerial duties were due to start at 2 p.m. I had to walk past the temptation of bars already rammed with fans in full song, to the Prater Park fairground where we were due to take on the Austrian veterans.

Despite the pitch being covered in at least six inches of snow, our hosts were determined to stage the game. However, and despite their status as a Vienna Sunday League Division Six team, they had forgotten to turn on the undersoil heating, or so they said. The next best thing was to clear a space big enough for a rough five-a-side pitch, although the two saplings growing in the central midfield area did cause a bit of confusion for the officials.

Normally we bring our own referee, Scunthorpe Dave, a legend among the England fans. He has been travelling to every game for well over two decades with his big Scunny flag. He is the official coach driver for the Scunthorpe United first team, which means that he has all the gossip from a small Championship team with which he never fails to regale us.

Ever wanted to know why the club banned spaghetti from the training ground menu, painted the away dressing room yellow or any other exclusives *World Soccer* magazine missed, then Dave's your man. On this occasion he had forgotten his shorts so he was unable to officiate, which meant we might have a chance of winning as his bias against some EnglandFans players is legendary, especially those who supported any other team from Yorkshire, Lancashire, Derbyshire – in fact, from anywhere apart from Scunthorpe; and Yeovil for some strange reason.

Many of the squad were either stuck in the UK because of the closure of Vienna airport, or in city centre bars after assuming our game would not be played because of the weather. The squad dropped from an initial twenty-five to eight, which made my job of picking a team very easy indeed. So easy that I was still in the bar doing my bit for Anglo-Austrian relations when the game kicked off.

I ventured out after fifteen minutes to see us 2-0 down. But with an inspired substitution, bringing on the Peter Taylor-lookalike British Ambassador, we were 3-2 in front at half-time. The young trees in midfield were now being brought into play at every opportunity, and they certainly had a hand in the fourth English goal. Our centre forward was definitely held back by the Elm and the referee had no option but to point to the spot. With the game ending 5-5, it was decided to finish proceedings with a penalty shoot-out which, of course, led to an English defeat.

So my record of never having managed a winning team outside the UK was extended and I took the plaudits accordingly, laughing off any thoughts that my position was once again in doubt.

Our Austrian hosts had arranged dinner and beers in a lovely little tavern in the Prater Park. If you have ever walked around an amusement park when it is officially closed you know exactly how Shaggy feels in most episodes of *Scooby Doo*. Every ride looks sinister, every clown face on the wall looks as if it is watching you and every arcade machine looks ready to jump out and assault you. We eventually came to a battered old hut that was transformed inside into a most wonderful alpine style chalet, like some real-life Tardis. Our hosts had laid on Stiegls by the litre and fantastic food, filling us up as if to say 'Don't go and watch the rubbish next door, stay here with us.'

As if to add to the temptation, they brought out the big guns; buxom young waitresses who made every effort to stick their cleavage in our faces when serving dinner. 'Marvellous,' said Barry the Millwall fan, summing up the day thus far. 'Life can't get much better than this, can it?'

After the formalities came a Mark Perryman quiz, featuring such questions as 'Which Austrian fifth-division team has a name with no vowels?' and 'On this day in 1973, which fourth-division team lost away at Blackpool 6-0 despite the home team having only eight players wearing Gola boots?'

Then came the highlight of our evening with the awarding of official team sheets (the proper players get caps; we get team sheets for representing our country) from the British Ambassador, my only chance to meet royalty – apparently ambassadors are higher up in the line of succession than us normal subjects. Then it was time for the match.

I was soon in a comfortable lounge with another beer, in front of a big TV showing the build-up to the game. Dilemma time. Stay here in the warmth and close to the bar, or go out, sit on a cold metal seat and look interested? Time to toss a coin: heads stay, tails go. After the flip, a long roll and a spin on its axis it came down tails and so it was out into the cold, but not before dropping my best friend, my Blackberry. I drop my phone on average twice a day. Every day I pick it up, dust it down and carry on using it. Today, with four or five Stiegls inside I kicked the blooming thing when bending down, which sent it flying over the railings of the stairwell to where the VIPs where eating. After recovering it from a bowl of salmon mousse, I attempted to turn it on, only to be met with a black screen, meaning no phone call to reassure CMF I was still alive, or tell her what time I would be home. More importantly, having made my own way to the stadium I had no idea where the return coach was – the details being on a text in the saved files. And the phone numbers of the people on the trip were stored on the phone! Even worse was to come in the second half – no Tetris and no music as by then the phone had given up the ghost completely.

Austria 0 England 1 – The Ernst Happel Stadium – 16th November 2007

So what is there to say about this pointless game? McClown decided to be brave and start with Scott Carson in goal, but why on earth did Sol Campbell get a recall? What about younger players like Matthew Upson or Jonathan Woodgate?

The back five looked second rate with Carson and Campbell being joined by Micah Richards, Joleon Lescott and Wayne Bridge. Not a formation to repel Eduardo and Klasnic the following week. David Beckham was recalled, although based on his first-half performance it wasn't worth the effort of flying halfway around the world from Los Angeles. Michael Owen lasted just over thirty minutes before a predictable injury which meant he joined the already injured Wayne Rooney in missing the Croatia match. At least Owen lasted a few minutes more than Austria's ex-Sunderland keeper Jürgen Macho, who was replaced by the ex-Arsenal Alex Manninger after being knocked unconscious in an accidental collision with Peter Crouch.

McClown not only got the defensive line-up wrong, he screwed up the midfield. Instead of playing the uninterested trio, he had the perfect chance to be brave and give the likes of David Bentley and Ashley Young a go on the wings, although both eventually got a run-out in the second half. The goal, when it came just before half-time, was from a predictable source. A David Beckham corner and Peter Crouch stood on tiptoes to head home.

The second half was pointless. Somehow Alan Smith and Wes Brown managed to win another cap each, coming on in the second period as a total of eleven changes were made, meaning the game was frequently stopped. These games are really devalued by such actions.

My idea for M. Platini or Herr Blatter would be that in international friendlies substitutions can be made only on the fifteen-minute marks (fifteen, thirty, forty-five, etc). That way the game is not stopped every three minutes. If a player is injured in between, then tough. Even more amusing if it is a goalkeeper, such as in this game.

Alan Smith's inclusion in the national squad astonished me. Is he a striker, who has not scored for nearly three years, or is he a midfielder, who cannot tackle, pass or head the ball? However, most of the forty thousand present for the first half had left by the time of Smith's entrance with fifteen minutes to go. The crowd figure was certainly disappointing for the Austrians who had hoped for a full house. But it seems that even the anticipation of seeing a potential appearance by Phil Neville is not good enough these days.

I lasted until Smith came on, when boredom finally set in and I went to find the coach, only to end up in a car park with more than one hundred coaches looking similar in the darkness.

Amazingly the first was mine, and more amazingly with fifteen minutes still to go before the final whistle it was almost full, as fans avoided the terminal boredom and the freezing cold.

Consequently, when the final three arrived five minutes later we were away before the end of the game, on the way back to Slovakia, sneaking over the border without a police escort, which was obviously still looking for lost American students (if you haven't seen the film *Hostel* this reference will pass you by). As our coach was ahead of the others the passage through Bratislava airport occurred without the disarray of Tel Aviv, Zagreb and Palermo. The Slovakians, sensing an opportunity to make some Euros, kindly opened the bars and the duty-free. The England fans duly obliged them, stocking up for the two-hour flight back home by quickly emptying both of alcohol.

CHAPTER

19

CHAPTER

THERE'S ONLY ONE BECKS AND IT'S NOT A BIT POSH

Christmas shopping in the home of beer, attacking football and Jack Frost

With CMF planning a day of Christmas shopping in Bluewater with the Little Fullers, the European football crystal ball was brought out. These day trips were becoming more and more infrequent and I wanted somewhere that a) was not already known to me, b) could be done in a day, c) had a game to go to, and finally d) would cost less than £100 (the amount CMF had to 'treat herself').

Putting all of those variables into the most advanced computer known to man, plus looking on WorldSoccer.com, one option popped up – Bremen.

My love for German football must be apparent by now. Beer, passionate fans, cheap tickets and normally some decent football add up to a great match day over there, so I was surprised that this cracking little city had not yet appeared on the Fuller list. A tasty last game before the long German winter break beckoned. Bremen were second in the Bundesliga, one position above their opponents, Bayer Leverkusen.

Ryanair for once not only had one pence flights available (really £19.40 for taxes plus a whopping £8 credit card fee but, hey, that doesn't have the same marketing message), but also flights out and back in the same day. So it was off to London Stansted on a cold December Saturday morning armed with just a trusty iPod. The airport was its usual organised self, with thousands of people trying to get through security.

Ryanair had taken their expansion plans seriously in Bremen, having built their own terminal in order to move their brainwashing to the next level. Not only was there the 'Bullseye Baggies' trance remix on the plane, but also at the queue for passport control, in the baggage hall and through customs. So far so good. The scheduled ninety-minute flight took less than an hour, and in the time it would normally take to drive to the in-laws up north I was in the home of Beck's beer. What a choice. Christmas market, Beck's Gold beer and decent football or throwing shopping trolleys in the River Trent.

Trams run every ten minutes from outside the main terminal into the old town, meaning that within twenty minutes of landing on German soil I was in the market square.

Bremen is underrated as a city. It has a mix of traditional German architecture and modern buildings, bars and restaurants. The Christmas market takes over the main square and the surrounding lanes with dozens of stalls selling all manner of food and drink. What was also impressive was that so many locals were bedecked in orange, green and white. Not colours you would readily choose for your front room but everyone seemed proud of their local football team.

The biggest-selling item in the market appeared to be orange, green and white Santa hats, which were, I was told by a Werder fan, roomy enough to hide four cans of beer that could be sneaked into the stadium. The club has never been shy in their kit design although the away strip of chocolate brown and lime green hadn't proved very popular judging by the small number of fans wearing it. Nobody could ever accuse the club of being traditional; colour-blind might be more relevant.

The problem with German Christmas markets is that they are all the same. If you have been to one in Hamburg, for instance, expect exactly the same in Stuttgart. Lots of wooden cabins that could double as sheds the rest of the year, selling the same items. During the 2006 World Cup they found a more exotic use for the sheds. They were utilised in temporary red light districts in a number of German cities to help fans cope with their 'needs'!

Bremen is small yet prosperous. The main industries are technology and beer. And is there a more famous German brand than Beck's? Stronger than BMW, more effective than SAP and liked by more men than Porsche. For centuries Bremen has proudly shown its name across the world on Beck's bottles. Bremen also means the opportunity to sample

117

the wonderful, yet rare Beck's Gold and Beck's Green Lemon. The Beck's we see in the UK is essentially an export brand. The decent stuff is kept for the locals to enjoy, and the fans were tucking into it in bars and cafes and on street corners.

What is strange about German football culture is the acceptance by the general public of the excessive match-day drinking. From 11 a.m. in any city centre on match day you see groups of men standing around a crate of beer drinking and discussing the forthcoming game.

Hardcore fans, with a myriad of badges sewn onto denim jackets, smartly dressed middle-aged men and young, scantily dressed women all take part in the ritual. In England such people would be given a wide berth had police had not already moved them on. But not in Bremen. No frills, no fanfare or trouble, just serious drinking and football chat, and, of course, ensuring the empties go into the correct recycling bin. This ritual carries on until kick-off when the fans simply finish their bottles outside the ground, enter the stadium and head straight for the bars to get more beer.

With so much alcohol consumed prior to the game and based on the failed logic of various British governments you would expect Germany to have the worst of football hooliganism problems. Nothing could be further from the truth. Crowd trouble in stadiums is very rare; indeed police are rarely seen in them.

The Weser Stadium, home to Werder for nearly one hundred years, is located in the south of the city alongside the river of the same name and most people cram (and I mean cram) on tram number three that runs from outside the old cathedral. A ten-minute journey drops fans at the Stadion stop where there is the smell of grilled sausages and the sight of loads of temporary bars serving ice-cold Beck's. Most fans get to the stadium early to sample the food and drink around the ground, joining in the club songs being sung with passion and verve.

Another strange feature of German football is the idea of fan co-operation. Essentially each club has a 'favourite' other team. And when they play each other the fans meet up for a big love-in. This co-operation is based around some kind of common enemy (in Werder's case this is Borussia Dortmund) or a common event (a match that saw one team stay up after a win over the enemy). Bayer Leverkusen were obviously a firm favourite of Werder Bremen fans as on every corner fans of both teams mingled and drank, while in the stadium there appeared to be no animosity at all. Hard to see this working at Millwall or Cardiff!

118

While the ground is one of Germany's oldest, it has been redeveloped a number of times. However, the club is falling behind the likes of Bayern Munich, Stuttgart and Schalke in terms of commercial revenues and they are considering relocating to a new sixty-thousand-capacity stadium close by. Currently there is room for forty-two thousand but on more occasions than not this is not enough.

Ticket touting is frowned upon in Germany and you will not find the hordes of Scousers hawking their wares as you do in England (and everywhere the English are playing). One reason may be that resale rules for football tickets in Germany are more liberal than in England, and they can be bought and sold freely on eBay.de, which is often the best way to pick one up for more popular games.

It will be a shame if Bremen do leave the Weser Stadium. Compact at the sides, traditional curves behind the goal and some strange floodlights give it a unique feel. But money rules the roost in German football, as it does in the rest of Europe, and if opportunities for match-day revenue can be made greater by moving then they will. When I visited, the club was one of Germany's big five along with Bayern, HSV Hamburg, Stuttgart and Schalke, and they had all benefited from investment in their stadiums during the course of the preparations for the 2006 World Cup. Any advantage Bremen can get off the pitch will help on the pitch in the long run.

Werder Bremen 5 Bayer Leverkusen 2 – Weser Stadium – 15th December 2007

With the sun setting early in the game, and the temperature barely rising above freezing (yet not one player wore gloves, let alone tights!), expectations of a defensive game were blown out of the water after thirty seconds as the Peter Crouch-lookalike Stefan Kiessling from Leverkusen went clean through the Werder defence only to fluff his lines. Werder Bremen's forward line of Markus Rosenberg, the revived Klasnić (who had lost a kidney just over a year before) and the mercurial Brazilian Diego seemed to have adjusted very well to life after Miroslav Klose's pre-season move to arch-rivals Bayern Munich and Bremen's astonishing home record of thirteen wins in fourteen games had not been earned by defending deep.

They soon went on the offensive and how the score stayed at 0-0 for more than five minutes was a miracle. All miracles must come to an end and so in the sixth minute the deadlock was broken. Werder Bremen's incisive break, which saw them with a three-versus-two attacking position, was quickly snuffed out after a stray pass and within seconds the ball was in the back of their net as with a shot from twenty-five yards Bayer Leverkusen ruthlessly exposed the Brazilian goalkeeper Naldo, who had gone walkabout.

The lead should have been doubled soon after when Kiessling missed a simple one-on-one with Werder's keeper when all the stadium, the TV cameras and most of the city stood waiting for the linesman to flag for a blatantly obvious offside. The legendary Bremen coach Thomas Schaaf acted swiftly, ruthlessly withdrawing captain and midfielder Tim Borowski with less than twenty minutes on the clock. Borowski was stunned to be taken off when not injured and he headed straight down the tunnel, but not without first seeing Klasnić stab in an equaliser.

With the clock running down at the end of the first half some dreadful play-acting (a headbutt that missed and a Bremen forward feigning injury as if he had been hit by Amir Kahn, Joe Calzaghe and Ricky Hatton all at once) should have led to a penalty and at least one red card.

The second half started with a bang. In the forty-sixth minute Bremen took the lead thanks to some Diego magic. Clemens Fritz made it 3-1, Klasni added a fourth and when Markus Rosenberg hit the fifth Bayer Leverkusen were understandably stunned. Four attacks in no more than fifteen minutes had resulted in four goals. Bremen had scored with every attack, getting every single lucky rebound, every break of the ball and every marginal decision.

Bayer Leverkusen didn't give up attacking, knowing that their luck had to change at some point, and eventually got one back as Kiessling's misplaced header looped over Bremen's goalkeeper Tim Wiese, much to his surprise and that of the forty-two thousand fans in the stadium.

The 5-2 win, coupled with a Bayern Munich draw, saw Werder Bremen join the Bavarians level on points at the top of the Bundesliga. Their home record was the best in Germany, and it it wasn't for an early-season defeat by Bayern Munich at the Weser it would have been the best record in the thirty-five-year Bundesliga history. After Werder Bremen's unexpected exit from the Champions League earlier in the week, when they lost 3-0 to Olympiakos in Athens, there was at least some hope for a swift return next year to the premier European club competition.

Less than thirty minutes after the referee had brought an end to one of the best games I had seen in years I was back at the airport, and with efficiency that would have had seasoned Ryanair travellers standing in awe, I was back Chez Fuller in time to see Same Difference get kicked off *X-Factor* at 9 p.m.

It should be added at this point that I gave up my season ticket for West Ham's home game with Everton to make this trip. Normally I hate missing West Ham games but based on the appallingly weak and pathetic exit from the Carling Cup at the hands of Everton earlier in the week, I could not face a repeat performance, and the decision proved correct. Another Alan Curbishley-inspired performance at home and another defeat grabbed from the jaws of victory. The cost of the trip to Bremen was less than £65. The cost of a ticket for Upton Park would have been £60. I know what I'd recommend.

TURKISH DELIGHT? YOU ARE HAVING A LAUGH

A weekend of muddle, mayhem and two games in two continents

Turkey holds bad memories. Dysentery struck on the second day of my only previous visit, in the early days of my relationship with CMF. For the next eight days I saw nothing other than the hotel ceiling and bathroom floor. After that incident I avoided anything Turkish. A Saturday afternoon Turkish Delight treat was no more, visits to the local spa were shortened as to avoid the Turkish steam room and Christmas dinner became a roast chicken.

So CMF reacted with surprise when in December 2007 I declared an intention of going to Istanbul for a weekend of football.

The reputation of Turkish football, both internationally and domestically, is characterised by chaos and violence on and off the pitch. A documentary by Danny Dyer in his *International Football Factories* series did nothing to dispel the myths or the fears for my safety. After reading an article in the *Sunday Times* about the rise in terrorism in Istanbul CMF went as far as asking for the secret location of the wills. However, I was confident of a successful mission, partly because the trip was being expertly planned by comrade Dennis and partly because lightning could not strike twice.

Nothing really prepares you for Istanbul. It is a mix of communist-style bureaucracy and backwater European poverty, with classic architecture thrown in. Everyone is either so friendly you think they are trying to rip you off, or is actually ripping you off. Take a taxi from the airport on three separate occasions, on the same route, with the same traffic conditions and at the same time of day and you will get three very different prices. Try walking down the street and counting how many times you have to say 'No thank you' to carpet salespeople and you will hit double figures within sixty seconds.

I arrived at the smaller but more modern Sabiha Gökçen airport on the Asian side of the city. The flight was one of the worst aviation experiences imaginable. Four hours on a budget airline, with no legroom and a set of passengers who did not understand concepts like 'one bag for hand luggage', 'stay seated when the seat belt sign is on' and the classic 'no smoking at any time' is part of my vision of hell.

However, equipped with a couple of films on the iPod and Marks and Spencer sandwiches I managed to blot out most of the noise, smells and disorder. The flight landed at 8.30 p.m., meaning an arrival into the city centre an hour and a half or so later, and a struggle to find the rest of the squad as they had flown out earlier in the day.

Turkey has strange entry requirements. After landing you have to queue up to buy an entry visa with your own currency. So if you hold a UK passport you have to pay £10. An Irish passport is €10. A US passport is $20 and if you are unlucky enough to hold a Canadian passport you will be charged $60 US! Many first-time visitors have landed without any of their own currency and been forced to work in the kitchens at the airport to pay off the entry requirements.

The other issue with the airport on the Asian side is the difficulty in reaching Istanbul's core, the area of Sultanahmet. Buses seem to go everywhere, but whichever way you cut it you have to take at least two types of transport, or take your chances that there might be a taxi driver who is only interested in slightly ripping you off.

After research and a touch of bargaining (the Turks like nothing better than a good old haggle), I decided to take a Havas bus to Taksim Square, the modern heart of the city. Of course, this was Turkey; nothing is straightforward. In most developed countries you would board a bus, buy a ticket and then the bus goes. In Turkey the process was different.

The start of the process was logical; board the bus, buy a ticket. So far, so good. Then the bus waited. Ten minutes, fifteen minutes and still no other passengers. After twenty minutes the driver got on, drove one hundred yards down the road, did a complicated three-point turn, which he managed in seventeen attempts, and then parked. He was replaced by a new driver and off we went towards the motorway. After two hundred yards it was around a roundabout and back to the terminal where we had started. At which point the original driver got back on and the new driver got off. Completely and utterly pointless.

An hour later, after disembarking in Taksim Square, I decided to walk to the hotel, which on the map seemed a mile or so. Taking off down the main pedestrianised street, it was a shock to see so many people out shopping so late in the evening. Crowds began to thin out as I walked north, and the shops turned into bars and restaurants before the real Istanbul started to show.

Broken paving stones, litter piled on the side of the street, feral cats, beggars and a blatant disregard for the rules of the road became more and more common as I walked to the water's edge and got my first sight (and smell) of the Bosphorus. The consolation for the long and lonely walk was the view across the Bosphorus from the Gala Bridge to the mosques on the European side of the city. Absolutely stunning are words I rarely use, but in this case they are obligatory.

After reading an indifferent review of the three-star hotel I'd booked, I swapped it for a four-star close to the station. Normally it's not worth taking notice of travel review sites such as TripAdvisor, but in this case the huge number of reviews with one out of five stars set off warning sirens. The new hotel overlooked a building site as the station was being refurbished. The first room I was shown ('A superb spacious double room with a view over the Bosphorus') was being redecorated, complete with paint, brushes and stepladder. Perhaps that was the deal; pay rock-bottom rates but have to decorate the room to your own tastes. According to the fire escape map the second room was the smallest on that floor, with a view over the fire escape and the back of the building.

'This is not my room – where is the view and what is spacious about this?' I asked.

The genial porter then declared that the hotel was full and for €20 a night my booking could be upgraded to a suite, the only other space left. On seeing the room, which could never have been described as a suite but had a view over the Bosphorus, it was obvious that it was exactly what I had booked. After the customary haggle we settled on €10 per night extra.

The following morning I left the hotel early after avoiding the grey breakfast. It must take real skill to cook breakfast and make it all the same colour. Eggs, bacon, sausages, toast and fruit had all taken on an unnatural hue. Just looking at it turned my stomach, let alone attempting to eat it. With memories of the bathroom floor eight years previously I settled for cereal.

Around the corner from the hotel was the Blue Mosque, allegedly one of the wonders of the world. On a dull drizzly day it was about as impressive as Centre Point in London, with no sign of the 'mysterious' blue glow. There was a much more impressive edifice with six minarets on the walk back to the hotel where the groundhopping squad, led by Dennis and hoping to fit in six games during an extended weekend, were waiting. I was only interested in the top league games and thus agreed to tag along for the Saturday.

The first game was a Turkcell Supalig bottom-of-the-table clash between Istanbul Büyükşehir Belediyespor and Rizespor. On paper there is nothing remarkable about the two apart from the home team's ridiculously long name. They are the municipal team of Istanbul created in the mid-1990s by a merger of several sides, while Rizespor are from the Black Sea port of Rize, hundreds of miles from the capital.

The game was being played at the eighty thousand all-seater Atatürk Olympic Stadium, venue of Liverpool's remarkable Champions League victory over AC Milan in May 2005. It's about fifteen miles outside the city in an area that would be described by optimists as a 'redevelopment zone' and by realists as a 'barren wasteland characterised by a white elephant of a stadium that is never used, with perfect views of a rubbish tip'.

The journey took in a train from Sirkeci, once the terminus for the Orient Express – and by the look of it not a lick of paint has been applied to the walls since those Agatha Christie days – for four stops to Yenikapi where we had to change to bus line 149T. Bus stops in Istanbul do not have maps, timetables or anything really apart from a sign that tells you it's a bus stop. Eventually a bus, so dirty that dried mud formed a 'tint' on the windows, arrived and for a sum of less than 40p (1.50 Turkish lire) we managed to get on and awaited the driver's call for the stadium.

We passed through suburbs, housing estates, farms, markets and industrial estates, as more and more people with bags and livestock got on. Eventually the driver announced the stadium and we stepped off the old crate to be left in a huge cloud of dust as it pulled away. As the smoke cleared all that could be seen was wasteland. Somewhere around here was apparently a huge football stadium. There was an hour until kick-off, and we had just disembarked from the only way of reaching it by public transport and yet there was no one else around. All of a sudden, over the hill, came our saviours. Three police vans, lights flashing, announced the arrival of the home team coach, and we followed the convoy up the hill. After a ten-minute walk, the futuristic arena came into view and it was certainly impressive. The main stand was topped with what looked like a flying saucer.

There were six coaches in the otherwise deserted car park with supporters disembarking and setting up stalls. It was odd that they appeared to be away fans who had made the long journey from Rize. Stranger still was that each of the twenty or so stalls was stocked with identical hats and scarves, yet every fan seemed to be already decked out in these colours. So who were their customers? Not the police, or the home fans; simply nobody. Apart from us. And on seeing us approaching with plain Primark hats that obviously shouted out 'Hello! I am English,' we were mobbed.

Match tickets were sold from a small booth on the edge of the car park and cost only TL10 each for the home or away sections (£3 in our language). Having seen the away fans being shepherded into the open seats behind the goal we decided to become home fans for the day.

Istanbul BBS 2 Rizespor 1 – Atatürk Olimpic Stadium – 10th February 2008

Five minutes before kick-off the stadium was hardly rocking. If fact we counted with some ease a crowd of no more than eight hundred, of which the vast majority were in the away section. Around us were a few hundred more away fans, who had opted to try and avoid the worst of the foul weather by having a roof over their heads. This would have been a great plan but for the hundreds of police who had turned up in full riot gear with two water cannons. They proceeded to wade into the crowd and extract any wearing away colours, marching them around the pitch to the away end. However, this applied only to those wearing away colours. Some other away fans, feeling lonely, decided they would rather be with their colleagues but as they did not have colours they were refused passage.

The game was poor, as you would expect from two teams in such lowly positions, playing in an unfriendly stadium with no crowd. However, on such occasions the unlikely can happen. And even more occasionally you get incidents that make you stare in disbelief. After thirty minutes the deadlock was broken. Istanbul BBS gave away a silly free kick halfway inside the Rizespor half. A very quick ball was played through to the centre forward who was at least twenty yards offside. But the linesman who should have flagged had his back to play. He was otherwise engaged arguing with the home bench about the validity of the original free kick and so missed the offside. With hilarious predictability, the centre forward went on to score.

All hell broke loose as the occupants of the home bench and the Istanbul team raced to surround the linesman, pushing and shoving him. This went on for three or four minutes, during which time the referee, confused about what had happened, lacked the courage to book anyone, let alone send someone off for dissent, violent conduct or simple barefaced cheek. Thankfully for Istanbul the lead lasted for only a few minutes and they equalised with a well-worked short corner move.

Halfway through the second half, with the scores at 1-1, Rizespor were offside halfway inside the Istanbul half. The players moved to the edge of the Rizespor box and after a hopeful punt upfield, the wind took the ball and carried it over everyone, including the goalkeeper, and into the net for what turned out to be the winner. I've seen a few goals from near the halfway line before, such as David Beckham's classic effort against Wimbledon in the 1990s, but this was without a doubt the longest 'shot' I had ever seen.

The game petered out as the cold started to bite, and we prayed for the final whistle so we could try to escape the Arctic winds. We had seen no sign of the so-called Turkish football fan mentality, but we didn't really expect it in such a sterile environment.

Mind you, as we walked round the stadium there was a group of around fifteen away fans taunting fifty riot police, who were armed with batons and shields. This stand-off went on for five minutes until the coaches drew up and the fans just turned around and got on board.

Back on the main road, and in real big-stadium style, we stood with a handful of other fans on the hard shoulder of the road, on a blind bend, waiting for the bus. Thirty minutes later it turned up and so began the marathon journey via bus, tram, funicular, metro and finally foot before we eventually emerged in Şişli, heart of the cauldron known as Galatasaray for their game with Manisaspor.

The Ali Sami Yen Stadium was the ground I was looking forward to visiting the most. Its reputation as a place from 'hell' is well known, and with a new stadium less than a year away from opening on the other side of the highway, the opportunities to experience its unique atmosphere were fast running out.

Coming out of the metro, we were met with the traditional Istanbul scene. Not Turkish Delight or locals being called to prayer and minarets poking into the sky, but traffic and misrule. Fans were everywhere. People shoved their way along the road but the sensible precaution of not opening our mouths to reveal we were English did not stop members of the group losing a wallet and a digital camera.

Fortunately the forward party sent out the day before had secured tickets in the Tribune stand. This was absolutely vital as being in such a crowd and waving money around to try and get a ticket does not bear thinking about.

Once inside, the stadium was revealed in all its rather basic glory. Despite the modest attendance, less than fifteen thousand for such an unimportant game, the noise was loud and atmospheric. No fireworks as the teams ran out, just synchronised chanting and scarf waving on a scale not seen in England since the death of the silk scarf tied around the wrist.

Galatasaray 6 Manisaspor 3 – Ali Sami Yen Stadium – 10th February 2008

The game itself was one of those that passed like a dream. Nine goals – six to the home team – did not tell the true story as the three goals scored by the away team were of the highest quality. Galatasaray were enjoying a magnificent season, topping the league with a single defeat after twenty games and their veteran striker, Hakan Şükür, helped himself to a hat-trick. It certainly wasn't the cauldron of hate I had been expecting, and the assumption must be that the real venom is reserved for visiting English teams.

Afterwards we opted for the long way back to the metro, crossing the main road to walk past the stadium and check on the traders selling fake Lacoste jumpers, fake Burberry scarves, fake Louis Vuitton handbags and fake goldfish. Well, a couple of carrots floating in a bowl of water can hardly be described as art and so they must have been trying to pass them off as goldfish to gullible children. After so much excitement in one day, I returned to the 'suite' after an obligatory doner kebab and a pint of Efes in the pub around the corner from the hotel, chumming up with the barman, who had once been to Upton Park, but didn't like the Coca-Cola served so won't be returning. Who said the Turks were irrational?

On Sunday the plan was to spend a few hours sightseeing before going to the football. Unfortunately the early spring heatwave England was experiencing had not made it a few thousand miles south-east and Istanbul shivered in temperatures close to freezing with monsoon-like rain. Getting soaked by a taxi that drove through a puddle led me to guess that the rain was unseasonal because council workers were woefully unprepared, with only mops to try and soak up the water. But it brought out the hagglers in force as they attempted to sell umbrellas and raincoats outside the holiest of mosques, the Blue Mosque, which I had discovered by looking in the guidebook was not the one I had thought was disappointing yesterday, but the impressive one with six minarets.

The destination early on the Sunday morning was Beşiktaş, with a stadium once described by Pele as the most beautiful in the world, thanks to its location on the banks of the Bosphorus. After getting a tram to Taksim, I followed the steep Inonu Cad road which snaked down to the water's edge. Inonu Cad is lined with embassies, and the importance of the country can be judged by the number of police officers on duty outside. Germany had half a dozen while Macedonia shared one fat old cop with the Chinese restaurant next door. In spite of the early hour, the stadium gates were open, and groundsmen were trying – not very enthusiastically – to clear pond-like puddles on the pitch.

On seeing me walk in they immediately started working with more vigour as if they thought some sort of supervisor had arrived. It was amusing for a few minutes, occasionally taking notes and shaking my head, but it's difficult to be cruel for long and I left them to return to their lounging ways.

Unable to get any wetter unless I jumped into the nearby Bosphorus, it was best to return to the hotel and rendezvous with the rest of the squad ready for another day's traversing of the city. The plan was to see two games, one in Europe and one in Asia, and Istanbul is the only place you can achieve this without the use of an aeroplane. Our first game was a bit of a mystery. We were sure a game was being played, but we did not have a clue at which one of three possible stadiums. So we went for the most obvious choice. The home team, Istanbulspor, came from the area of the city called Ataköy and we could see on Google Maps that there was a stadium next to a railway station named after the Ataköy Stadium. Thirty minutes later we were standing outside a ground which was locked, and with an hour until kick-off it was obvious, even in this crazy city, that no game was going to be played there.

So, reverting to Option B we hopped on the No. 38 tram in the direction of the terminal beginning with a Z that nobody could even try to pronounce. Here we crossed the tracks and got on the light transit line. Why they couldn't just continue the line I don't know. It went in the same direction yet appeared to have been constructed by two different companies who decided on different gauge rails. If the Channel Tunnel builders had used such an approach, we would have had two tunnels where passengers would have had to change under the middle of La Manche!

We alighted at Yenibosna, three stops from the airport, to be met with a huge car park, full of buses at least thirty years old, tower blocks as far as the eye could see, hagglers, hustlers, beggars and all the signs of a post-communist society. In the distance, towering over the mess, was a solitary stand which looked to have people sitting in it. That must be game number three of the weekend featuring Istanbulspor against Orduspor, a second-division game of little or no importance.

The visitors were from a small Black Sea town, hundreds of miles away, so we expected a small crowd. After crossing the main road, we went past a B&Q, complete with the Turkish version of Neil Morrissey advertising patio furniture, and up the hill.

The stadium sits in a residential side street which stirred memories of some older UK grounds such as Gillingham's Priestfield or Ewood Park in Blackburn. Now, either the Turks have so little to do on a Sunday that a match three hundred miles away is such a pull that the whole town decides to attend, or the Istanbul chapter of the Orduspor fan club is thousands strong.

Not surprisingly we found the usual chaos. The stadium – or I should say, stand – had two gates, each of which had a small ticket window, with hundreds of away fans crowding around waving TL20 at the face behind a grill. Deciding bravery was the best option we dived in, using our considerable combined bulk to reach the front and grab the tickets. For all the bluster and front, it seemed that such a brute-force approach was alien to the away fans and they cleared a path for us to hand over the required amount of tatty notes.

Next we had to push our way to the turnstile where the steward took the ticket, let us in and then gave the ticket back to the man behind the grill to resell! At least this offered a kind of crowd control. Other fans simply ran into the stadium, climbed the steps to the top and then threw their tickets to others in the crush below. Stadium control is not big on the agenda in Istanbul and there was no way of judging when the capacity had been reached.

Istanbulspor 0 Orduapor 1 – Bahçelievler Stadium – 11th February 2008

The feeling that the single-stand stadium had not seen such action before grew quickly as within twenty minutes it was full with four thousand away fans, and at least three people supporting the home team!

At last the club realised that they could not continue to sell the same seat more than twice, and, with the dugouts the only seats left, they stopped letting people in. Fans unable to get in shinned up trees, hung on lamp posts and scaled the ten-foot wire fences in scenes not seen since the 1970s English FA Cup. It was inevitable that the game itself was average.

Orduspor's single goal, halfway through the second half, was enough to win it. However, I would love to have been in the dressing room to listen to the Istanbulspor manager talk to the young centre forward, who not only had a very bad game but also a very bad hair day. He had obviously left his hair dye on too long and his locks had taken on a strange orange colour which matched his jet black bushy eyebrows a treat.

He was caught offside fourteen times (the team's total), hit the post when clean through on goal, was booked for dissent after kicking the ball away when ruled offside and finally, and certain to be included in the annual Turkish lower league 'bloopers' DVD, managed a miss of epic proportions. From a free kick swung in from the left, the Istanbulspor centre back towered above the defence and headed the ball goalwards. Nothing could stop it except a teammate, the man with orange hair. Standing on the line, he managed to divert the ball over the bar from two yards out when had he left it his team would have scored!

After the game it was back to the Bosphorus where we were to get the boat across the water from Eminönü dock. For 45p (TL 2) you cross one of the busiest shipping lanes in the world to Asia, and the port of Kadiköy. We arrived to a 1930s docks scene, with old porters lugging cases and packages around, and rows of buses and taxis awaiting fares. And people, hundreds and thousands of people, not going anywhere, just bustling from place to place. We were there to visit Turkey's wealthiest club, Fenerbahçe and their newly redeveloped stadium, which hosted the 2009 UEFA Cup final.

Fenerbahçe are the country's playboy club. Alex and Roberto Carlos provided Brazilian flair, Kežman the goals and they were led by another Brazilian legend, Zico. The previous season they had taken the title with ease, but this year Galatasaray had managed to turn draws into wins and apart from a controversial victory at the Ali Sami Yen stadium, cheer had been thin on the ground on the Asian side of Istanbul.

The stadium is on top of the hill running up from the port, a street heavy on clothes shops, but very light on bars due to the strong Muslim community on this side of Istanbul. After fifteen minutes it came into view, rising above the surrounding buildings. Unfortunately because of a date with Luton's finest, I had to miss the match but still managed to sneak into the stadium for a look. A fifty-thousand all-seated arena, with the four stands offering an identical two-tier viewing pleasure, it was certainly impressive. And although the match was on TV at the airport, my one regret of the trip was not seeing the game. Fenerbahçe had invested wisely in a bid to join the European elite. They had made massive strides both on and off the pitch and their performances in the Champions League had seen them become a feared opponent. The stadium is one of Europe's finest, and without doubt the best in Turkey; fully worthy of staging the 2009 UEFA Cup final.

But my time in one of the craziest places on earth was coming to an end. With two hours to go before the Easyjet flight, I hailed a cab outside the stadium and asked to go to the airport.

'Atatürk, yes.'

'No,' I tried to explain to the bemused taxi driver, 'not Atatürk,' but he seemed hell bent on going back to Europe. With one option left, apart from bailing out of a moving vehicle as he accelerated away, I uttered the magic words 'Hakan Şükür'. He screeched to a halt, turned to me and, before he could swear in my face for trying in the Fenerbahçe area to raise the anti-Christ, I thrust my boarding pass at him and pointed to the airport name.

'Easyjet, yes? We go now, chop chop,' and that was it.

With Turkish Lire running a bit low, haggling in Euros was necessary. The official exchange rate was 1.75 lire to the Euro and the final meter read TL46. I drew out €30 and he proceeded to open the negotiations at €80.

'1 lira is €2, yes?' was his argument, a fiscal policy move that would solve any credit crunch at a stroke. After two minutes I'd had enough so he was the beneficiary of my final TL50 note reserved for a last few Efes and I headed into the terminal to watch the remainder of the game on TV.

Apart from the usual idiots who had never flown before and decided to start queuing at the aeroplane door while the plane is still on the runway after landing, it was a relatively uneventful flight. CMF welcomed me back with a wry smile, asking if I was feeling ill yet. There were, of course, presents for all the Fullers.

'Turkish Delight! You are having a laugh,' quipped CMF when seeing what I'd brought her. I couldn't have put it better myself.

RUNNING AROUND DENMARK WITH A CARLSBERG AND A SAUSAGE

My attempt at a world record five games in one day

The 'Hop' is a specially arranged day during the season when a group of like-minded football fans will try and see as many games as possible in a single day. Such is the appeal of these 'hops' that many non-league teams will arrange a round of games especially, even providing transport to each match. While these games tend to be in the lower reaches of the football pyramid, fans still plan the trips months in advance, poring over maps, railway timetables and CAMRA guidebooks.

The opportunity to take in more than one game in a day in most major European leagues is rare. Arranging games for the benefit of fans rarely registers in today's commercial world. However, occasionally the scheduling of TV games can throw up unique opportunities. For instance, the 2008 FA Cup sixth round gave travelling fans a chance to see Manchester United against Portsmouth and Barnsley versus Chelsea the same day.

My record had been stuck at two games in a day for many years. Crewe and Port Vale in 1997; Atalanta and AC Milan in 2004; Denmark versus Senegal and Uruguay versus France in South Korea at the 2002 World Cup (the most impressive as the distance between the two was almost 300 miles); and in the 2004 European Championships in Portugal when I watched England v Switzerland and France v Croatia on the same day. However, as luck would have it, a work trip to Copenhagen turned into a 'hopper's' heaven. Five games, all in Copenhagen and all within the Danish professional league structure. I checked, rechecked and triple-checked the fixtures before putting in a call to the *Guinness Book of Records* who promised to get back to confirm whether the category was indeed valid (I am still awaiting their response).

Denmark is one of the few European countries in which Maundy Thursday, the day before Good Friday, is still a public holiday, and through the sponsorship of Carlsberg 'probably the best football-watching day in the world' was arranged. Taking in two Superliga games, two from the first division and one from the second in just eight hours it was a marathon trip, but with careful planning, fortunate scheduling and a warm coat it was certainly going to be worth it.

Copenhagen is small enough to get around with ease, although it has a number of interesting attractions that will sidetrack you for hours if you are not careful. The myth that everything is very expensive is just that – a myth. Sure, food and drink are expensive, but more important things like public transport and tickets to the football aren't.

How about this for a comparison:

Metro (underground) ticket to go anywhere in the central area of Copenhagen: £1.25

Underground ticket to go anywhere in the central area of London: £4

Ticket to see IF Brøndby in the Danish Superliga in a seat behind the goal: £14

Ticket to see West Ham in the English Premier League in a seat behind the goal: £45

So five games in eight hours at a cost of less than £50, including travel, was too good an opportunity to miss. Preparation was the key, and a Wednesday night out in the city drinking Carlsberg Special with Big Ben was probably not the best preparation for an event that could put me in the record books.

There are a number of stories that English ex-pats in the United States tell about American girls in cities such as New York falling for Hugh Grant-type accents in the bars. Unfortunately this theory does not translate to Scandinavia. We shy and retiring Brits, full of strong Danish beer, do not really cut the Hugh Grant cloth, let alone Bobby Grant, with such beautiful people. And the more you drink, the more pretty girls you see, and the braver you get.

One bar merged into another, and in each one we tried a different approach. The first idea of pretending to be dolphin trainers went out of the window to be replaced by human rights lawyers, sponsorship managers for Twentieth Century Fox, location managers for the next James Bond film, script writers for porn films and finally casting agents for the next *Big Brother* programme. Still it passed a few hours, and then a few more until the sun was coming up over the harbour. There was no option left. Copenhagen does not have twenty-four-hour public transport so with no night buses, no metro and no taxis around, Copenhagen's bike-sharing scheme was the only option at 5 a.m. Two miles at silly o'clock in the freezing cold has a remarkable effect on sobering you up, although the comfy surroundings of the hotel at the company's expense was a welcome end to the evening.

The plan for the following day was to take in games at Hvidovre, Frem, Lyngby, B93 and finally IF Brøndby in the Superliga; the stadiums ranged from the very basic athletics ground at Frem to the ultra-modern twenty-nine-thousand capacity stadium at Brøndby, a ground that would make many Premier League clubs jealous. The itinerary had been planned for weeks in minute detail and I spent the hours before dawn going over the facts again just to convince myself I was mentally ready for such a task. My 'football bag', containing essentials such as a notebook, pens, family pack of Mars bars, Danish phrase book and the most important item, an A-to-Z of Copenhagen, was packed.

Football in Denmark had been on its winter break since late November, and this was to be the second round of games after the mid-season holiday, so it was not only me who looked forward to its return. Nothing could spoil the day, except snow. December, January and February had passed without so much as a single flake falling, but come Easter week the temperature fell significantly and by the time I ventured out of the hotel after breakfast light snow had settled.

Lower-league football is not as advanced in Denmark as in England. Undersoil heating is unheard of. So at 10 a.m. the games started falling like ninepins.

First Frem was cancelled, then the Superliga game at Lyngby and finally B93 at the Østerbro Stadium next to the national stadium at Parken. With my trusted Blackberry, I was at least able to work out an alternative plan which meant taking in KB, FC Copenhagen's second team, which would fill in a gap during the day.

The day's first game, between Hvidovre IF and Akademisk Boldklub, or to abbreviate them, HIF versus AB, was the nearest to the hotel. The suburb of Hvidovre is a fifteen-minute train trip from Dybbolsbrø station which was opposite my hotel. While this may have been seen as a game between two mid-table lower-league teams, the two clubs between them have won the National League on twelve occasions. Both have a claim to fame as well. The home team were owned for a number of years in the 1990s by Peter Schmeichel and this was where he started his career in 1984. He went on to make nearly eighty appearances and score six goals as the club's penalty-taker. AB are one of Denmark's oldest football clubs, having been formed in 1889.

Hvidovre IF 0 AB Copenhagn 0 – Hvidovre Stadium – 20th March 2007

This was one of the aforementioned athletics stadiums with one single large stand, and wooden benches running around the edge of the running track. The snow had stopped falling by kick-off with the grey sky being replaced by a bright blue that made a mockery of the decision to cancel all those games.

Families with young children sat in the sunshine enjoying the public holiday atmosphere, although the football was dire. It is always amusing to see how footballers interpret 'fashion', especially those in the lower divisions. For instance, the AB goalkeeper decided on the Bjorn Borg circa 1975 look, with long blonde hair falling down his back, a black headband and a ginger beard.

Obviously he was seen as a figure of fun by the HIF hardcore fans or, to be precise, the teenagers who started throwing paper aeroplanes at him. The highlight of the second half came when one got lodged in his hair just as he went for a cross, which he fumbled. Thinking he had been hit on the back of the head by an opponent he proceeded to roll around in agony, until the referee pointed out the screwed-up piece of paper on the ground next to him.

Both teams struggled with the conditions. The players who started with hats and gloves soon got rid of them and while the pitch was far from a carpet, there was no excuse for the amount of time the ball spent in the air. This was a completely forgettable game although it was a shame when the final whistle went as it woke everyone up from their pleasant midday snooze.

On to game number two. While the club goes by the name of KB, they are officially FC Copenhagen's (or København if you want to impress Danish girls) second team, who were in the third level of Danish football. Their history is a bit more complicated.

Kjøbenhavns Boldklub, to give them their full name, was formed in 1879, making them the oldest club in continental Europe. They have won the national title fifteen times in their own right but in 1991 they merged with B1903 to form the club now known as FC Copenhagen.

KB 2 FC Holbæk 2 – Peter Bangs Vej – 20th March 2007

Due to the frozen pitch at their Frederiksberg Idrætspark ground (another athletics track with a small stand), the game had been switched to FC Copenhagen's training ground just down the road. A twenty-minute train ride from Hvidovre via the central station to Peter Bangs Vej station, and then a short walk, takes you to the training complex which was open to the public to wander in as they pleased.

The game was being played on an open pitch with a rope around the edge, as it was the only one playable. Imagine the likes of Carlisle or Brighton in our third level playing on such a ground in a league match.

However, it was refreshing to be so close to the action, although why there was a need for a speaker system in each corner that wouldn't have looked out of place in the Ministry of Sound was difficult to understand. Arriving a few minutes into the game, I counted a crowd of twenty-three plus two dogs. So why was it necessary for the announcer to give us a running commentary, interspersing the action with sound bites (Blur's 'Song 2' every time there was a corner was a bit too much after the sixth time)?

The first half was cagey, but it was apparent that certain players did not like each other, judging by the sly kicks and insults which could be heard by everyone. The second half started with FC Holbæk taking an early lead, although the goal celebration, which involved running to the two away fans, was a bit over the top.

The turning point was a seemingly uneventful punt upfield by the KB keeper. The ball was being shepherded out by the Holbæk centre back when the KB forward did what we'd all like to see happen more often in these cases of blatant obstruction: he booted the defender up the backside as hard as he could. Cue histrionics on the edge of the pitch, and a straight red card for the forward, who left to a chorus of laughter and cheers. Within five minutes the lead had been doubled to 2-0 as a defensive error was capitalised on by the Holbæk left back, possibly the fattest professional player I had ever seen.

The game seemed dead and buried, but tactical substitutions by the KB coaching team saw them get a well-deserved goal almost immediately as a corner was headed into his own net by the player who had been involved in the sending-off offence. Stupid incidents in football, Number Two. Why do forwards rush to get the ball from the net when they are chasing the game? It is the team that has just conceded that has to kick off and so that mad rush and bundle in the goal is absolutely irrelevant. In this instance the Holbæk goalkeeper picked up a stupid yellow card for stopping the retrieval of the ball by lying on it in the net.

With time running out, KB earned a free kick thirty yards out, and they equalised with one of the best strikes you will see anywhere. It led to a frantic last two minutes as both teams looked for a winner. The referee blew for time, and in traditional Sunday League style the home team had to go and take down the nets before they could have a shower. Two games down, and two draws.

The final stop of the day was a personal favourite: a visit to the west of Copenhagen to watch IF Brøndby. As with many of Denmark's major clubs, Brøndby were formed quite recently through a merger of a number of local teams. In their short history they have risen to the top of the pile, played in the Champions League and nearly gone bankrupt before finding their feet more recently with sound financial backing and a spanking new stadium.

The one thing about football grounds in Denmark is the imagination used when naming them. In the north you have the NRG stadium in Aarhus, and the wonderfully named Essex Park in Randers. FC Copenhagen play at the national stadium, Parken, yet Brøndby, having spent millions of pounds rebuilding their stadium, could only come up with the name 'Brøndby Stadium'.

Getting there is an adventure in itself. Hopping on the train out of the central station for twenty minutes to Glostrup takes you only part of the way. The journey is completed by bus unless you fancy a twenty-five-minute walk. Normally the Danes are very much like the Germans when it comes to queuing in that they are organised and orderly. That is except when it comes to football crowds. Then it's every man for himself, and the fun really begins. Cans of Carlsberg are passed around, the singing starts, and the bus is rocked from side to side. The Danes know a thing or two about football songs, simply because they have stolen all ours! 'Stick the Blue Flag', 'Blue Moon' and 'You'll Never Walk Alone' are all staple songs, sung word for word in perfect English.

The first half of this season was a disaster for Brøndby. If it wasn't for the fact that Lyngby were so far out of their depth, they would have been in the relegation zone. A run to the semi-finals in the Danish Cup was their only redemption. However, they went away to Horsens in their first game back the previous weekend for a rescheduled game and won convincingly. Now they took the game to the Superliga surprise package, FC Midtjylland, from the start.

IF Brøndby 2 FC Midtjylland 1 – Brøndby Stadium – 20th March 2007

With just ninety seconds on the clock Brøndby took the lead as a misdirected shot from a poorly-cleared corner was diverted into the net by one of the away team's defenders who had been too slow to run upfield. This was the cue for wild celebrations as plastic glasses full of beer were launched in the air in the Faxe Tribune behind the goal and at the stewards at the front of the stand.

A flare was fired on to the pitch and the stewards looked at each other, seemingly unwilling to venture onto the turf to put it out. It was left to one of their number who had obviously enjoyed the grilled sausages a little too much. He ambled on to the field while play was proceeding, tried to stamp it out, managed to drop his cap, then his bottle of water and generally do everything apart from extinguish the flare. Just as he managed to kick it from the pitch, Brøndby scored again. This time the fans launched beer, paper aeroplanes and practically everything they could get their hands on at the hapless steward, causing him to drop the sausage he had been tucking into a few minutes before when there was calm.

After such an appalling first half to the season, Brøndby could not believe they were 2-0 up against the league leaders from Herning in the middle of Jutland. Obviously, as the team had not been in such a position for so long they reverted to type, going back into their shell. They started to defend very deep, inviting FC Midtjylland to come at them. How they made it to half-time without conceding was one of the wonders of modern football.

A tradition at half-time at Brøndby is for the fans to break into song, prompted by the PA announcer. This week it was their turn to impersonate Elvis and his song 'Can't Help Falling In Love'. It was expertly sung and a stirring anthem to welcome the teams back on to the pitch. The rest of the game was quite low-key with a single last-minute goal by the visitors the high point, although it did lead to a number of worried faces among the under-pressure Brøndby coaching team.

With more snow, this time falling hard, the journey back to the airport was always going to be a challenge. The original plan was a bus to the station, then into the city before getting to the airport by train. However, the Brøndby fans decided it would be more fun to try and tip the bus over rather than board it, and I had to get a taxi. The taxi driver laughed off the snow now settling on the roads, and as if auditioning for a part in *Speed 3*, did not go below eighty miles per hour all the way to the airport, throwing in a couple of handbrake turns in the car park for good measure.

So I failed in my world record attempt of five games in one day, but did achieve a personal best. The three games had produced little in the way of excitement but plenty in the way of two of my three favourite ingredients of life in Copenhagen: Carlsberg and sausages! Still, there is always another year, and with one more team from the city in the First Division six games could yet be on the cards!

CHAPTER
22
CHAPTER

PARIS, PARIS, WHY IS IT ALWAYS IN PARIS!

Ten reasons why the City of Love is really Hell on Earth

Am I the only person in the world who genuinely hates Paris? Many people say they love it – including some who have never been there, my parents included – but for everyone who falls in love with the beauty of the Eiffel Tower, or the paintings in the Louvre, there will be someone else who, after receiving the kind of service that would make 1970s Moscow seem like Disneyland, will vow never to return.

What gives me the right to judge the city? Well, I had to spend a day and a night a week working there for more than a year and I've been dozens of times for rugby and football. Every time I vow never to return, yet every year I am back. December 2003: Stade Français versus London Wasps in the Heineken Cup; March 2005: again to see London Wasps; September 2005: Paris Saint-Germain versus Lyon; and May 2006 for the Champions League Final. In 2007 France hosted the Rugby World Cup finals, and after gaining a media pass for the tournament I made visits to the city on four separate occasions to watch England. The first three trips passed without incident, meaning I was due for a nightmare. So what better way to suffer one than for the Rugby World Cup Final weekend.

I appreciate that most of you want to read about football, but please humour me for a short while and get a flavour of what the city is really like. September is a busy month in Paris, with tourists still flocking there in the hope of enjoying the late summer sunshine (*Reason No. 1 why I hate Paris is it is either very hot or very cold. There is no such thing as a temperate time of year*); add to the mix more than one hundred thousand English rugby fans and there is a recipe for a logistical nightmare. The media pass was confirmed a week before the match so the travel had to be sorted. Direct flights to Paris cost more than £1,000 return, and with only first-class tickets left Eurostar wanted the best part of £1,200 for the journey. Alternatives had to be looked for.

I decided to take a Ryanair flight to Tours, seemingly the smallest airport in the world. Approximately halfway between Paris and Nantes on the west coast, Tours then serviced only one Ryanair flight a day; what a job the firemen there must have. Passport control was in a marquee attached to the terminal, the check-in counters double as seats in the cafe when they are closed, and once you passed through the door (security) there were no shops/duty-free in the departure gate (a sitting room basically). The plane parallel parks against the terminal, adding to the informal feel. A simple tick list ensures all passengers are on the plane. From Tours a regular SNCF train to Paris takes less than two hours. For once I managed to pull one over on Ryanair who had not correctly figured out their yield management model, and so had a bargain return for less than £50.

What was going to make the trip even better was that I was going to be joined by part of the 'Old School Crew', Mr Grumble (Joel) and Ginger Pete (so called as his name is Pete and he has ginger hair). They were arriving on the day of the game via Charleroi (also with Ryanair), then by train to Lille before picking up the SNCF line to Paris Gare du Nord where I would meet them. What could possibly go wrong?

My Friday afternoon flight was perfect. Arriving early and with a taxi waiting, I was on the train just thirty minutes after landing. The Friday evening match was the third and fourth place decider between France and Argentina at the Parc des Princes later that evening and it seemed to be a good idea to go first to the hotel (*Reason No .2 – Hotels are a rip-off. They are fifty per cent more expensive than comparable ones elsewhere in the world yet the rooms are fifty per cent smaller*). Great thinking, only the metro drivers had called a wildcat strike (*Reason No. 3 – Public workers strike all the time over the smallest thing and the government just shrugs and extends their lunch breaks*) and travel across the city was almost impossible. Of course, there was no information at the metro stations about which lines were running so I had to wander from line to line (*Reason No. 4 – The concept of an interchange does not exist and you can sometimes walk for twenty minutes between lines at stations*) hoping to find a train with a driver who had been bothered to make it into work. A twenty-minute journey took two hours. The 'top-of-the-range' hotel, costing €150 per night, was in fact an Etap affair, more budget than a Budget Inn and less quality than a Quality Inn, which normally offered rooms for €39 per night. Handing over my credit card there seemed to be a problem. The credit card machine had broken and the hotel wanted payment by cash.

'Could I pay on my card tomorrow as I have no cash on me?'

'Non, monsieur. We must have cash or we will release your room.'

And of course the nearest cashpoint was a fifteen-minute walk away (*Reason No. 5 – Cashpoints are never where shops, bars and restaurants are in Paris. They are in the most inaccessible and insecure areas*).

Leaving for the game around 5 p.m., I decided not to take my laptop to the press area as the last time someone tried to steal it (*Reason No. 6 – The Metro system in Paris is one of the most crime-ridden in the world as most stations have unguarded entrances, allowing undesirables to travel freely across the network*) and prepared to board the smelliest, most crowded and most inefficient transport system in the world (*Reason No. 7 – The overpowering smell of the Metro, especially in the summer months, is not one you will forget in a hurry*).

Obviously fearing global shame, the Parisian authorities had shipped in a number of English drivers and so some trains were running. I jumped on one to Boulogne, home of Longchamp, the ladyboys of the Bois de Boulogne and my old office in Rue Thiers where I spent many unhappy hours in 2001 and 2002.

To compound the misery, someone on the packed train managed to press the call button on my mobile while it was in my pocket, resulting in the battery being drained flat by my destination of Pont de St-Cloud. Great timing; with a complicated day of arrangements to come I would not be contactable. Absolutely typical. Arriving at the media centre I tried to find a payphone to call CMF but there was no such thing. After all, they were only catering for hundreds of the world's press.

My seat was in the back row of the upper tier of Parc des Princes. But although this was the press area nobody seemed interested in writing about the game. My neighbour launched into a massive rant about the tournament, the facilities and the French in general. It transpired he was the chief rugby correspondent for a major British newspaper. After kindly letting me make a call home ('Call Timbuktu if you want, the *Daily X* are picking up the bill') he told me about his night out the previous evening when a group of the 'press pack' managed to 'do' more than €1,000 in four strip clubs and a brothel.

'Marvellous,' he said. 'What a job I've got. They pay for me to shag my way around Europe.'

Nice. But worse was to come when the national anthems of France and Argentina started.

'If there are two countries I hate more in the world today than these two I don't know who they are,' he said, proceeding to boo and whistle the anthems.

I asked him who he wanted to win.

'The referee. What I want to see is a massive fight and both teams have all fifteen players sent off.'

He very nearly got his wish in a surprise Argentine win.

After an uneventful night in the Pantin region of the city (think London's Hangar Lane and you won't be too far off the mark) I set out early for Gare du Nord to meet Ginger Pete and Mr Grumble. Obviously they had no way of contacting me so I waited like a forlorn lover as each train arrived. With hundreds of ticketless fans on the concourse it was chaotic. I had to resort to finding a payphone to call CMF and get her to act as the intermediary. It turned out that the Ryanair flight to Charleroi had circled over Brussels for an hour because of ground fog before heading to Ghent. It surprises me that in this modern era when aeroplanes can fly without any human intervention, they still cannot land due to a bit of cloud. It also transpired that none of the passengers were told they had been diverted to Ghent, and knew it only when they saw the signs on the top of the airport terminal.

Of course Ryanair, being Ryanair, had laid on absolutely nothing for their stranded passengers. The boys, not knowing their Belgian geography very well, jumped in a taxi and headed for Charleroi. The hour-long cab ride cost them €130 and deposited them at the station just in time to catch the TGV that had started some thirty minutes earlier in Ghent!

Eventually we met and went straight for the bars opposite the station. The bar owners, sensing that the fans might want a drink ,were selling pints of Kronenbourg at €15 (*Reason No. 8 – What gives them the right to treble the prices of their beer for major events?*). But the atmosphere was excellent. With so many non-rugby English fans heading for Paris for the day it had a different feeling to a normal rugby match. There were no South African fans and soon the party had taken over the whole street. The bar owner tried to get into the spirit by putting on a plastic policeman's helmet and waving a flag of St George while jumping up and down on a car (*Reason No. 9 – There is nothing worse or embarrassing than seeing a Frenchman pretend to be British.*).

South Africa 15 England 6 – Stade de France – 20th October 2007

After a pit stop at the hotel we left early to take in the atmosphere at the stadium. I had not had a proper media desk all tournament but on picking up the ticket I was astonished that 1) I had been issued with a press conference AND mixed zone ticket, and 2) the seat was not only a proper media seat with a desk and its own monitor but two rows from the front on the halfway line. Not only was it a plum view, the likes of Jeremy Guscott and Paul Ackford were neighbours. Of course, my laptop was back at the hotel so I did what any respecting cub scout would do, and pretended to make notes on the programme.

The last laugh was mine as the press were so busy trying to file copy at the end of the game that they missed events on the pitch and had to ask me what was going on as the ageing English faded gradually.

Still with no mobile, I had no clue where the boys were, which meant a game of cat and mouse ended with a tired and unemotional meeting in the hotel foyer at 3 a.m. Joined by Ginger Pete and Joel, I left for Tours on Sunday morning, reflecting on a better than expected tournament and also for the opportunity to catch up with the chaps. At least it meant no return to Paris for a few years. Or so I thought.

Later in 2007, the Football Association announced that England would play an away friendly against a 2008 European Championships qualifier the following March. As they were already due to face the old enemy, Germany, in November 2008 it couldn't be them again, surely? They'd also played the Netherlands just a year previously so it seemed likely to be the Czech Republic in Prague, Italy in Rome, perhaps Sweden in Gothenburg, or France. And France it was. Typical! At least it could be somewhere like Toulouse or Lyon and, of course, there was always the Marseille Velodrome. But no, it had to be Paris, bloody Paris.

It was going to be a very quick trip – a crossing via Eurotunnel for 2 p.m., returning at 2 a.m., meaning only a half-day off work.

My travelling companions all shared a deep loathing of the city. The original plan was for Rob the Red, his mate Jonno, Knighty from work, Karl the Yid and CMF to join me. With six in the car the trip's cost, including the ticket, would be less than £50 a head, acceptable even for such an unfavourite place. The talk leading up to the game was whether Fabio Capello, in only his second game in charge, would grant David Beckham his hundredth cap. The biggest surprise was that West Ham's Robert Green had been called into the squad for the first time in nine months. Green was recognised by most who watch the Premier League on a regular basis to be the most consistent English goalkeeper, yet in the previous nine months he had been overlooked in favour of thirty-seven-year old David James, Paul Robinson, Ben Foster (still to play a game for Manchester United in the Premier League) and Scott Carson (He would be overlooked again later in the year in favour of Manchester City's Joe Hart and Peterborough's nineteen-year-old Joe Lewis).

Due to last-minute childcare issues CMF was unable to travel so the rest of us left SE9 at lunchtime on the Wednesday. The England Fans' forum was already full of stories about ridiculously-priced beer, people being mugged and absolutely no atmosphere in the centre of Paris. There had been a big fan party arranged, in an Irish Bar, of course, and it seemed people were complaining it could have been anywhere in the world. Doh. It's ironic that when groups of mindless fans get together abroad they always go for an Irish Bar, drink Guinness and sing 'No Surrender to the IRA'!

The journey was textbook. With little traffic on the motorway to Paris, we covered the two hundred or so miles in less than three hours and arrived at the stadium three hours before kick-off. I had pre-booked parking at the stadium via Francebillet.com. However, it appeared a ticket had to be picked up from the 'shop'.

What shop? Where did it say that? I showed the steward the email confirmation but he simply shrugged his shoulders and refused to let me pass (*Reason No. 10 – Eighty per cent of French people are rude and obstructive*). Why couldn't the ticket be printed online? Too simple and straightforward. A kindly man (must have been a Belgian) took pity on us and gave us a spare car park ticket for underneath the stadium.

On a match day the area around the stadium is populated with temporary bars, and because few England fans had booked rooms at the hotel chains in the area and were still drinking in the centre of Paris, it

147

wasn't too busy. To avoid the anticipated last-minute rush we entered the stadium with an hour to kick-off. I had seen it only from the upper tiers and press area and could not believe how much of a dump the lower tiers were. Toilets overflowed with urine, rubbish was piled everywhere and there was hardly anywhere to eat or drink. Add to this the overpowering taste of tear gas and you could have mistaken it for a riot zone anywhere in the world.

France 1 England 0 – Stade de France – 26th March 2008

Beckham was in, Rio Ferdinand was named captain as our Italian coach rotated the armband, and the rest of the team almost picked itself. David James was in goal, and I had bad memories from the last time he kept goal against France in the 2004 European Championships in Lisbon when he brought down Thierry Henry in the last minute to hand victory to the French. And sure enough, history repeated itself as he tripped Anelka midway through the first half and Franck Ribéry slotted away the spot kick.

Despite the likes of Rooney, Gerrard, Barry and Joe Cole occupying the midfield, England did not create one chance in the first hour, and it took the introduction of David Bentley, Peter Crouch and Michael Owen to spark them into life. Unfortunately one shot on target in the whole game was hardly a great effort from a team that promised so much. With the four-and-a-half-thousand England fans counting down the minutes until they could get back to the bars, it was no surprise that the players were as lethargic as the supporters.

The game ended with a whimper and there were the inevitable queues to get out of the stadium. Our timescale was tight. There were three hours to reach the Eurotunnel terminal in Sangatte and the traffic jams around the stadium did not help. Eventually we made it onto the motorway and put our faith in the hands of a TomTom satnav. It took us in completely the wrong direction, then told us to turn around, which led us back into the traffic jam at the stadium. Time was ticking away and drastic action was called for. Bribery. We needed to turn left off a slip road, otherwise we would be funnelled back into the stadium car park. A policeman was directing the traffic right so we bribed him with a €5 note. He turned a blind eye and it was back to where we'd started some thirty minutes before. Two hundred miles in just under two hours proved quite a challenge. Not only was I tired (after all it was now after midnight) but the French toll system means speeding is difficult. The toll booths work out average speed and alert the authorities if it is excessive. It was a balancing act, speeding on the roads with no tolls. Making the crossing with ten minutes to spare, we were lucky to board the Eurotunnel train first in the top row, meaning that when we disembarked some thirty-five minutes later we officially became the first fans at the match to get back to England (not counting those with private jets, of course). After a few drop-off points I was in bed at 4.35 a.m. Was it worth it? Not for the football, not for the travel and not for the time wasted but it had been an enjoyable afternoon and evening of football banter.

One thing was certain though – based on this performance England had missed the 2008 European Championships on merit. With almost a first team on the pitch at the start they had failed to create one single chance against one of the oldest defences to have qualified for the European Championships. With no Plan B, Capello would struggle to achieve anything with this group of players. Still, only ten years to 2018 when we might qualify as hosts!

GOULASH, A BLIND MASSAGE AND SYLVESTER STALLONE

A visit to two film sets in the course of a weekend being a pest in Buda

The Danube is one of the world's most famous rivers. The longest in Europe, it flows through ten countries on its way from the Black Forest in Germany to the Black Sea in Ukraine. No city has had its history shaped more by the Danube than Budapest. The river splits the city into two: Buda on the hills and Pest on the plain.

People have raved about Budapest for years, especially since the budget airlines started flying there when Hungary joined the European Union in 2004. Its stunning architecture, beautiful people and cheap beer make Hungary one of the fifteen most visited countries in the world, and the capital is the fastest-growing tourist destination in Europe.

But I'd never been there. One reason was the relative lack of quality in their domestic game. The city has six big clubs, five of which played in the Hungarian top league, yet no club had been able to dominate the Soproni Liga in recent years. However, all of that was about to change, or so the daily sports press would have you believe. In 2007 the chairman of Magyar Testgyakorlók Köre, or MTK for short, announced that his club would dominate the game for decades to come.

Such statements called for investigation and so I swiftly put together a weekend trip, picking a weekend where four of the five top Budapest teams were at home and West Ham were away at Sunderland.

CMF was unmoved about going with me, although I was convinced she was confusing Budapest with Bucharest, which she had recently read about as one of the most boring places on earth. But Football Jo was keen, especially when told that Hungary exports more hardcore pornography than any other country. Her quest to track down the most unusual films is the stuff of legends, and she quickly compiled a list of titles that would shock even those with the broadest mind. If the Hertfordshire Rotary Club knew of her double life, she would be excommunicated.

Unfortunately, as with most football schedules these days, television interfered and matches started to be moved. Saturday's early game at Újpest was switched to Friday and another afternoon option, Honvéd, became the Monday evening game. That left two games to choose from, at MTK Hungária, the current league leaders, or Rákospalotai EAC (REAC), who had been promoted the season before.

Less than a week before the due date, the Hungarian FA announced that REAC's opponents, FC Sopron had filed for bankruptcy, which meant their game was cancelled. Thus the original four-game weekend had been reduced to one. Still, at least it made the choice obvious.

After a ridiculously early start from south-east London, Jo and I arrived at London Luton airport at 5 a.m. London Luton! Now there's a laugh. I live in London, which, of course, is one of the biggest cities in the world, but to reach this outpost of sophisticated modern travel I had to drive through three counties – and that's the quickest route. From Charing Cross, the point from which all London distances are measured, it is thirty miles as the crow flies, hardly a London airport. But then again where is? London Gatwick is more than twenty miles away, London Stansted is twenty-nine miles away and a few years ago London Manston Airport, located on the shores of the English Channel at Ramsgate, handled flights by EUJet, yet was technically nearer Ostend in Belgium than Charing Cross.

Luton may not have been convenient but it did offer a chance to pack in all the necessary components of a good weekend trip, namely football, food, beer and a bit of sightseeing.

The first impressions of Budapest were good. A smart new airport terminal, good signage in English, and quite a few locals who could have been models. Having started watching *Hostel 2* on the plane, I was nervous about boarding the ancient train from the airport when it finally arrived, especially when I took a look at the locals. The simple three-point

151

plan, the trusted course of action all over the world to avoid getting into difficult situations, was required. First, don't talk. Second, refrain from pulling out phone/camera/iPod, and third, on no account get out a map and look lost.

All was going well for at least thirty seconds before Football Jo leaned over and said loudly that 'someone smells of Gorgonzola' and could she borrow the map to see where the hotel was as the GPS on her phone wasn't picking up a signal. Perfect. We could not have attracted more attention to ourselves had we worn Chelsea away shirts and walked in playing the trombone. Faced with the option of disowning her or playing along with the tourist façade, I reverted to looking at fantastic views of factories, car-breaker yards and rubbish dumps as we passed through the council-estate-riddled suburbs of Pest.

The central station goes by the memorable name Nyugati Páalyaudvar and apparently hasn't changed much since the days when the Orient Express would pass through on the way to Istanbul. Beautiful wood-panelled waiting rooms, antiquated signage, beggars and piles of rubbish (can you see a theme here?). We did stumble across the fantastically named Club Cool, still open and complete with a scary bouncer outside and a number of cheap-looking women trying to drag in passing tourists – at 10.30 a.m. on a Saturday morning!

Our hotel was in a side street close to the historic Oktogon area of Pest, on the right bank of the Danube, and it turned out to be a brand new serviced apartment block, with our 'Gold' suites each having a dining room, kitchen and bedroom. It provoked one of those moments when you need to go into the corridor just to check you have the right-numbered room! Amazing value for less than €100 per night and the only shame was that there wasn't enough time to arrange a candlelit dinner party.

There was no time for idling. We were off to the home of Ferencváros, the most feared and famous club in Hungary, to watch a match at lunchtime. Confession time here. When I first saw the fixtures I was disappointed that the mighty Green and Whites were playing away on this particular weekend. However, according to the Babel Fish translation, there was a game due to start at 12 p.m., although they couldn't give a translated answer to the question about which team was playing.

However, Ferencváros has such a history and tradition that a visit to their stadium was a must, even had it been just for a match played between mascots. The club still grabbed most sports headlines in the city despite being in the second tier of Hungarian football. Things went wrong for them in 2006 when they were relegated after being embroiled in a financial scandal that threatened to topple the government.

Our first trip on the metro passed without incident, although it was very noticeable that they took security very seriously. Instead of ticket barriers they had big men, with big dogs, who checked everyone in and out as well as every bag. Outside the metro station at Néepliget, opposite the ground, we found a market, or so we thought. It turned out to be a Hungarian offline eBay with the inhabitants of nearby tower blocks attempting to barter old clothes, bric-a-brac and other worldly goods. Football Jo was tempted by a pair of strange yellow tennis shorts and a single slipper but she had nothing with which to barter other than a Gucci handbag and nobody wanted to trade.

The Stadion Albert Flórián, to give it its proper name (the Üllöi úti if you want to be more informal), is unique. It is located on the corner of two main roads, and the raised highway heading south towards the airport gives drivers an excellent view of the stadium. It is bedecked in green and white benches, with executive boxes bolted on top of a stands. At the south end there is a statue we guessed was of Flórián Albert, the great Hungarian centre forward, European footballer of the year in 1967, five years after he was top scorer at the World Cup finals, although there was no plaque saying who it was. Behind this were VIP seats protected by glass windows.

It was here in 2005 that Millwall fans suffered the kind of beating they have been used to dishing out for years. Ferencváros was significantly censored by UEFA, and would have been banned from European competition if it wasn't for the enforced relegation. In the weeks leading to our visit the club were once again thrust into the limelight as, in a bizarre move, Kevin McCabe, the Sheffield United chairman and owner of a company called Esplanade, purchased the club and stadium in the hope of developing young talent to add passion to the South Yorkshire club on and off the field.

We were trying to find a way in to watch this 'game' of football that in theory had already started. As with many stadiums in Eastern Europe, if you walk around and try enough doors eventually you will find one that has been left unlocked. In this case we did not expect it to be one that said 'Players' Entrance'. Walking through it and straight out of the tunnel onto the pitch was not exactly what I expected but that's what happened.

There was no game, but there was a full-blown first-team training session going on.

On seeing a couple of bag-carrying tourists, the whole squad stopped and stared. I did what any self-respecting person would do when walking into a strange place, obviously not supposed to be there. I took out my notebook and started writing.

'Act as if we are scouts, and we will get away with this,' I said to Jo. Sure enough, within ten seconds the players had returned to their squat thrusts, star jumps and hopeless free kicks from forty yards.

Judging by the state of the stadium it was difficult to envisage what McCabe had seen in terms of potential. It was in a desperate state of repair. Everywhere was overdue a lick of paint, the roof of the one and only covered stand was full of holes, and the pitch was worse than my back garden.

We stayed for all of five minutes, getting up with an obvious shake of the head as if to say 'You're shit and you know you are' and went out the way we had come in. Leaving the car park, we could see a women's game in full flow on one of the training pitches, so wandered over.

What was remarkable was that all twenty-two players had ponytails. Was there some unwritten rule in Hungarian female football that all hairstyles had to conform? Had we stumbled upon a secret society? Football Jo used to play right back for Luton Ladies, which probably explains her complete lack of knowledge of the offside law, and she critically assessed the performance of the teams over the next ten minutes. A few things struck me about the female game in general though during this brief period, such as:

When a player kicked the ball a long distance they made a grunting sound, not dissimilar to the noise made when serving by most women tennis players.

When one team scored, everyone clapped, including the goalkeeper who had just conceded the goal – and the referee.

Whenever they ran with the ball they did so with their arms outstretched like some strange aeroplane impressionists.

Jo was able to explain this last point. It was necessary for balance as apparently 'women have bigger chests than men' and as these stuck out they would fall flat on their faces if they didn't use their arms for balance.

Realising that the game unfolding at a snail's pace in front of us was the mysterious twelve o'clock kick-off I had to think fast as Jo was getting into the match. I had no intention of letting the fact I had actively sought out a women's game in order to visit a new stadium become common knowledge. So I told her that Hungary was on BST plus two hours and we would miss the main game's kick-off if we didn't leave there and then.

We returned to the city for a quick peek at the national stadium, conveniently located next to Stadionok metro station, three stops from the centre of town on the red metro line two. The Ferenc Puskás stadium (previously the Nep) is the biggest arena in the country and, while it is home to the national side, it is a long time since it has been more than half full. As we approached there were rows of security men. In Eastern Europe security men are easy to spot. They are all five feet tall and five feet wide with shaved heads, and they wear huge black puffa jackets with 'security' on the back, which is the universal language in these countries for 'I am carrying a Glock.' This crack team were busy protecting the entrance to Budapest's Green Show, an exhibition next to the stadium and full of *Viz* magazine's Malcolm and Cressida types to whom sneaking in for free would be as alien as a day out deforesting. As we went to walk past the entrance, the thug squad blocked the way, saying that the exhibition was ticket only. Filled with disappointment at missing out on such a cultural high point, we carried on towards the stadium on a road that passed what appeared to be another market.

Having already seen the Soviet-style architecture in the suburbs, this small market was right out of what I imagined life was like in the old Soviet Union. Scores of people were setting up stalls, selling what is best described as rubbish. Think back to when you last walked along the street in England and saw an odd trainer, a discarded T-shirt or a strange pair of trousers? Well that was what these people were buying and selling. People had also set up stalls selling food. Not hot dogs or burgers. They were purveying what appeared to be pieces of dead birds, grilled over oil-drum fires. Bottles of strange yellow fluid were being passed around.

The overwhelming characteristic of the area was the smell. There was a distinct pong of urine, and the reason was evident around the corner. Instead of toilet facilities, a nearby wall was serving as a public (very public!) convenience for trader and consumer alike. All very well, except it was at the top of a small incline and so all the pee ran down the road into the market and was beginning to puddle around the feet of the food vendors. Not too be outdone by their male rivals, a few women had got into the right spirit by hitching up their skirts and squatting down to have a go in full view of shoppers. This was not an attractive sight and even Jo, with her bizarre taste in night-time entertainment, found the whole scene disturbing.

We eventually found the stadium entrance and had a wander around. A vast empty bowl, with no roof for most spectators, and a genuine feeling of underuse and neglect. The stadium, named after Hungary's most famous ever footballer, Ferenc Puskás, has been full only once in the past decade, and that wasn't for a football match. It was used by Steven Spielberg as a double for the 1972 Olympic Stadium when filming *Munich*, the story of the Black September terrorist attacks on the Israeli Olympic team. It still had all the signs of a classic communist arena with towering and imposing floodlights, plenty of stark statues around the outside of the stands and uncomfortable seats.

Time was getting on and with the main event of the weekend looming we boarded a number fourteen tram which appeared to be running in the general direction of MTK's stadium. At this point I had no idea where we were going, most unlike me. No map showed the Hidegkuti Nándor Stadium but I figured that as they were the current league leaders and biggest club in Hungary the crowds would guide the way.

At the tram stop there were no signs of football fans apart from a sullen teenager wearing a Torquay United shirt, who clearly wasn't a football fan or had any taste. This assessment is based on the one and only Torquay fan I know, Luge Pravda, who runs our New York office. Not only has he one of the best names in the company, he is also one of the funniest guys you could ever meet. He regularly emails with his footballing views, completely unbelievable and always linked back somehow to Torquay. Ask him for his opinion on where Cristiano Ronaldo will be transferred next summer and he will have a fully constructed argument why he will end up on the Devon Riviera.

We did see a chap with a scarf and so comforted ourselves that the rest of the crowd must be in the stadium already, arranging a passionate display of support.

The tram rattled down the Hungarian Utca for five minutes before we saw the crumbling ground on our right and hopped off. From the outside it appeared it had been abandoned years ago and had been left to the vandals. The ticket office had a small, broken window in the outside wall and even with no Hungarian language skills I managed to pay 160 Forints, or around £7, for two top-range seats in the main stand. It became clear that the ticket office also doubled up as the women's toilets and that to dispense his wares the seller simply locked himself in a cubicle before kick-off.

MTK Budapest 3 Bodajk Siófok 0 – Hidegkuti Nándor Stadium – 29th March 2008

We were in the back row of the main stand, which offered a good view of the action, in theory the best seats in the house. The stadium was used in the film *Escape to Victory* in 1981, and it is ironic that the last time it underwent redevelopment was for the purpose of making it look forty years older for the film's final scene where the Allies, inspired by Pele, Bobby Moore and, of course, the world-class goalkeeper Sylvester Stallone beat the Nazis. The small MTK 'firm' were stood below us in the five-row paddock, and opposite our stand was an open terrace with blue and white seats, completely empty apart from a group of Swedish fans looking completely out of place flying their blue and yellow flags with pride.

The game was entertaining. It took some time to work out which team was MTK as every time there was an attack a small section of the crowd cheered. We eventually worked out they were the blue team, not the pink team. This was based on the ball boys quickly throwing the balls back to the blues as opposed to ignoring it when the pink-shirted team won a throw-in or corner.

Being a neutral made a refreshing change, especially having sat through so many disappointing games at Upton Park in the past season and a half. A strong second half performance by MTK saw them score three times in quick succession, although one miss will live forever in my memory. After earning a penalty, MTK's centre forward picked himself up, dusted himself down and blasted the penalty against the bar. As the goalkeeper lay prone, the centre forward followed the ball towards the goal and with the net empty and from just five yards he managed to hoof it over the bar.

The game strengthened MTK's lead at the top, the chairman's prediction of making an impression in Europe close to becoming a reality. Unfortunately, despite winning the title, they were humiliated by Fenerbahçe in the Champions League qualifying rounds, losing 5-0 in Budapest to complete a 7-0 aggregate defeat.

With such a small crowd, public transport was hardly bursting at the seams and we were back at the hotel within twenty minutes of the final whistle. Having yet to see any culture the city had to offer we decided to visit Buda and take in a few major sights.

Football Jo had a dilemma. She wanted to watch the Manchester United versus Aston Villa game to get her weekly portion of Cristiano Ronaldo, but she had not yet found any of the titles from her over-eighteens' wish list and wanted to track them down in dodgy back-street shops. The agreement was that we would go into whichever came first, a bar showing TV or a porn shop. Fortunately for me it was a good bar behind St Stephen's Cathedral and we settled for food, beer and some Rooney appreciation. This area was what I expected from such a historic city. A very attractive waterfront, dominated by the castle on the Buda side, and the parliament on the Pest side, linked by the Chain Bridge which was lit up as the sun went down, sending thousands of reflections on to the still Danube.

After a decent three-course meal, a few beers and spending less than £20 a head we went back to the apartments. Jo still hadn't found a shop of ill-repute and I was too tired to care, so making my excuses I made sure I sat on both sofas, each seat at the dining table and, of course, on the balcony – just to get my money's worth!

Sunday morning brought glorious sunshine and after an early swim we were ready to face the city. Football Jo wanted to try one of the famous thermal baths, and as I had no intention of stripping naked and being pummelled to death by a large Hungarian, I left her to it, deciding to head north to find one or two of the other grounds for research purposes. I had a rough idea where to go, but after forty minutes wandering around the same neighbourhood it was back to Plan B to find the Stadion Rudolf Illovszky, and that was to call home! With the PC fired up, CMF managed to find directions to FC Vasas's stadium in the Budapest's 13th district.

If MTK was a dump, then Vasas SC was a whole refuse tip. Most of it was boarded up, but what was left of the main stand (I assume it was the main stand as it had half a Perspex roof on it) was just rough benches bolted onto the terraces. And this was home to another team in the top division. Certainly not a stadium to rush back to, and it prompted the feeling that if it was in England, even at the Blue Square South level, it would be condemned and closed down immediately.

Back in Oktogon, I heard Jo's tale from the baths. Her best chance of some action for the whole weekend had disappeared even though she found herself wearing a only a small towel in a locked massage room with a large Hungarian masseur.

It seemed a great opportunity for some romance for my friend from Luton, but unfortunately he was blind and spoke no English. She did give him the eye and struck suggestive poses before realising his disability. Was it worth it? Her comments about the roughness of the massage and the lack of any 'male totty' made it seem that wandering the suburbs of Budapest looking for a fifth-rate football stadium was actually a better use of time.

After a quick lunch (Hungarian for a BK Whopper is 'Whopper'; amazing!) we sought more culture at Budapest's most visited tourist attraction – The House of Terror. After the Second World War, the building in Andrássy Utca became the home of the AVO, the secret police, and was the scene of the murder of hundreds of dissidents. It was very interesting, and the trip in the purposefully slow lift to the dungeons with the voice of the executioner playing was very disturbing. I am not normally one to feel 'presence' in places like this, unlike my dear mother, who can feel a presence in the fruit and veg section in Waitrose, but the basement area was very spooky and unnerving.

With a couple of hours left we had a few beers in the city park before it was back to the airport, and a snooze all the way to Luton. One of the better trips of the past few years, and certainly a place to recommend as a great weekend destination. As luck would have it I would be back within six months, this time on company expenses, for more fun, but for now there were lasting memories of grand buildings, rundown football stadiums and that awful sight of that old lady squatting in the market.

CAN FOOTBALL GET MORE DEPRESSING THAN THIS?

Life in the land of a pope, a palace and a passionless crowd

Watching football in most European countries is an introduction to some real nutty fans. Passion often overflows into madness in continental Europe, as anyone who has been to a Rome derby or Feyenoord against Ajax can testify. The Turks are another nation deeply passionate about their support, but for all their bluster their domestic game is relatively tame.

One nation, however, which still has a major issue with football-related violence is Poland. And in the quest to get to the real heart of the sport I had still to visit the country. I had planned to go earlier in the year to Warsaw and Łódź (pronounced Woodge), Poland's two biggest cities, but a combination of flight delays, poor weather and a better offer from CMF meant the trip was abandoned at the last minute.

However, with West Ham playing one of the most pointless games in the history of football, away at Premier League-chasing Manchester United (not helped by our clueless manager Alan Curbishley, who stated in the run-up to the match that United deserved to be champions), there was an opportunity to organise a weekend away in Poland to sample that overzealous support. The most logical destination was Kraków, a city with two clubs who had been at each other's throats for decades.

What made it even better was that I was to be joined by not one, but two beautiful angels. With the children safely installed in front of the television, CMF won the equivalent of one of Willy Wonka's golden tickets and agreed to come with me, after exhausting all potential excuses not to go. Unfortunately at the last minute the second angel, Charlotte Church, pulled out as Gav still hadn't managed to figure out the recipe to make Chicken Super Noodles. But fear not, a quick call to Luton's favourite sister of sin and Football Jo was on the plane quicker than you could say Szeczin correctly.

Kraków was chosen for a number of reasons. It gave the opportunity to see a game, have some decent food, see a little of the country and explore the history of a city that has become synonymous with good and evil. OK, I admit it was also a chance to get some decent vodka down my throat and experience some Danny Dyer-inspired Polish hooligan-fuelled football.

Flights were sorted to Katowice, one of Poland's most industrial and ugliest cities, where the huge steelworks of Chorzów dominates both the skyline and the environmental agenda. From there we would pick up a car and drive the forty-five minutes or so down to the birthplace of Karol Józef Wojtyła, better known as Pope John Paul II, who had once stood on the very terraces we would be visiting the following day.

However, first we had to negotiate our way through the airport and endure what would become a recurring theme of the weekend, the Polish concept of customer service. Queuing for passport control, waiting for baggage, going through customs was always the same. Every passenger was viewed with the same suspicion, fear and loathing.

The plan was to drive to the hotel, around fifteen miles south-west of Kraków, dump the bags and sample Polish hospitality in the city. We had landed on Constitution Day, one of Poland's national holidays, and we saw how proud the Poles were of their country. Every lamp post displayed a flag and everyone was in their Sunday best on their way to church. The drive took longer than we thought, mostly due to Football Jo's navigating skills. I was convinced she thought we wanted to know where the Battle of Zagbre took place, and where Javok Milojka lived but, at the expense of unimportant issues such as 'take next left', or 'head onto the A44', that was probably not the best form of navigation.

The forty-five-minute drive became a one-and-a-half-hour laugh-a-minute comedy romp. After all, we all know how easy it is to get used to driving an unfamiliar car, on unfamiliar roads, with unreadable road signs while your passengers discuss major issues of the day such as 'Angelina

Jolie or Madonna – who is a better mother?' and 'Why do men have such a hang-up with the fact I have seven handbags?'

I had promised a real special treat for our accommodation – a nineteenth-century hunting lodge in the middle of the countryside – although I had lied to Jo on the flight over that it was the hotel used in the films *Hostel* and *Hostel 2* to try to stop her talking about the forthcoming Cambridge Folk Festival. The Paszkowka Palace Hotel was used by one of the crown princes of Poland and was as impressive in real life as it was from the pictures on the internet.

The smell of food was wonderful, and after a long trip from Luton we decided to delay our trip into Kraków until we had eaten. With the 'when in Rome eat like a Roman' theory strictly enforced, we opted for a range of soups – asparagus, chicken and beetroot – and a selection of local meat, all washed down with vodka. With West Ham already 3-0 down after twenty minutes there seemed little point in following the original plan of finding somewhere to watch the humiliation, so we settled down for a few hours of chat. Well the girls did, continuing their thought-provoking conversations such as 'Gordon Brown should be Prime Minister because he looks like a lost puppy', 'Why there aren't enough magazines for women' and 'Why the *News of the World* and *Heat* are the only places where the truth is written.' I had a snooze.

After an hour, and another Manchester United goal, we were shown our rooms and found the swimming pool, fitness suite and spa. Hmmm – not quite as in the brochure. The swimming pool was being filled from the fire hose in the corridor and was due to be ready 'sometime on Tuesday'. The fitness suite was two bicycles fixed to the floor and some dumb-bells which were being used to hold open the door, and the spa was no more than a garden pond with a SodaStream by the side!

Kraków beckoned, and remarkably, despite Jo's directions, which included fantastic statements such as 'Oh look, there's an IKEA. Do you think they do meatballs?' and 'Is the no entry sign the same in Polish?' we found Błonia Park, which separates the two football grounds in the west of the city centre. We walked around the Wisła Stadium, to which we would be returning the following day for their game versus LKS Łódź . Huge barbed wire fences, crumbling terraces and Stalinist architecture. Graffiti covered the stadium's outer walls, while every accessible window had been smashed at some point and not repaired.

Overcome with joy at the prospect of attending a game there in less than twenty-four hours, I told the girls that this was as good as it got in terms of Polish football and demonstrated the point by taking them across the park to the home of Cracovia. Three of the stands were open to the normally harsh Polish elements and behind each goal the basic terraces had become overrun with weeds. We are now so used to modern all-seater stadiums in England that a visit to a place like this is a real eye-opener, especially when it could easily have been hosting Champions League football in less than four months' time.

On the way back to the city centre we passed the Astro Hotel (now the Orbis) which sits squarely next to Cracovia's stadium. The hotel is a relic of the communist age. A huge concrete block, its interior is a slate shade of dull grey, with I would imagine customer service to match. Yet it was heaving, with dozens of coaches lining the car park and disgorging their passengers. Oh how they would have laughed as they looked out of the Astro's grimy windows across the park to the Radisson SAS opposite, with its impressive glass exterior and Mercedes filling the car park.

The old town has a huge square similar in design (and crowds) to St Mark's in Venice or Grand Place in Brussels. With only a couple of hours to spend, we needed to get the most from the visit so we chose to take a Golf Cart tour. After finding a driver who spoke no English, we set off at a pace, the two girls sitting behind the driver and me at the rear of the vehicle facing backwards. Initially this was fine as it provided great views as we whizzed through the crowded back streets.

Every so often the cart would stop, the speaker above our heads would crackle into life and an American voice would spout a line of commentary about a particular building, a commentary punctuated by the driver pointing at something in the distance. This was OK until we reached the ring road and began driving at the vehicle's top speed, which seemed to me, hanging on at the back with no protection, to be around twenty-five miles per hour. This was bad enough, but having Polish lorry drivers accelerating towards you was enough to scare anyone witless.

The tour lasted for ninety minutes and included a visit to Oskar Schindler's factory, a derelict building with a temporary sign saying it belonged to Oskar Schindler and was currently closed for refurbishment. It was in such a bad state of repair that it seemed it will be 2050 before it reopens. Although we were feeling weary after the long ride around the sites, Jo sprang to life as we passed along the outer ring road. It was her cultural highlight of the day, a strip of sex shops with a DVD clearance sale. But, despite her best attempts, our driver did not understand what 'stop' or 'porn' meant and all she could do was look ruefully at the long line of English stag parties wandering into live sex shows.

CMF wanted to make the most of the night away *sans enfants* and enjoy a good meal with decent company. A few years before, we all (CMF, Football Jo and the Little Fullers) went to Valencia for a weekend and stayed at a brand new five-star hotel built for the America's Cup. That night I drew the short straw, agreeing to look after the children while the girls went for a candlelit dinner in the posh restaurant. We enjoyed a family bag of Doritos and watched *Jaws* on pay TV. Judging by the funny looks and comments CMF and Football Jo got from the hotel staff they must have assumed they were in a relationship and that I was the nanny.

This time I joined them and we tucked into a full Polish banquet, featuring at least four different types of dead animal and enough potato products to feed our troops in Iraq. The girls decided to try the local wine, but attempts at ordering it resulted in them being served either vodka or water. They could, of course, have decided to send both back but at every opportunity they downed the glass and called for more. Someone was going to suffer in the morning and it wasn't going to be me.

Sunday morning was initially going to have started with a leisurely trip to the spa before visiting Auschwitz, one of the most infamous places in the history of the world. However, two of the party were feeling the worse for wear and could not face surfacing early. So we went west to the scene of one of the biggest crimes ever committed against humanity.

I will not dwell on Auschwitz. I had expected a peaceful place where it would be possible to reflect on the horrendous crimes committed there. Instead there were dozens of tour buses, full of snap-happy tourists taking pictures. The site is divided in two. Auschwitz was the original camp, and is much as it was when liberated in 1945. The buildings are still in place and exhibits had been set up in brick-based outhouses. However, with the sun shining, people wandering around in shorts, and children laughing and playing, the mood was completely different to what I expected. What no one can be prepared for, though, is the immense size of the second camp, Auschwitz Birkenau, around a mile away. While most of the buildings were destroyed after the war you could still see the sheer size of the concentration camp, and only imagine what horrors went on here.

Although irked by the atmosphere, I was glad to have made the visit, and my overwhelming memory wasn't of the conditions or the despairing stories but a lonely man sitting on the steps of a detention block with his head in his hands.

Now I might have read the situation completely wrongly. Maybe he was overwhelmed by the oppressive atmosphere and the history of the place, but bearing in mind he was wearing a Leicester City shirt and ten minutes previously their relegation from the Championship had been confirmed, I reckoned it was because he would have to go to Division One grounds next season. But why on earth would you choose to go to a place like Auschwitz on such a day and in a Leicester City shirt?

It was now time for more classic Polish customer service in a restaurant. This time you ordered at the till and waited until someone held up a plate and shouted something completely different, at which there would be a scrum to get to the dish. The waitress would then shout 'no' a few times and give it to the meekest person in the crowd. I left it to the girls to get the food by smiling sweetly, and sure enough within minutes we were tucking into a strange grey meat platter that should have been chicken.

It was time for Wisła's game with Łódź . Although a seasoned traveller, I am sometimes surprised at the location of places in relation to others. Before visiting Slovakia I had an impression it was further east than it really is; that Macedonia was further south and Luxembourg would be interesting. Wrong on all three counts. However, less than two hours' drive eastwards from Kraków is the city of Lviv, one of the biggest settlements in Ukraine. Ukraine is almost in a different continent and here it was on a road sign. I almost had a *Thelma and Louise* moment and considered driving on past Kraków and heading for the land of Chernobyl, Dynamo Kiev and tall, stroppy blondes.

We stopped in the same spot at the north of the park we had visited twenty-four hours earlier and, with the sun still shining, sat on the grass to enjoy the weather and a beer. So this was where Danny Dyer thought it was 'gonna get a bit naughty' in his *International Football Factories* series. Wisła fans, families and couples sat around rejoicing in the sunshine. No one was running amok as Greenwich's finest had described. However, one fact did ring true. We had not seen a single non-white face, apart from the tourists at Auschwitz and in the city centre. Racism in Polish football is a real problem, and with few non-white fans attending games the situation is spiralling out of control.

The queues at the ticket windows were non-existent, as if the fans had simply decided to boycott the game in favour of a barbecue at home. With my Polish now coming along in leaps and bounds – well, I had printed a map of the stadium, written the number three on it and an arrow to where we wanted to sit – we acquired three main stand tickets for less than £10, although with the stadium redevelopment only fifty per cent completed, the main stand is not as luxurious as it sounds.

Wisła Krakow 5 LKS Łódź 2 – Wisłly Stadium – 4th May 2008

Wisła were still hoping they might stage matches in the 2012 European Championships, although they were not on the original list, and reckoned their stadium would eventually be a modern, fully functioning arena when complete, but for now we had to make do with two modern single-tier stands that ran down the sides of the pitch. The old main stand was now behind one of the goals as the pitch had been rotated ninety degrees when building work started. There was no roof, although with an early-evening sunset this was no problem. At the far end, the away terrace had seen many better days and was one of the most inhospitable sections I have seen: crumbling terrace steps, barbed wire and high fences. Not a problem, though, as LKS Łódź had brought only seventeen fans.

The game was a cracker but my overwhelming memory wasn't the comical defending of both sides, or the unbelievable decision by the linesman to award a penalty to Wisła for a handball that a) hit the defender in the chest, b) was a cross from a forward in an offside position and c) was at least two yards outside the penalty area, but the racist abuse dished out to one of the away team's substitutes when he warmed up.

The fan on my left said it was the same for every team; even Wisła fans had booed and racially chanted at their own players in the past. With less than four years until Poland is due to host a major tournament you have to wonder how these fans would react at seeing the likes of Micah Richards, Thierry Henry or Ryan Babel. The BBC had shown a report from Legia Warsaw concerning this issue, and the so-called 'experts' from our media said that seeing such players as Henry and Drogba (I wondered if the 'expert' realised the Chelsea striker plays for Ivory Coast, who are not part of UEFA!) would turn them immediately into non-racists! Life must be seen through rose-coloured spectacles in the offices of some newspapers.

I had expected a more passionate level of support from the home fans. But there were no flares, little in the way of organised singing and chanting or waving banners. Perhaps it was the weather or that it was a relatively meaningless end-of-season game but the fans acted as if on medication. Perhaps it was the wrong day, but my impression of Polish football was that it had no more passion on or off the pitch than a game from the League of Wales.

So, after a quiet drive back to Katowice with both girls asleep and thus not talking bollocks about Kerry Katona and why her marriage was destined to fail, we came to the end of another cracking weekend away. CMF was pleased we had spent quality time together, although she still blamed me for spiking her drinks the previous night. Football Jo was sad she hadn't had time for one of her shopping trips.

Marks out of ten for Krakow as a weekend venue – eight.

Marks out of ten for Polish football – two.

To borrow a phrase from Bob Hoskins in *The Long Good Friday*, 'Polish Hooligans – I've shit 'em!' And Mr Dyer, in future try visiting some of these games in the summer when people are a tad more relaxed and not worried about losing their fingers to frostbite!

CHAPTER
25
CHAPTER

WISH YOU WERE HERE – TOO BLOODY RIGHT, McCLOWN!

A neutral's view of the world's second biggest tournament, without England

When a very damp and disconsolate England team eventually left the Wembley pitch at 10 p.m. on Wednesday 21st November after losing at home to Croatia, most fans could not begin to imagine the pain they would feel when the 2008 European Championships kicked off in Switzerland some seven months later without England. Some fans vowed not to watch the tournament, disgusted that a team of our so-called quality failed to qualify.

However, over the next few weeks a number saw the silver lining in the defeat. If England were not taking part, a trip to see a few matches would be significantly cheaper than expected. For me there was the bonus that applying for a media pass was much easier because of minimal interest from the British press.

There would be a number of short trips in the first round and the anticipation of enjoying the football, the food and the festivities without having to listen to endless out-of-tune renditions of 'The Great Escape' from the scourge of the English team abroad, the FA Band.

The opportunity to sample a tournament as a media representative, without having to worry which English player would be the next to humiliate himself from the penalty spot, was enticing, and so as soon as the media pass had been confirmed I booked the trips.

First, the good news. For most games flights were cheap and easy to arrange. A return on UneasyJet to Geneva was a bargain £45 return, some £200 cheaper than when England visited in November 2005.

The bad news was that hotel rooms were impossible to come by, especially in Switzerland. However, all was not lost as, thanks to the generosity of the organisers, first-class train travel was free for the tournament's duration, so a couple of trips were planned with the concept of using a train seat as a hotel bed.

Trip One was to Geneva to watch Portugal versus Turkey.

You'd be hard-pressed to find two other countries hated so vehemently by England fans as Portugal and Turkey. The reasons are so diverse. To lose to one team on penalties in the quarter-final of a major competition is unlucky but it takes some doing to do it twice in two years. But Portugal managed to put one over on England in Lisbon in the European Championships of 2004 and then two years later in Gelsenkirchen at the 2006 World Cup finals. The matches are remembered for the early exits of Wayne Rooney, a broken metatarsal in Lisbon and a petulant stamp that led to a red card in 2006.

On the other hand, for many fans Turkey conjure up a return to the dark days of football violence, and the hatred for some inexplicable reason still runs deep. And here were our two 'enemies' facing each other.

The midday flight (leaving late of course) got to Geneva at 3.30 p.m. on the opening day of the tournament, and after crossing the motorway (quite literally; after all, who wouldn't risk a five per cent chance of death on a major road to save a thirty-minute walk?) I checked in at the hotel. Thirty minutes later I was at the Stade de Genève, officially a member of the press corps. Most major organising committees give the media a free gift, but it is hard to guess what it will be. Some give away bags for a laptop, others polo shirts, but there is always the risk that it will be a golf umbrella or something completely impractical to carry. In the 2007 Rugby World Cup it was a fantastic Heineken beer glass shaped like a rugby ball which was almost impossible to take home without breaking.

UEFA conformed to standard and handed out a bag, with lots of pockets to stuff with as many free copies of the official tournament programme (normally 15 Swiss francs) as possible. These were being listed on eBay within days. With a few hours until the kick-off of the tournament in Basle it was time to see what other freebies could be blagged. Media centres sound very exciting but they are normally nothing more than a big marquee with rows of tables where journalists sit typing away on laptops with the intent of filling thousands of column inches. Geneva was no exception but there were a few familiar faces from the Rugby World Cup.

Geneva's stadium is in the middle of nowhere. Sandwiched between a railway line and motorway, with a shopping centre at one end, it is not blessed with good public transport access. In fact the official guide recommends a fifty-minute 'fans' walk from the city centre, taking in many of the city's main sites and passing the official Fans' Village.

The idea of cramming the fans into one area (essentially a compound) with toilet facilities that were almost non-existent, food and drink that were overpriced and where there was no shade from the sun or cover from the rain seems like fan hell, but they are very popular, especially with locals, who can pretend they are at the game. The one in Lisbon during the 2004 European Championships at the old Expo site was brilliant. Not only did it have an arena constructed like a small stadium, where matches were shown on big-screen TVs, but it also had some excellent games such as 'Can you shoot as hard as Roberto Carlos' and the football equivalent of 'Hole in One' with a goal floating some fifty yards out in the harbour, the idea being to try to score three goals.

At the 2006 World Cup in Germany, the organising committee took it one stage further by building mini-stadiums in many cities just for the games. Many an unsuspecting fan was fooled into buying a World Cup final ticket on eBay only to find they had a seat in the twenty-thousand-seater arena built by Adidas.

Geneva's version was no different, although as the opening match was the game between Switzerland and the Czech Republic it was not surprising that the place was packed and hardly the most pleasant place from which to watch. Instead I was off find to a small French restaurant and to meet Howard (and his dad).

Howard is one of a dozen or so fans who have not missed an England game, home or away, for more than twenty years. He even travelled on a day trip to Tel Aviv in 2007, only hours after the birth of his first child, just to maintain his record. He didn't have a ticket but had the money with which to negotiate so we had a decent meal, a couple of beers and headed for the stadium for Portugal v Turkey. With so many sellers, the market was certainly in his favour and within minutes he had snared a ticket at face value.

Portugal 2 Turkey 0 – Stade de Genève – 7th June 2008

The Stade de Genève was alive with noise and colour as both sets of fans tried their best to outdo each other. The dull-looking stadium had been transformed into a sea of red and maroon by the fans, and with the grey clouds hanging over the mountains in the distance, everyone waited patiently for what promised to be a cracking game. The earlier offering between the Czechs and the Swiss had been disappointing, but this game started at a real pace with the Portuguese using Ronaldo wide on the right to attack the weaknesses in the Turkish backline.

The first half had plenty of incident as the Turks played to form, diving to the floor at every opportunity, and with only one yellow card issued it was arguable that the German referee was turning a blind eye to most things. Pepe thought he had given the Portuguese the lead in the nineteenth minute but his header from a Deco corner was ruled out for a push. Pepe and the Portuguese bench appeared not to have heard the referee's whistle as they carried on celebrating for a good thirty seconds while play continued around them, making them look particularly stupid. Ronaldo, sporting what could only be described as a baby mullet, hit the post with a free kick late in the first half.

The second half started much as the first half ended, with Portugal continuing to pump cross-pitch balls to Ronaldo, and he continued to beat defenders with ease. The veteran Nuno Gomes hit the post in the fiftieth minute after the referee played advantage following a clear foul on Simão in the penalty area.

Pepe eventually got his goal after an hour following a great one-two with Deco. Although there was still half an hour to go, the goal essentially destroyed the Turks, and apart from a couple of ludicrous penalty appeals they ran out of steam with ten minutes left. Thanks to the brain and quick feet of Deco, substitute Raul Meireles finished off the game for the Portuguese in injury time after rounding the keeper.

Three points for one of the tournament favourites, and game number one on the UEFA gravy train under my belt. With a strategically well-located hotel I thought it would be an easy journey back. How wrong could I be? This was proof of why Switzerland and Austria cannot host big events. I even waited in the media centre for an hour after the game to allow the crowds to disperse. On leaving the stadium it was north to Lancy, the nearest point of civilisation to the ground, to wait for a tram. And wait, and wait. After twenty minutes one turned up absolutely packed apart from the end carriage. Those of us waiting at the stop boarded, only to be hit with the smell and sight of vomit on most seats. This wasn't an 'I feel a bit sick and cannot hold it in' type but an 'I am going to make sure I cover every inch of the tram with this baby.'

The tram took ages to crawl through the streets as Portuguese fans in their cars were driving like maniacs, beeping their horns as if they had won the tournament, as opposed to beating the twentieth-best team in the world (according to the FIFA rankings anyway).

The tram eventually got into Cornavin, the city's main station, from where the train for the five-minute journey to the airport was due to leave. But the 'extra' trains laid on through the night for fans meant that there was one every two hours instead of the usual three. It left a difficult decision. Walk the three miles, wait in a very long line for a taxi or try to find the bus. After waiting more than thirty minutes for a taxi prepared to go such a short distance I gave up. And then a miracle happened. A number five bus signposted to Aeroport/Palexpo drew to a halt on the opposite side of the road. Without any care for the traffic or other pedestrians, I sprinted across, confirmed it was going my way and settled back for the ten-minute journey.

Hopefully I would be at the hotel by 1 a.m., and four hours' sleep would have to do before I returned to the UK. After twenty minutes' driving around the northern suburbs we arrived at the deserted exhibition centre known as Palexpo, where the driver told the dozen or so passengers who also wanted to get to the airport that he was terminating the bus and we had to get out and that another bus would come 'in about an hour' to take us the remaining mile to our destination.

So much for the 'transport experience you will never forget' which the Swiss had promised us. What made it all the worse is that the airport was clearly visible a few hundred yards away, with only an eight-lane motorway in between. So, with a choice of waiting another hour or trying to find a way across the road I once again chose the latter, much to the surprise of everyone else, who must have guessed I was English and thus either drunk or mad, or both. A twenty-minute assault course was all it took to realise my hotel backed on to the Palexpo car park, and my bravado had all been in vain. A quick turnaround awaited me in the UK as I prepared for a return to Salzburg, home of Mozart, Red Bull and chocolate, salty marzipan balls!

When Greece were announced as one of the two first seeds for the tournament, alongside the Netherlands (after hosts Austria and Switzerland were automatically given top billing), everyone wanted to be drawn in their group. However, when the dust settled on Group D there could have been few able to predict the final positions, as all four had a chance. The ever-improving Russians were so reliant on their midfield maestro Andrei Arshavin, who would be missing from the first two games after a needless sending-off in their final qualifying game away to Andorra, and many thought that they might struggle in the early games; perennial underachievers Spain had at last found the attacking balance that would surely see them reach at least the last eight; Greece had been written off as flukey winners four years ago but had bounced back from missing out on the 2006 World Cup in Germany to dominate their qualifying group, and Sweden were buoyed by the return from his second international retirement of Henrik Larsson to partner one of the most impressive players in Serie A, Zlatan Ibrahimović.

The first round was being played in Innsbruck and Salzburg, two of the most attractive cities in the Alps. I'd got a media pass for the Greece versus Sweden game in Salzburg and, ideally wanting to take just one day off work, I booked a ridiculously early flight back from Munich (ninety miles west of Salzburg) – 6.30 a.m. the morning after the game.

The plan was to be back in the UK by 7.30 a.m. and into the office at 9 a.m. At 4 a.m. on match day I was on the way to Stansted for a monthly slice of customer service Ryanair style. Having become an expert in 'Customer Experience', it amazes me that the airline can keep on going considering the number of complaints it receives. On this occasion they started their in-flight advertising at 6.30 a.m. and who (aside from the Scots) would want a double rum and coke at that hour? Apart from the stewardess waking me to ask if the magazine I was holding was rubbish (thanks for that, and guess where I'd have stuffed it given the chance!) the flight was relatively uneventful. Not surprisingly the plane was full of exiled Swedes and Greeks on their way to Austria for the game.

With nearly twelve hours to kill, and after just four hours' sleep, I wondered how I could stay awake for the rest of the day. There was the cinema, a possible venue for a few hours' sleep, but I decided to visit parts of Salzburg not seen on previous adventures. That meant breakfast

173

at Hangar 7, the impressive home of the Red Bull racing team, across the runway from the airport terminal, where you can peruse Red Bull branded jets, racing cars, helicopters, planes, trains and just about anything else that can be branded and raced.

Next it was off to fetch the press ticket. Public transport in Salzburg is efficient, and within fifteen minutes I was at Salzburg Europark, the huge out-of-town shopping centre, which has an IKEA and the railway station, the departure point for Munich later in the evening.

Amazingly there were no signs for the stadium. Having been here only nine months before I knew where it was – no more than a ten-minute walk away. But the locals, in keeping with the rest of the tournament, had decided such signs were irrelevant. Which meant the walk took twice as long, but from the stadium the media centre was so badly signposted that it took another twenty minutes to find it.

After a couple of hours of cool recuperation on a day when temperatures hit thirty degrees in Salzburg, it was time to check the FanZone in the city centre. The centre of Salzburg is not particularly big and it had become overrun with Swedes. Big Swedes, small Swedes, fat Swedes, thin Swedes, drunk Swedes and very drunk Swedes. The Swedes rank with Estonians and Danes in terms of beauty and what better way to show off fine feminine figures than dressing in football kit. Always does it for me. The Greeks were small in number, hairy, fat and ugly.

An Abba tribute band was on the huge FanZone stage getting everyone in the mood. It was like a hen night in Magaluf. Beer was flowing, songs were being sung and the sun shone down on the righteous. As if by some divine intervention, Abba-esque exited stage left, then the rain started and out came the extras from *My Big Fat Greek Wedding*. How to kill the dreams of five thousand men! The music was awful. 'Zorba's Dance' is about as far as Greek music goes on the world stage but these guys were intent on murdering any song they could get their hands on. Surely the organisers had seen the crowd of five thousand had dwindled to about thirty, and even the most ardent Greeks had fled to the bars instead of listening to Stavros and his goat.

Soon it was time to leave for the stadium to watch the rest of Spain versus Russia on TV. The media centre was packed but the Carlsberg remained under lock and key. What is the point of having a fridge full of the stuff if it's not there to be drunk?

With Spain cruising to a 3-0 win, I popped into the bar for a Coke and bumped into two footballing legends. First it was Franz Beckenbauer, who was very pleasant, asking if I was enjoying the tournament, who did I think would win and did I like Salzburg? As a parting note he said to say 'Hello' to everyone in England. Then I spotted someone with a bright red face and thinning ginger hair. It was McClown himself, our recently departed England manager. He refused to give a word for the blog, saying he was 'watching the Russian defensive formation in the game'.

Quite right, mate. But if you'd done it last year we might have been properly prepared for the game in Moscow and not lost. Then it would have been England here and not Russia. What exactly was McClown doing here? What possible expert opinion could he offer to anyone after the tactical failures he imposed on England? As a colleague said, it was good news for Blackburn Rovers fans as interviews for their vacant manager's job had taken place in Lancashire earlier in the day and he obviously hadn't been shortlisted.

There weren't a lot of press in Salzburg, and after climbing up the Lego Technics towers to the media area it was obvious most had gone west to Innsbruck for the Spain match earlier in the day. It seemed a shame, though, that so many real fans were missing the chance of seeing this game while some fat journalist couldn't be arsed to cancel his seat. The UEFA media team had put in place a system of red and yellow cards for non-attendees. One no-show and it was a yellow card by text and email, a second and it was a red card and an immediate one-match ban.

Greece 0 Sweden 2 – EM Stadium (aka The Red Bull Arena), Salzburg – 10th June 2008

It was good to see that the Swedes had taken over the stadium, and were making all the noise. I love the Swedes. They are passionate about their country, love a beer and have some of the best-looking fans in the world – which makes crowd watching an enjoyable pastime. That's what I spent most of the first half doing as the ultra-dull Greeks started playing for the draw as early as the seventh minute. Try as Sweden did, with Larsson, Ljungberg and Ibrahimović up front, the Greeks stifled the life from the game. It was only the Swedish fans singing their hearts out, and jumping up and down, that kept me awake. One passage of play summed it up. A string of more than thirty consecutive passes is normally a sign of a team in total domination, but when the passes were between the three

Greek centre backs in their own half, under no pressure from the Swedes, you will understand how desperate the champions were. 'Total Football', Greek Tony texted me.

I tossed a coin to decide whether or not to leave the press room for the second half and lost, but at least the first fifteen minutes of the second half justified the return. Greece threw on Georgios Samaras, the ex-Manchester City striker, to try and get the ball into the penalty area but it was the Swedes who struck with a goal that immediately started the competition for the goal of the tournament. Zlatan Ibrahimović picked the ball up near to the left-hand touchline, took one touch and blasted it into the top corner of the Greek net with their George Clooney lookalike goalkeeper floundering. For a player who had been so prolific in Serie A, one of the toughest defensive leagues in the world, it was astonishing to hear this was the Swede's first international goal for more than two years.

A serious cock-up from the Greek goalkeeper, now acting as well as looking like the Hollywood heart-throb, allowed the Swedish centre back Petter Hansson to bundle the ball home for their second goal.

The 2-0 scoreline was a fair reflection of the game. Sweden had been average, Greece very poor and with all sixteen teams having played a game it was obvious that neither of these two would be upsetting the apple cart later in the tournament.

After the game it was the slow train to Munich. It was surprisingly full, with fans attempting to sleep. But this was impossible as police with dogs were patrolling, looking for anyone drunk and troublesome. We arrived in a deserted Munich central station at 3 a.m. Most towns and cities in Germany operate twenty-four hours a day so it was a real shock to find nothing at all open. After enquiring from a policeman what time the S-Bahn to the airport started, it transpired there were two hours to kill. He gave me two suggestions. The first was to go to an address he scribbled on a bit of paper. Ring the top bell and when the door was opened, ask for Silvi. Once inside I could 'take my choice from the girls on show, and even have a shower' – or it was off to Burger King. While I was on a 'no fast food' diet I did not think that CMF would be too happy with the alternative!

It was never going to be an easy trip but some eleven hours later, when I walked through the front door at work, I realised that planning to avoid an hotel stay and 'sleep on the hop' on a train from Salzburg to Munich, at Burger King in Munich, on the S-Bahn at 3.30 a.m. to

Munich Airport and finally at the airport was a tad ambitious. All for the love of the game.

Next was Romania against Italy in Zurich and the Netherlands versus France in Berne. Romanian football has hardly set the world alight since Gheorghe Hagi, Ilie Dumitrescu and Florin Răducioiu retired after leading the team to prominence in the 1990s. But beggars can't be choosers and so the opportunity to get another game under my belt in the Euros was too good to miss.

After round one of the pool games, Romania had pulled off one of the surprises of the tournament with a dull 0-0 draw with France. Italy on the other hand had come into the tournament as world champions, and with an impressive qualifying record. Although they were in the so-called group of death with Romania, Netherlands and France they still expected to finish in the top two. However, they did not expect to be on the end of one of the best Dutch performances in living memory. With a combination of attacking flair, ruthless midfield efficiency and some excellent goalkeeping, the Italians were blown away. The only consolation was that because of France's 0-0 draw with Romania, a win and a draw from their final two games would take them through.

Despite being only a hundred miles or so from the Italian border, few fans decided to make the trip to Zurich. And as Romania were one of the poorest teams in the tournament, and the concept of following the team away had not yet reached Bucharest, this was a game in which the atmosphere was bound to be muted, or so I thought.

Zurich is a strange city. It is possibly the most typical of Swiss cities, which sounds odd, but any visitor to Geneva will testify that it cannot make its mind up whether it is French or Swiss. Basle thinks it is German but Zurich is in the middle. It is also one of the most business-orientated cities in Europe, meaning hotel rooms are at a premium at the best of times. Factor in a major sporting event and even Expedia had run out of rooms (bar a suite at the Four Seasons at £1,340 for one night!).

Zurich is home to two clubs separated by a railway line running south towards Lucerne. To the west of the tracks you will find Grasshoppers, one of the most famous Swiss clubs in the 1980s. They were rebuilding their Hardturm stadium as a 25,000-capacity football-only arena.

Their local rivals are FC Zürich, one of Switzerland's most successful teams from the past decade. Their Letzigrund stadium had been rebuilt for the championships, although it still had an athletics track which basically meant views from many seats were poor. The presence of a huge gap between the pitch and the stands somehow always leads to a rubbish game. I don't know why but I cannot remember a decent game played in such a stadium.

With businessmen doing deals worth millions of Swiss Francs in the city centre, there was little room for fans to enjoy themselves properly. A FanZone had been opened close to the lake, as far away from the business centre as possible, but at 5 p.m. there were few fans with enough cash to be in there. One reason is that the price of food and drink inside the FanZone was far more expensive than the bars outside, and considering how expensive the city is that took some beating.

At the stadium the touts were out in force, which was a surprise considering the teams involved. In my experience, touts come in two categories. First, there is your lovable English tout, normally a Scouser, who walks quickly up and down the road outside the stadium saying 'buyandsell, buyandsellanytickets'. He will normally pay you in fake £20s if you are seller or get his mates to rob you of your ticket a hundred yards down the road if you are a buyer. Second are the foreign touts who seem like extras from *The French Connection* and simply want to rob you blind. In the tournament so far there had been very few of the former and loads of the latter. An hour before kick-off they were doing a roaring trade for a game which on paper appeared to have little interest. One even offered to buy my press accreditation, despite the fact that my fat, white face didn't match his countenance.

Media centres for the tournament had so far been a mixed bag. A big wedding marquee in Salzburg, a series of temporary buildings in Geneva, but Zurich won the award for the best yet. Underneath the main stand was a huge room used as a warm-up room for the Weltklasse, athletics' most famous yearly meeting, and this had been converted into a press centre for more than five hundred journalists.

Next door was the warm-up track, a sixty-metre blue synthetic surface that had been converted into the mixed zone for post-match interviews. Access to the stands was up a Batman-like secret staircase that deposited reporters at the top of the main stand and offered a great view of the city. In terms of press areas Zurich got a nine out of ten so it was disappointing to report that sweet and sour chicken with boiled potatoes was not the kind of Swiss cuisine expected and so they lost marks in the Fuller guide to press freebies.

The stadium was absolutely packed, although it did look as if Romania had more fans, even without the noise they generated. The Italian fans, not known for following their team with passion, made do with a few 'Forza Italia's but nothing to suggest they really believed in their team's ability to progress in the tournament.

Italy 1 Romania 1 – Letzigrund, Zurich – 13th June 2008

Romania started the brighter, and obviously thought they spotted a weakness with Gianluigi Buffon as they peppered his goal with shots in the first half. One free kick in particular from Cristian Chivu took a wicked deflection and nearly found the net. However, Italy soon came back into the game, and, with Romania losing Mirel Rădoi to a nasty facial injury sustained in a clash with one of his own players, they were forced on to the back foot. Luca Toni went close twice and would have had a hat-trick were it not for the inspired goalkeeping of Bogdan Lobonţ, and a linesman's erroneous flag ruling out a header. The first half ended on a high for the Romanians as again Buffon had to pull off a top-drawer save from a long-range effort.

The game came to life in the fifty-fifth minute when the Italian coach, Roberto Donadoni, obviously unhappy with his team's performance, brought on the talismanic Antonio Cassano. However, it was the Romanians who stunned Italy and a fair percentage of the rest of world football when a poor defensive back header let in Adrian Mutu to put them one up. Only thirty-eight minutes for Romania to hold out and world champions Italy would be going home. Could it be? Of course not. Just three minutes later from another dangerous Alessandro Del Piero corner, the evergreen Christian Panucci tapped home from close range after fellow defender Giorgio Chiellini outjumped the Romanian defence to create the chance.

Romania were not to be put off their quest for a victory though, and they poured forward in numbers, showing no respect to the world champions. With fifteen minutes left to play Daniel Niculae was bundled over in the penalty area by Panucci and the referee pointed to the spot. Adrian Mutu snatched the ball before anyone else could get close and hit his spot kick true, but Buffon saved it, and undeniably kept his country in the tournament – just!

So honours were even. The Italians headed back to the city centre for coffee, ice cream and to pray for a Netherlands win. The Romanians' destinations were Club Paraguay and the Erotik Shop just up the road from the Letzigrund which advertised 'the only glory hole in Zurich'. Let's just hope they had a better aim than their star striker.

My day, however, was far from over. There was a mission to complete and just seventeen minutes to get to the main station for the 8 p.m. train to Berne. After I made it with seconds to spare, the train passed through some uninspiring scenery. Whoever said that Switzerland was all cows, fields and cuckoo clocks was obviously on drugs. All I saw was railway sidings, graffiti and motorways. However, the train did get to the Swiss capital just ten minutes after the Netherlands versus France game had started.

My intention was to see if there were any no-shows for the media seats. So far there had been dozens of empty seats in the press areas so far, but that didn't mean they would give them out. If no media seats were available the idea was to wait until the security people weren't looking and sneak into the arena. Once there I was not going to move until the final whistle.

With earlier results in the tournament having gone their way, the Netherlands came into the game knowing that a win would guarantee top spot in the 'Group of Death' and a place in the last eight. They also knew that a draw would take them through, barring a freakish result in the Italy versus France game. However, they were hell bent on winning the tournament in style for their departing manager Marco van Basten, who was off on the 1st of July to try and resurrect Ajax after a decade of doom.

France, on the other hand, had been slated back home. They either purr with brilliance, or run round and round in circles like headless chickens. There was so much pre-tournament hype about Franck Ribéry and Karim Benzema but they had been rubbish in the first game and now was the time for them to step up to the plate.

Netherlands 4 France 1 – Stade de Suisse, Berne – 13th June 2008

The taxi dropped me at the ground with Holland 1-0 up thanks to Liverpool's Dirk Kuyt. The next job was to blag a seat from the Media Manager. No can do, he said, but a kindly Brit, the UEFA Technical

Services Officer (whatever that entails), sorted out a standing place so I could at least watch the game. Yes, it was good to see that in this age of all-seater stadiums you could still stand at the back. 'Just don't get in the photographers' way.' Trying to find a decent vantage point was hard though, and it wasn't until half-time that I ventured down to pitch-side to find a vacant seat. Once there I was ushered onto the pitch by a steward who thought I wanted to interview one of the subs warming up. I took my chance for a quick snap for the history books of me on the pitch and swiftly ventured back into the stand before the steward could realise his error and throw me out.

Marco van Basten was obviously trying to kill France off early in the second half, bringing on Robin van Persie and Arjen Robben to attack the ageing French full backs. Thierry Henry had a great shout for a penalty turned down after a Dutch hand seemed to block his goal-bound shot, but not for the first time in the game fate proved a fickle friend as with pace and incision the Dutch broke away to the other end. Robben drilled the ball across and van Persie slotted home (well, the keeper got a hand to the ball and it trickled over the line). Two-nil down, with his tournament disappearing down the Mont Blanc tunnel, Raymond Domenech played his final card and brought on Le Grand Sulk, Nicolas Anelka.

Within five minutes Henry had pulled a goal back with a neat backheel, but Robben restored the lead within a minute thanks to another breakaway that he finished by slamming the ball into the roof of the net from an impossible angle. With a minute left in time added on, another of the stars of the tournament so far, Wesley Sneijder, lobbed the French goalkeeper from the edge of the box to make it 4-1. Undoubtedly the Dutch were favourites not only for the tournament but also with neutrals. With the three Real Madrid stars, Robben, Sneijder and Ruud van Nistelrooy, dominating the second half you have to wonder why Real Madrid were pursuing Cristiano Ronaldo.

The Netherlands could now lose to Romania in the last group match and put out both France and Italy in one fell swoop, which led to a plethora of conspiracy theories in the press in Paris and Rome.

The last leg of this journey involved another overnight train to Geneva airport, followed by an hour's sleep in a corner of the terminal. However, bedlam reigned at Berne station as the Orange Army took over every single inch of the platforms. This fanatical support is as passionate as the

English and certainly more colourful. Berne's population in the ten days of the tournament had trebled after the Dutch invasion; there will be more than a few bar owners who rued the end of their best summer in living memory.

As the train pulled into a deserted airport train station I felt the tournament had been exciting on the pitch but relatively sterile off it. It had been a good event for the neutral, which proved there was a silver lining in England not being there. Travel had been smooth and my only regret was not being able to spend more time going around on non-match days. However, as I am reminded on numerous occasions by CMF, being a family man means doing family things. With an exciting weekend trip lined up in just seven days' time to Chessington World of Adventures I could hardly wait.

SWEDISH FOOTBALL THROUGH THE EYES OF A FIVE- AND AN EIGHT-YEAR-OLD

How to win the hearts and mind of young children through football, beer and roller coasters

Every year in the Fuller household we have a tradition. During the school summer holidays I transport the Little Fullers away for a night somewhere in Europe, taking in a bit of culture, a game of football and a theme park or funfair. They look forward to these mini breaks as if they were huge, expensive holidays, packing and repacking their cases weeks in advance, and looking up the destinations on the internet. In the past we have been to Paris, Berlin, Amsterdam and Copenhagen. This year it was Sweden, with the Littlest Fuller and me going to Gothenburg, and a few days later travelling to Stockholm with Lolly.

So Trip One saw us landing in the middle of the western Swedish countryside outside Gothenburg on a scorching hot Wednesday afternoon in early August. Having taken this very journey the previous year with Lolly, I knew what to expect on arrival in the city centre.

We walked to the hotel, dropped off the bags and headed to Liseberg, Scandinavia's biggest theme park, which attracts more than three million visitors annually, before taking in a Swedish Superettan (second division) game at the Valhalla Stadium, home to Gothenburg's third team, Örgryte.

On the way to the hotel we walked past the building site of the new Gamla Ullevi, which is the new home stadium for IFK Gothenburg and GAIS and was completed in April 2009. The original Ullevi, still the biggest ground in the country and the preferred home of the national team, is across the road from the new arena and its future was under discussion at the time we were there. Two clubs sharing meant it was used on a regular basis, although crowds were far from impressive. The new stadium, with a capacity of just under twenty thousand, is a much more intimate football venue.

Littlest Fuller had already decided to be brave and go on every ride she could, so I tested this resolve by taking her on the fastest I could find, which completely changed her view. The temperature had hit the other side of thirty degrees, and we had to punctuate our rides with drink breaks before going back to the hotel for a mid-afternoon snooze.

Unbelievably, the hotel had no air conditioning, scandalous for a four-star, and we had to rely on a small fan to try and keep us cool. Needing provisions, we popped across the road to the supermarket. I really object to paying silly money for minibar beer, and as we were in Scandinavia the prices were Timmy Mallett silly at more than £6 for a small can.

The theory was that I could get a couple in the supermarket and keep them cool in the fridge. Wrong! Sweden has the kind of alcohol purchase regulations you get in strict Muslim countries such as Saudi Arabia. You cannot just walk into a supermarket, pick up a four pack of Carlsberg and pay for it. You can purchase beer only from a licensed shop and only if it is three and a half per cent proof or less. Even then it is only four cans per adult. So I had to bite the bullet and stump up £6 for a lukewarm can of Carlsberg from the minibar. To make matters worse I fell asleep within ten minutes, leaving the can on the window ledge. Forty minutes later Littlest Fuller woke me up to say the beer was smoking. The sun, magnified by the window glass, had heated the beer so much that it had begun to evaporate.

Örgryte 1 Jönköpings Södra 0 – The Valhalla Stadium, Gothenburg – 31st July 2008

The Valhalla Stadium, home of Örgryte, was a five-minute walk from the hotel, and with the game due to start at 6 p.m. we didn't leave the room until 5.45 p.m. The stadium certainly sounded busy when we walked along the road, very impressive for a club which averages just over a thousand fans. Queues were stretching down the road, and it seemed we had stumbled on a game with some meaning for the home fans.

In fact, as my Swedish translation skills kicked in (well, a bloke in front told me in English actually) I discovered that the game was a complete sell-out, the first in more than a decade at the Valhalla. The reason was one of those stories that rarely reach the media, similar to Aston Villa's last game of the season in May 2008 when they visited Upton Park to play West Ham United with Olof Mellberg playing his last ever game for Villa. In a wonderful gesture he bought every single Aston Villa fan who travelled, which was more than three thousand, a replica shirt. Yes, the shirts were going to be replaced at the start of the next season, yes, he probably got a discount, but even if they cost him £5 each he stumped up more than £15,000 out of his own pocket. How many Premier League footballers would donate even a tenth of that?

Anyway, back in Gothenburg the reason for the huge crowd was that Marcus Allbäck, the ex-Aston Villa and FC Copenhagen striker, had returned to Örgryte, his boyhood team, to play a final season, allegedly without payment. His contract promised him just a share of the gate money. So the crowd had come out on this sunny day to welcome him back. A great gesture, but where did it leave me and Littlest Fuller? In all of my years of watching football I had never been 'sold out' of a game. Sure, I have had to buy tickets on the black market, and on one occasion in the World Cup in Germany, when Portugal played Iran in Frankfurt, I walked away from a game, refusing to pay the going rate of €250 a ticket from the touts.

With kick-off approaching a decision had to be made. There was no way I was going to miss the game after travelling so far. Sure, Littlest Fuller wasn't too bothered and we could have just gone next door to the Ullevi where IFK Gothenburg were playing FC Basle at 8.15 p.m. in the Champions League second qualifying round. But I had come to visit the Valhalla, and that is what we were going to do.

So we moved next to the entrance gate and I whispered in Littlest Fuller's ear: 'If you start to cry then I will buy you candyfloss when we go back to Liseberg.' Right on cue she started sobbing that she wanted to watch the football. She almost ruined the moment by asking which teams were playing but overall her performance would have earned a BAFTA.

185

After five minutes there was a tap on my shoulder and a steward handed me a ticket, winked, opened a gate and we were in.

A brief stop for ice-cold drinks and a sausage and we took our places in the main, and thankfully covered, stand. The game was a few minutes old before the home team took the lead, reading the bounce on the artificial pitch when the Jönköpings Södra defenders were dithering. After just five minutes Littlest Fuller was fast asleep. She still doesn't really get football and I had packed a bag with books and an iPod loaded with a few children's films for the anticipated boredom requests. However, the sleep meant I could concentrate on the game.

It was hardly a classic, comparable to League Two in England, full of huff and puff but little in the way of invention. The artificial pitch didn't help, nor did the Mediterranean temperature. Neither team seemed willing to up the pace in the second half, and it ended up making a testimonial game seem like a championship decider. Allbäck departed on the seventy-minute mark to a standing ovation, and with him went the vast majority of the crowd.

Littlest Fuller slept right through, including the half-time break, waking in injury time and upset that she had missed it all. I didn't want to push my luck by suggesting we went up the road for the IFK game and it was back to Liseberg instead.

However, I had a cunning plan to combine visiting the theme park with seeing some of the game at the Ullevi. In the middle of Liseberg is a huge observation tower, with a revolving passenger cab that slowly climbs to a height of more than one hundred metres, revolves for a few minutes at the top, giving magnificent views of the city, before slowly descending again. Bribed with the candyfloss the Littlest Fuller and I spent thirty minutes revolving at the top. Together with several other men, I walked around with the turn of the cab to watch the game at the Ullevi in the distance. Our kids sat patiently and the attendant pocketed a few kronor to keep us up there.

All good things come to an end, and the phone rang to tell the park employee to take the cab down and let other people have a go. With darkness falling rapidly and Littlest Fuller getting tired, we were back at the hotel in time to phone home.

After a restless night of temperatures in the mid-twenties and absolutely no breeze, it was back to the UK for a few hours before unpacking and repacking, putting the Second Littlest Fuller in the car and returning to Ryanairland for the mid-morning flight to Stockholm.

Of course, this being one of the least customer- (sorry, self-loading cargo as they like to call passengers these days) focused organisations we didn't land in Stockholm. It wasn't even in the same region as Stockholm. I had to check the map to make sure it was Sweden and not Norway. Skavsta Airport is close to the town of Nyköping, some sixty miles south-west of the capital and linked to it by a regular ninety-minute bus service.

Coincidentally, I caught up on the bus with one of the guys with whom I had travelled to Turkey (see Chapter 20) in February. He and a couple of others were on a whistle-stop tour of stadiums in the area. There was really only one game in town on the Sunday, IF Hammarby at the Söderstadion, or so I thought. These guys are dedicated and they had a list of matches in the Swedish second, third and fourth divisions that were within an hour of Stockholm. They planned to get in games at 2 p.m. and 4 p.m. before the Hammarby game kicked off in the evening. They did ask if I wanted to accompany them, but I had promised Lolly that we would do 'fun' things in the afternoon. My plan was actually to go to the Olympic Stadium, home of Djurgården, to see if it would be possible to take photographs.

Nearly all of my dealings with Scandinavians have been positive. They return calls and emails promptly, and if they cannot help they point out someone who can. All except Djurgården. I wrote and called to ask for a photo of the stadium for the *Fan's Guide* book. At first they seemed helpful.

'Sorry, but we don't actually have any available but what about if I take one myself and send it?'

Perfect. But days turned to weeks and with a publishing deadline approaching, the fallback was a poor-quality stock image. Before this trip I contacted the club asking about taking pictures. No reply, so Lolly and I travelled to the stadium, which is only fifteen minutes from T-Centralen on the fantastically named T-Bana, the Stockholm underground.

The stadium was hosting the Nordic Classic, a veterans' tennis tournament featuring the likes of Chris Evert and Mats Wilander, on a specially built court at the far end of the ground, which meant there was no problem in taking as many photographs as I liked. More importantly they had bouncy castles and climbing walls for Lolly. In fact, after half an hour it was difficult to prise her away and she commented on what a wonderful surprise it had been. Good planning indeed!

We headed to Globen, an area growing in popularity year by year. The journey from the city centre takes just ten minutes and six stops on the T-Bana. Globen is the name of the futuristic development consisting of a shopping centre, bars and restaurants, a hotel (in which we were staying), the Söderstadion and the Globen Arena, the world's largest spherical arena and the main concert hall and indoor sports stadium in the city.

After checking in, Lolly was pleased to see that the opposition for the game, Ljungskile SK, were also staying at the hotel, which has an excellent view of the Globen and the football stadium behind it. It is a rare treat to find a hotel so close to a football ground, where sanctuary can be enjoyed until minutes before kick-off and you can watch the crowd build outside, and then be back in your room within moments of the final whistle.

In England, some of the newer football grounds include integrated hotels such as that at Bolton Wanderers' Reebok Stadium, which has a few rooms overlooking the pitch (although you don't get any crowd noise when watching the game from the room) and West Ham United's Upton Park where the hotel rooms are converted into executive boxes on match day. So we didn't need to be in the stadium until five minutes before kick-off and fortunately we were under cover as the sky was starting to turn a nasty deep purple.

IF Hammarby 2 Ljungskile SK 2 – Söderstadion, Stockholm – 4th August 2008

The stadium is strange, and there is talk of the club moving to a new one closer to the heart of their support in Hammarby around three miles to the east. It has one open end, with temporary seating, two single-tier covered stands running along the sides of the pitch with the other end consisting of six rows of seats with office buildings above. It was inevitable that it would rain and that those in the temporary stand would be soaked. Cue an operation of military precision by stewards dishing out free plastic ponchos to the fans. What made it even better was the standard of the stewarding. No English-style characters who look like bored students, fat controllers or failed policeman. These were female, mostly blonde and absolutely stunning. Worth the admission fee on their own.

Meanwhile on the pitch, third-placed Hammarby struggled to break down the low-lying opposition from Ljungskile. A goal against the run of play put the away team into the lead midway through the first half. It was their only visit to the Hammarby penalty area in the first thirty minutes. The home team rained crosses into the penalty area for the remainder of the half, but failed to realise that in order to convert such opportunities you need someone in the penalty area who can jump and head the ball. But the goal did come eventually as their centre forward and top scorer, Freddy Söderberg, took a half-chance after the visitors failed to clear a free kick, and at half-time it was 1-1.

The second half was more of the same, although my attention was drawn to the arrival of riot police below us. It was not that there was a particular incident, but that the six were female, blonde again and looked as if they had walked off an adult film set, complete with handcuffs, truncheons and filthy looks. It wasn't just me who had his attention diverted from the game. Most guys around me clearly felt the same, as did the assistant referee, whose attention wandered so much that he missed a blatant penalty for handball. The riot police seemed completely oblivious to the attention and it took a scrambled goal by the visitors to refocus attention on to the pitch.

With three of the four minutes of injury time played we made for the exit with most of the home fans, but a huge cheer saw most run back up the stairs, causing disarray in the stairwell as fans tried to see who had grabbed the equaliser while those in the know went the other way. It was Söderberg who had saved a point for Hammarby to keep them in touch with Elfsborg and Kalmar at the top.

Post-match it was off to the Katarina Lift, an old container crane that has been converted into a viewing platform, and is also one of the best restaurants in the city. The view from the top was fantastic as the sun set and storm clouds gathered over the city centre, providing excellent photo opportunities. The forecast for the following day wasn't good, and with rain starting to fall and hunger making its first appearance of the day, we went back to the hotel for food and *'Allo 'Allo* on Swedish Television (dubbed into Swedish!).

The following day's destination was Gröna Lund, Stockholm's amusement park on the island of Djurgården. Dressed in T-shirts and shorts, we took a ferry in bright blue summery conditions. After going on everything at least twice and lunch in the Bavarian restaurant (of course, when in Sweden, eat German food) we were off to the Vasa Museum to give Lolly some culture and to try to explain the reason why in 1628 the world's biggest ship sank a hundred yards into its maiden voyage. When she asked the simple question 'Why', I blamed it on using wood riddled with woodworm which meant that water seeped in as soon as the ship entered the sea. I couldn't really think of any other logical answer.

At five o'clock the rain started falling heavily but despite the weather Lolly was excited to be going to the first and most famous Ice Bar in the world. It was time to leave when her hair started to freeze and go distinctly crispy. The rain continued to fall well into the night, turning a pleasant sunny day into one of Stockholm's worst summer storms in the past decade.

Tuesday morning meant boarding another bus, this time for Ryanair's second-best attempt at an airport in Stockholm – Vasteras, which is only (!) seventy miles and ninety minutes away by public transport. The concept of priority queuing for the flight again went out of the window as the ground staff boarded anyone they fancied. However, I put a new tactic into play, and it worked a treat. We waited until last, and, of course, there were only single seats left. But due to Ryanair's rules on unaccompanied minors we had to be sat together and so we still got adjoining seats while someone who might have fought their way to the front, or paid £8 to board first, had to move.

We landed slightly early (cue the appalling Ryanair fanfare to announce they had managed to get a flight on the ground on time) but, of course, this being Britain we had to endure a forty-five-minute queue at passport control.

My adventures with the little ones had come to an end for another year. Two games, four stadiums, two theme parks and God knows how much junk food and additives saw them deposited back with CMF, and me in the good books as a great dad with children as cool as the Ice Bar in Stockholm for another year.

ALL RIGHT IN
WHITE RUSSIA

A long day in the dullest capital city in the world,
surrounded by smiling faces and boots galore!

Since the final whistle had blown in the Maksimir Stadium in Zagreb on the 10th of September, the optimism surrounding the England team, and more importantly our chances of reaching South Africa (or will it be Germany, Herr Blatter?) in June 2010 had risen dramatically. The four weeks between the Croatian game and the next set of matches with Kazakhstan at Wembley and Belarus in Minsk had been awash with talk about whether Fabio Capello was going to break up the winning team, replace Gareth Barry with Steven Gerrard or bring back Michael Owen.

The loyal fans, however, were more worried about trying to sort out visas to travel to Belarus and decide in which bars to drink.

Belarus usually gets just under four thousand visitors a year from the UK so this game was very high-profile. It would deliver almost the annual total into Minsk in a forty-eight-hour period. With only a couple of weekly direct flights from England, most fans had again to look for alternatives. The most popular routes were via Lithuania and Poland, which would mean a cheap night out in the likes of Vilnius and Warsaw, before a train to Minsk. It looked so easy on paper.

However, every single train trip into Belarus (and, of course, out) required a stop at the border where the carriages needed to be lifted off their wheels and transferred onto a new set because the Belarusian rail network uses a different gauge. Historically this was to stop invaders trying to use the rail network to invade the old Soviet Union, but now it just acted as a massive inconvenience, taking up to two hours. And this was always done in the middle of the night so that any sleepers (excuse the pun) would be woken up. Of course, once the work was done and people returned to their slumber they would be woken again by border guards needing to check visas and entry papers.

Talking of visas, it is worth a little comment about this anarchic process. Why do we still need to jump through hoops just to get a stamp to enter a country in these days? The two- page application form for a visa, which would see me in the country for less than sixteen hours without an overnight stay, asked questions such as wife's maiden name and the names of our children? Why? Were they planning to send birthday cards or check CMF's GCSE records? After going through the pain of trying to get a Russian visa two years previously I intended to use the services of a private company.

Due to work commitments and a reluctance to let go of my passport, it was late September before I applied for a visa, by which time the Belarusians had realised that they had been charging only £19 whereas when Belarusians visited the UK they paid £63. Not surprisingly, but without warning, the price trebled and I had to pay almost as much for the visa as for the whole trip. Guess how I felt when landing in Minsk when they told me that they could have processed one there and then for $30?

When the Soviet Union fell in 1991, the Belarusians were the least prepared state in the old empire and struggled to cope with life not being tied to Mother Russia's apron strings. Today, the country has changed, but it still retains some Soviet scepticism. Minsk has more police per capita than anywhere else in the world simply because it is one of the safest jobs in the country. This trip was always going to be an excuse for them to come out to play.

The only real option open to me was the Thomas Cook day trip from Gatwick. It meant a 3 a.m. start from SE9 but spirits were high, both from the senior team's 5-1 win against Kazakhstan the previous Saturday, and the Under-21s' 5-4 aggregate victory over the Welsh at Villa Park the previous evening which meant they achieved something the senior team hadn't for nearly four years – qualifying for a major tournament.

Rob the Red was in the car to Gatwick Airport for this one, along with Dennis, making his EnglandFans away debut. Thomas Cook had recently lost their franchise to print money via the England fans and this was their last official trip. From November, the German firm TUI would take over ripping off the fans.

We landed in Minsk, on time for once, but it was one of those really annoying flights. Obviously Thomas Cook were trying to get as much money out of credit crunch hit fans as possible before they lost the franchise, because from the first minute they went to work on us. Headphones to watch the in-flight movie (£2.75), a blanket and pillow (£5) and of course all the usual duty-free crap. All announced by a stereotypical camp steward who spent most of the time telling passengers off for 'leaving their rubbish in the seat pocket', 'talking too loudly' and 'leaving their seat belt undone'.

He also started a witch-hunt at one point, suggesting that someone's phone was on, and asking to see everyone's MP3 player! Sleep was impossible but at least we could have an early-morning beer. Wrong! Thomas Cook had decided this flight was 'dry', although they were happy enough to sell us duty-free alcohol towards the end (which could only be picked up on the return flight just in case we downed a litre of vodka on the way out) from Mr Trolley Dolly's dolly trolley.

As expected we were met by dozens of Belarusian military personnel, all sporting outsized hats and grim faces. However, they had at least had the forethought to put some better-looking people behind the immigration counter. And although they tried not to smile, many couldn't resist typical English humour, which led to a few faces cracking, none more so than when a number of fans passed 'remarks' the girls understood all too well.

'Ah, so you must be man with the small penis,' was a quip to one over-familiar fan.

Thirty minutes after landing we were on the coaches. The so-called fuss and delays did not materialise and it was gratifying that there was a general lack of people trying to exploit us as had happened in Zagreb, Skopje and Moscow. The presence of a couple of British Bobbies was the major story, and throughout the day locals queued to have photos taken with them, laughing at their strange hats – pot, kettle and black as they say. The coaches left with a full police escort, powering down an empty motorway which bisected fields in which rural peasants, using old-fashioned equipment, tended their crops. It seemed that this motorway had been built to serve the airport, as we drove for miles without passing another car on either carriageway.

It took thirty-five minutes to reach the city's outskirts and soon we were transported back to what I always imagined the 1960s Soviet Union was like, huge, ugly, grey concrete housing developments, people queuing at bus stops and every few hundred yards strange kiosks offering all sorts of home-brew treats. Everyone stood and stared at our convoy. It must also have been one of Minsk's biggest police operations for many years. They revelled in the opportunity to speed along, closing off roads with rolling roadblocks and displaying their weapons.

The coaches parked opposite the stadium and we were herded across the main road. Tania, our guide, who promised to show us a 'good time' in Minsk, actually meant directions to the nearest cashpoint, McDonald's and the Irish Bar, as she had been told that was what all England fans wanted. Rob and I passed the stadium, noticed the gates were open and diverted inside. Soon the rest of Tania's party also decided the good time would start with a wander around the stadium, much to her disgust; obviously she was on commission from the numerous bars into which she was going to take us.

Dagenham Dan and Shents were in the stadium and, after a quick tour, during which we took the opportunity to sit on the bench – one brave soul even decided to run on to the pitch – we trudged down the main drag to the nearest ATM, which, of course, didn't work. However, in the shed – well it was a wooden structure, and had a felt roof – next door was a bank. We were greeted with a sweet smile and a flash of legs as the blonde behind the counter sat back on her chair with her feet up. Twenty pounds got me 38,900 Belarusian roubles, including two 10 rouble notes that were worth the equivalent of a quarter of a penny.

The four of us continued five hundred yards up Niezaliezhnasci, the main road through the city centre, looking for a place to eat. So far England fans were thin on the ground, although to be fair there were not many bars in the area. But there were hundreds of women walking around wearing tiny skirts and long boots. Obviously the arrival of two and a half thousand England fans had caused them to dig out their Sunday best and go on full husband alert. They seemed to love the attention. We saw them at various points during the day, casually walking backwards and forwards past bars full of fans, stopping in the middle of the street and bending down as if to pick up something. Basically they were doing anything possible to draw attention to their fine assets.

It was not just bars that were missing; there weren't many restaurants either. Close to the main square, Kastrychnitskaya, was a major junction

194

with a McDonald's, a TGI Friday's and a local restaurant. We ruled out McDonald's as it would have meant crossing a very busy main road, so we flipped a coin and it came down in favour of TGI Friday's. Big mistake. There were only about a dozen tables and all were taken by England fans. After ten minutes we got menus; another ten minutes and they took our drink order (four Cokes). Ten minutes after that we were told there were only three Cokes left and could we change our order. Another ten minutes and they took our food order. Thirty minutes later Rob's and Shent's food turned up. Twenty minutes after that, following numerous complaints, Dan's and my meals arrived, looking suspiciously as if they had come from McDonald's across the road (including the obligatory pickle inside the burger).

By this stage the restaurant was full and they announced there was no more Coke, Fanta, Sprite or, eventually, bottled beer. Amid this confusion I saw a familiar face. In one of those bizarre 'Fancy seeing you here' moments, I saw my postman, Jamie, sitting at the bar. Granted I knew he was an EnglandFan and that he travelled, but you never really put two and two together in such situations. At least it gave me the opportunity to berate him about the post for our next-door neighbours that keeps getting put through our letter box.

After nearly two hours in TGI Friday's we tried to get the bill. People on other tables had simply given up the ghost and left after waiting too long for their food, yet the waiters still brought it out and placed it on empty tables as if they expected the diners to return. We decided eventually to walk out without paying, although we knew Belarus was the only country in Europe to retain the death penalty (a fact kindly pointed out in the FA's information pack), and that probably they had a statute that made leaving a Western chain of restaurants without paying a capital offence. Our move had the desired effect and as we reached the door a burly manager appeared to proffer a bill. We gave him a 100,000 rouble note for the 87,000 roubles (or £20) bill and he 'assumed' that the 13,000 roubles was a tip and that we didn't want any change. Customer service at its best.

With eight hours to kick-off we planned an afternoon of sightseeing. One warning we had been given by the authorities was that taking pictures of the KGB building and Palace of the Republic in Kastrychnitskaya was a strict no-no. So, of course, if you wanted to find out which building this was you had only to head for the one which had England fans standing outside with their cameras!

Across the square was the highlight of the city centre, the Belarusian State Museum of the Great Patriotic War, depicting the struggle of the nation between 1941 and 1945. I appreciate that few English speakers visit it each year but without any English text we had no clue about the exhibits.

The four of us were followed around the museum by a party of giggling schoolgirls, probably seeing an opportunity to try and snare a husband early in life. And that was the high point of the sightseeing. We wandered around for another hour, more in awe of the skirt/boot combinations than any other sights. After our 3 a.m. start, tiredness was beginning to take effect and we spent the rest of the afternoon watching snooker on Eurosport at the Hotel Planeta, where Dan and Shents were staying.

We had travelled more than a thousand miles to a country very few people visit and we ended up with a couple of cans of beer watching snooker with a German commentary in a small hotel room. The crazy world of England fans abroad.

Managing to sneak on to a coach laid on by the hotel for fans going to the game, we were delivered back outside the Crowne Plaza hotel, home to the England team. I bet the players had never stayed so close to a major stadium before, as we paced it out as one hundred and fifty paces from hotel steps to stadium entrance. But, of course, the FA decided to do their bit for the environment by arranging a coach with police escort.

As we waited around, Rob the Red was approached for his autograph. On being told it was because he was an England fan, 'the best fans in the world', Rob duly obliged and more and more people came over to get his signature, much to his bemusement. Outside the hotel our two bobbies were again the centre of attention and lining up for pictures with the locals. It must have made a change from ducking bullets in Southwark.

The temperature was dropping when we went to find our entrance to the stadium but any local ladies attending the games still kept to their dress code despite the cold.

We were thoroughly frisked, tickets checked twice, and then searched again before we were allowed into the away fans' 'compound'. One small refreshment stand, one tiny souvenir stand, selling all the balsa wood accessories you never wanted, hundreds of portaloos and . . . prostitutes! The authorities clearly felt sorry for us so that with ninety minutes to go to kick-off they had laid on entertainment. With so many portaloos available they obviously fancied their chances of a nice little earner before the game but no one was buying and with time ticking down to kick-off the 'girls' trooped off to another part of the stadium, obviously looking for a local customer.

Belarus 1 England 3 – Dinamo Stadium, Minsk – 15th October 2008

The authorities had allocated seats along the side of the pitch to the England fans, which gave us a great view. They also did their bit to get the crowd going by pumping out very loud techno-rock from huge speakers right in front of our section. Just before kick-off, they filled the pitch with children with bunches of balloons that were released as the teams lined up for the national anthems. The band then threw us a curve ball. Not only did they play the anthem slowly, so that by the time we finished singing they were only three-quarters of the way through, but they added a second verse. With few knowing 'O Lord our God arise' the majority reverted to verse one.

With Ashley 'Boo Who' Cole and John 'I respect referees' Terry still out, the team was close to that which had started on the Saturday. My concern about Ashley Cole is that, apart from being one of the most hated footballers in England, he is an average left back. Replacing him with Wayne Bridge, at the time his reserve at Chelsea, suggests we are desperately short of cover in this area. Add the continuing presence of Wes Brown at right back and the whole footballing world could see how weak we are at full back. Barry, Lampard and Gerrard had been included in midfield with Rooney and Walcott adding pace down the flanks and the born-again Emile Heskey ('He used to be shite, but now he's all right') acting as the link man.

Belarus soon showed why Capello had been wary, creating a number of good opportunities in and around the box. However, it was England who took the lead on eleven minutes with a classic Steven Gerrard shot from twenty-five yards beating the diving goalkeeper. England then sat back, inviting the Belarusians to attack, so it was no surprise when they equalised after a good move left Pavel Sitko, the central midfielder, unmarked in the penalty area and he headed home.

In the past England might have folded but this new squad under the Italian are made of sterner stuff, and they buckled down, carrying the game back to the home team. One-all at half-time was no disgrace and the travelling fans appreciated that. The second half started with the home fans turning up the atmosphere a notch. It was never intimidating like in Zagreb, but it was certainly loud and passionate. However, England struck another blow in the fiftieth minute when Rooney finished smartly from close range to score in his third consecutive game. Twenty-five minutes later and the impressive Heskey broke clear of the defence and set up Rooney to score the third and put the game to bed.

The authorities said they would keep us in for fifteen minutes and they were true to their word as right on the dot we were on the coaches and waiting to leave. Except one of our passengers was missing. To make it worse his mate hadn't seen him since lunchtime and still had his jacket, containing his camera, passport and mobile phone. After thirty minutes without progress, during which the Thomas Cook staff called hospitals and police stations, we set off.

After a much-needed hour's trip on the snooze express, I woke up at the airport to start the process of going through security. Initially we'd been due to depart at 12.30 a.m., but it was already 12.45 so the best we could hope for was 1.30. However, we had not factored in the thoroughness (or was it just bureaucracy?) of the authorities. We were all asked to queue outside the security area, and then they invited us in one at a time. Getting into Minsk was easy; getting out less so.

Step One – check boarding card for signs of forgery (bear in mind the seat numbers had been written on in pen by Thomas Cook at Gatwick earlier in the day).

Step Two – put bags and coats through X-ray machine.

Step Three – check boarding card against passenger list.

Step Four – hand over passport and have visa stamped.

Step Five – hand over passport to another immigration officer to remove landing card.

Step Six – check boarding card against passport.

Step Seven – put bags and coats through smaller X-ray machine.

Then it was announced that under no circumstances were we to take Belarusian roubles out of the country. Fortunately they had opened the duty-free especially and took pleasure in offering us the finest potato vodka and the latest Belarusian scent, Tractoria! Most people just wanted to get on the plane and go to sleep but it took another hour before we departed, some three hours late.

The missing passenger had turned up by this point. Apparently after one too many beers at lunch he had fallen asleep in a disabled toilet in a bar. He consequently missed the game, had his wallet stolen and then, after getting £100 wired to a Western Union office, had to pay for a cab to the airport to catch us up. The evils of alcohol in a foreign country!

Someone had obviously had a word with the steward as this time around he arranged for food to be served as soon as we were in the air and then shut up.

It was 5.25 a.m. when I opened the door of Chez Fuller and crawled into bed, needing to be up in less than three hours. CMF rolled over and asked the killer question: 'Was it worth it?'

If I thought of the dull buildings, the lack of food and drink, the depressing conditions in which the locals live and the simple lack of anything to do then the answer would be negative. But if I think about the passion they showed for the game, the performance of the England team, the smiles on the faces of some locals and those boots, then it was definitely an 'oh yes'.

SOFIA LOREN

When all the elements of a perfect football weekend come together

The nature of my job means I am used to getting up early. Frequent travelling on budget airlines has led to an acceptance of 3 a.m. alarms with 4 a.m. check-in times on an almost weekly basis. I don't like early starts or lack of sleep, but it's part of life. However, as the years roll by, the longer the recovery time becomes. It may be that I miss our big warm bed and the allure of CMF, but getting up is becoming harder and harder. So after the twenty-six-hour day in Minsk I had hardly returned to a normal sleeping pattern before three days later it was another 3 a.m. start for a very early morning flight to Sofia.

This was a trip that had been paid for essentially by easyJet after their screw-up in the summer when they delayed a flight to Geneva by three hours. And as they do, they nearly ruined this one as well. At 5.30 a.m. I sat with a couple of dozen other passengers at Gate 25 in Gatwick's South Terminal only to be told that the gate had been changed to 34, and was in the process of closing. According to their maps that was a twenty-minute walk.

I hate Gatwick Airport with a passion. It is very poorly designed, with blind corridors and long walkways that are no help to passengers. We took off at full speed, making it eventually to the gate only to be told we were too late to board. With more and more passengers arriving, all telling the same tale, they had to back down and allow us to get on.

When the trip was booked, the plan had been to take in the Levski v CSKA derby, one of the most passionate in European football. I tried for weeks to find out about it and, more important, how to get accreditation, but none of the emails to either club or the Bulgarian FA were answered. I asked a friend from work, whose husband was Bulgarian, to call the club and he was told that there was no guarantee the game was being played on that weekend at all as CSKA 'didn't feel up for it'.

So a few weeks later it came as no surprise to see the fixture list had changed, and my idea of seeing games at both Levski and also at Lokomotiv Sofia were replaced with nothing. That's right, no games at all. They had been pushed back to 4 p.m. on the Sunday, some two hours after I was due to leave Sofia. There was a game in the B-League, at Akademik Sofia, one of the city's older clubs, but that wouldn't have been worth a weekend away.

I toyed with the idea of moving the flights but could not see how an extra night's accommodation, plus the risk of flying with Hungary's finest, Wizz Air, was worth the cost, so consoled myself that second-division Bulgarian football might not be that bad. And, of course, I could try to get photographs from the city's other stadiums for the website. But four days before departure a brief check online showed that Levski Sofia had moved their game back to the Saturday and so the trip had some meaning again, with a double-header on the Saturday and an opportunity to do some groundhopping on the Sunday morning.

Sofia is a capital blessed with football clubs. At that time there were four in the top division, Slavia, Lokomotiv, Levski and of course CSKA. Add to this a couple of second-division teams and a traditional national stadium close to the centre and you have a great destination for catching a game or two on most weekends. There is also a low-cost economy, with cheap and plentiful (if a bit old and slow) public transport, excellent basic food and a mix of post-communist and Ottoman architecture – the perfect recipe for a great weekend.

The three-hour jolly jaunt on Luton's finest touched down at Sofia's old Terminal One just before 11 a.m. local time; plenty of time for sightseeing around the old city, checking in at the hotel and even the opportunity to watch the early Premier League game at a suitable Irish bar before the first game kicked off at Akademik in the south-east of the city.

I had been warned that ticket inspectors were prevalent on buses to and from the airport, so was determined to make sure I had a valid ticket. Problem number one. Where to buy it? The airport arrival area was swarming with taxi touts, all looking to make a fast Euro from newly-arrived and uneducated visitors, yet there were no signs for public transport.

I approached a number of locals, all of whom shrugged their shoulders and walked on by. Deciding authority would be best, I approached a policeman, who, taking me under his gun-laden wing, marched me to a small kiosk in the departures hall. He pushed straight to the front of the queue and demanded the man behind the counter provide a ticket 'for my English friend'.

So for 4Lv, or the equivalent of £1.60, I had an all-day pass for the city's public transport.

The No. 84 bus departed from outside the terminal and drove past crumbling motorways and building sites that appeared to have been abandoned apart from, right in the middle, a huge Porsche showroom, complete with armed guards. So far the notorious ticket inspectors had not appeared but as we approached a stop on a housing estate, an old lady got up as if to get off before suddenly brandishing her shield in my face, a move of which any FBI agent would have been proud.

She tutted disappointingly when I showed her the ticket, but she did not have to wait long before she found some unsuspecting ticketless Englishmen and took great glee at fining them 7 leva each.

As the bus continued on its way through the outskirts, the huge Mount Vitosha loomed overhead with its first patches of snow already visible. The communist influence was clear in these areas with huge tower block estates, intermingled with local markets with hundreds of people buzzing around. The old and creaky trolley buses were full to bursting as they travelled up and down the main highway into the city, belching pollution in their wake.

The first stop was the Borisova Gardens, home to the national stadium, the Vasil Levski, and that of CSKA Sofia, the ex-army team. The gardens were a wonderful mix of tall trees, turning golden in the middle of autumn, and perfect picnic lawns. The smaller of the two stadiums, that of CSKA, was wide open, with people wandering in and out as the team mingled with supporters, ready for their coach trip to their game the following afternoon. The stadium was a prototype ex-Soviet structure with tall, imposing floodlights, sweeping banks of seats behind the goals and one solitary roof that covered the VIP section, as if the climate here was Caribbean rather than eastern European.

CSKA had been one of the most feared teams in the 1970s and '80s when they won the Bulgarian title eleven times. They frequently made it into the latter stages of the European Cup, including the campaigns in 1981 and 1982 when in the latter year they met Bayern Munich in a classic semi-final. After a 4-3 home victory hopes were high that they would become the first ever Bulgarian team to reach a major European final. But the team crumbled 4-0 in the Olympic Stadium.

Just a minute's walk north through the trees is the Vasil Levski. A few days previously it had hosted Bulgaria's match with Italy when Italian fans had caused controversy during the game by burning a Bulgarian flag. The Italian authorities quickly tried to distance themselves from the incident, blaming Italians from Sofia, as if their own house was entirely in order.

The stadium is also used for Levski Sofia's bigger games, including the derby against CSKA and their frequent games in the Champions League. However, the season I was there, a surprise defeat to BATE Borisov of Belarus in the final qualifying game denied them a place in a money-spinning group with Real Madrid and Juventus.

The stadium, on the edge of the city centre, is perfectly framed by the mountain in the distance, and in good weather watching football there would be a real pleasure. The stadium is similar in design to the majority of those in Eastern Europe, although the fences and running track partly obscure the view of supporters in the lower seats. Just across the road is the Orlov Most Square where the Soviet Army Memorial dominates the skyline. From a distance the tall memorial looks impressive but up close you get an impression of what makes this city so strange. The memorial is covered in graffiti, some not so polite but at least demonstrating that the locals grasp some of the finer points of the English language.

The park was in desperate need of repair. Most benches were broken and huge holes on the paths were left uncovered. The reason for most of the debris was apparent on the corner of the square as a poster showed that this would be the site of a new metro station, 'Coming soon in 2006'. So only two years behind schedule!

Sofia is one of Europe's oldest capitals, founded around 7,000 years ago. It is also capital of a country that everyone has heard of yet many would struggle to find on a map. I had never been near this part of Europe until a few years before, but had become hooked on places like Macedonia, Romania and Serbia as they struggled to come to terms with the new Europe and shed some of the bureaucracy of their communist past.

Leaving the stadium behind, I continued north-east towards the city centre, passing impressive buildings including the university, the Bulgarian Parliament and the most imposing building in the city, the Alexander Nevsky Cathedral. This is without a doubt the city's most magnificent landmark. It was designed by Alexander Pomeranstev, an architect from St Petersburg who fashioned it in the style of Greek and Russian buildings, complete with huge, gold-leaf-covered domes. Outside a small market had been established to tempt tourists with memorabilia from the communist days, including 'genuine' KGB hip flasks, fighter pilot helmets and cases full of fake Rolex watches.

The city is full of parks and gardens, littered with statues, benches and unfinished monuments. It has the feel of an outdoor city, although it was the only capital I could think of not to have a major river running through it.

The east of the city centre is home to the major administrative buildings, including the National Theatre, Opera House and the Presidential Palace. It was also where my hotel was, which had an excellent view of the Party House. I left shortly after checking in because I wanted to find the Lokomotiv Stadium, which appeared to be just off the map.

The compact commercial centre is well served with trams and buses, and there was a feeling that the country was on the edge of economic freedom. Looking around at the cracked pavements, potholes, cheap shops and the miserable faces you can understand why the European Union had pushed back Bulgaria's membership. The concept of 'no win, no fee' litigation obviously hadn't reached Sofia, judging by the lack of investment in the pavements, and I would hate to think what burden is put on the health service by injuries caused by the paths.

The number twelve tram went north, past the main railway station and into the housing projects. It deposited its passengers in what could only be described as a factory car park, with huge chimneys and heavy machinery littering the roadway. Apparently the stadium was close, so I relied on trusty Google Maps to show the way. Unfortunately, on the day the satellite passed over this area of the city, the pollution from the factory spread a cloud over the whole area. Brilliant! Back on the main road I turned northwards, looking for a tell-tale sign. As luck would have it a set of monstrous floodlights showed in the distance. They were indeed the floodlights of Lokomotiv Sofia, and after a ten-minute walk I was there. In keeping with the rest of the outskirts it was almost in a state of ruin.

Practically every window had been broken, every wall covered in graffiti and every entrance showed signs of fire damage. Welcome to twenty-first-century Bulgarian Premier League football. Inside it was a different story. Two covered stands swept from corner to corner, smartly lined with red seats. Behind each goal was a bright red bus, painted with the club's logo. Despite this good housekeeping, it is difficult to imagine why stadiums like this are allowed to host domestic games, let alone European ties as it did in 2007–8 when Lokomotiv Sofia reached the UEFA Cup first round, losing to French club Rennes.

Time was pressing and the first game of the day was in the south-east suburbs, close to the airport. I needed to change buses a few times but managed easily, and even though the route was convoluted it was only thirty minutes before I was outside the home of Akademik Sofia for the second-division game.

FC Akademik Sofia 1 PFC Vidmia-Rakovski Sevlievo 0 – Akademik Stadium – 18th October 2008

The stadium was just one big, covered stand with bench seats and a few rows of terracing behind each goal. Entry was free and so most 'locals' who had turned up were there to kill a few hours. They included a dozen chavs, complete with Burberry baseball caps, and their token girl, who from the back looked like Rod Stewart, complete with a 1970s wig. She was obviously not fussy who groped her, as long as she got her cigarettes which she chain-smoked. At frequent points during the dull first half she disappeared downstairs with one of her companions, returning a few minutes later smoking another fag and looking ever more dishevelled.

Having visited the gents before the game, it was difficult to believe she would choose this as the place for a romantic, or even commercial, liaison. It was possibly the most appalling convenience I have ever used. If you have ever seen pictures of prisons in the Far East, such as the Hanoi Hilton, that will give an idea about the decor.

The stadium has a perfect view towards the airport and with the fare on display so poor, watching the planes coming and going was the high point. Having played as one for many seasons, I am familiar with typical Sunday League players. In front of me now were twenty-two of them. The pitch didn't help as it was full of divots, and nor did the huge open areas behind the goals.

The stadium didn't have dugouts for the coaches and reserves. Instead there were park benches and parasol umbrellas.

The game itself was completely forgettable, and in fact the small, almost silent crowd gave me no idea which team was which or even what the away team were called. The only notable point of interest in the first half was a late tackle which resulted in two opposition players being stretchered off. The resultant melee saw the goalkeeper sprint seventy yards to become involved and get the game's first yellow card.

The only goal came just after half-time when a mistake in the dark-blue-shirted defence allowed the light-blue centre forward to head home. Queue that Ricky Martin song, which drove the little trollop wild, giving her another excuse to jump on one of the gang.

At full time I ready for game number two.

Levski Sofia 2 PFC Belasitsa Petrich 0 – Georgi Asparuhov Stadium – 18th October 2008

The journey back north looked complicated. There is no direct public transport between the stadiums, and a dirty great railway line provided a formidable barrier to a thirty-minute walk. The number twenty-two bus dropped me on the edge of a motorway slip road and the railway, and not for the first time on a trip abroad, I just followed the locals, traversing the railway tracks and stepping over the electrified rails.

Levski Sofia are the best-supported team in Bulgaria, and the most successful of the modern period. Their twenty-five national league titles have been spread over an eighty-year history, and they were the current form team after winning the title five times since 2000. They have also been a regular in the Champions League, even making the group stages in 2007 when they faced Barcelona, Werder Bremen and Chelsea, although they played games across town in the Vasil Levski Stadium.

It's obvious from just one visit to their place why they cannot host such high-calibre games at the Asparuhov Stadium.

At the start everything looked relatively normal. Lots of police in riot gear patrolled the park outside, but when approaching the ticket windows either side of the main entrance to the west stand I saw the police there were more interested in throwing paper aeroplanes than crowd control. There were few fans and approaching the ticket windows it was obvious why.

Despite my best efforts at establishing details about the game, the kick off was in fact at 7.30 p.m. and not 6.30 p.m. So, after buying a seat in the covered main stand for a laughable 4 leva (£1.60), there was nearly ninety minutes to kill. Fortunately the supporters' bar next to the entrance offered a real log fire, grilled kebabs and a bohemian atmosphere.

With kick-off fifteen minutes away, I took a seat one row from the back of the stand, in a completely empty section. To the left were the away supporters. I have no idea where Petrich was, but as only one supporter had made the journey it can only be assumed it was in some faraway corner of the country with no public transport. A few minutes before kick-off something happened that could have come from the BBC's *Fast Show*. A couple decided that, of all the seats in an empty section of about a thousand, the ones directly behind me were best. And there they stayed, munching bird seed throughout the whole game.

It was obvious why they chose my section. It was the best of a bad bunch. Weeds grew through the concrete steps and many areas of the stadium would have been condemned in England. The stadium was opened in the early 1960s and didn't appear to have been modernised at all.

On paper the game was going to be a cakewalk for Levski. Coming into this game, Belasitsa had lost eighty per cent of their games (the other twenty per cent being draws) and had only scored one goal. Levski, on the other hand, were second and had scored seventeen times. And so the parade started. From the first whistle Levski pounded the Belasitsa goal. Chances went begging as time after time the impressive Soares found space down the right and put in excellent crosses. In the eighth minute a header from the Levski centre forward Georgi Hristov hit both posts and bounced away, only for the resulting clearance to find its way back into the box for the centre forward to head home at the second attempt.

Belasitsa simply could not get the ball into the Levski penalty area and the poor home goalkeeper must have been absolutely freezing as he sat against his goalpost for long periods, clearly bored. It was forty-three minutes before the ball came to him and this was a back pass from the halfway line. It was under-hit but he left his post quickly enough to clear his lines.

Levski's Brazilian midfielder Soares was definitely the star, coming very close to doubling the lead with a fantastic overhead kick from the edge of the penalty area that was stopped by an equally good save. However, he scored the second on twenty-six minutes with a smart volley from a rare left-wing cross. Two-nil should have been the start of something more impressive, but Levski huffed and puffed without creating anything else.

In the second half Belasitsa came more into the game with their central midfielder having a horrendous time. He was Beto, a Brazilian in the mould of Patrick Vieira. He was also the most fouled player on the pitch, being regularly hacked down without any protection from the referee. You can only speculate whether the colour of his skin had anything to do with the referee's leniency towards his transgressors, but the abuse he suffered from the Levski fans behind the goal when he went to take corners was insufferable.

With less than two hundred fans in this part of the stadium, how on earth could the club ignore such blatant racism? Yet time after time the choruses of boos and monkey chants could be heard everywhere in the stadium.

What with the chants and the cold, I'd had enough and it was back down Reka Veleka towards the tram stop, taking care not to fall over broken manhole covers. There were ladies of the night parading on the side of the road. They were hardly stunning, and very poorly dressed. Perhaps the local men had a fetish for Croydon facelift hair, Sam towelling tracksuits in purple and yellow and complexions that could have only been achieved using a Black and Decker sander, but they certainly didn't appeal to me.

Fortunately the tram took only ten minutes to reach the Hotel Arte. Central heating stuck on high made for a very uncomfortable night and on waking up early on the Sunday, I resisted the urge to try and sneak in a visit to 'just one more stadium'. Instead it was a big armchair in Costa Coffee opposite the National Theatre for a latte and a ham and cheese panini.

As with everything concerning travel that weekend the return timing was perfect. I arrived at the Airport Bus terminal and a bus immediately turned up. Even the flight was on time.

DEUTSCHLAND DEUTSCHLAND WO FÜR KUNST-TAUSEND DEUTSCHLAND?

Sausages, beer and mayhem in the capital of culture

What can you say about a trip to your country's greatest rivals in one of the world's greatest cities when you come away with a win although fielding almost a second-string team? Quite a lot actually, so here goes, without the need to rely on *Top Gun* (or The Mobiles for those who remember the one-hit wonder in 1982) song titles.

This was always going to be the top England away trip for the past few years – well, certainly since Amsterdam in 2006. There's no need to dwell on the history of games between the two great foes, but there is enough in the payback bank from World Cup 1990, the European Championship in 1996 and of course Munich in September 2001 to ensure it was more than just a friendly.

As soon as the game was announced, and the venue confirmed as Berlin, the anticipation among fans was immense. The German FA allocated nearly eight thousand tickets to England fans and most were snapped up well in advance, ensuring that the atmosphere was going to be tip-top. But it wasn't all about the possibility of a mouth-watering game.

Berlin itself was a great result as a venue. Whatever the visitor is looking forward to, he (or she) will find it somewhere in the city. One only has to mention the KitKatClub to draw a knowing smile (go on, you know you

209

want to google it now – just wait until the children or your boss are out of the room though) from a lot of people.

There are a number of great things about Berlin including:

- There is no real centre to the city which means that crowds are dispersed and it is never too busy.
- There is history galore, and most of it is free to see.
- There is German beer and sausages.
- It's full of German women who are not backward at coming forward.

But there are a number of bad things too:

- Because there is no real centre to the city it means attractions are quite far apart.
- There is a lot of 'sensitive' history that attracts the wrong type of visitor.
- Too much beer and sausage makes you very poorly.
- It's full of German women who are sometimes too forward in not going backwards.

A balanced scorecard then, although most people who visit Berlin vow to return time and time again. I'd been on three occasions and captured its forever changing face. In 2000 I surprised CMF with a birthday trip and we wandered around Europe's largest ever building site, which today is the impressive Potsdamer Platz development. Three years later I was back to see a game at the Olympiastadion, which at the time was in the middle of a huge upgrade in time for the World Cup finals in 2006, and finally I went on a day trip with Football Jo so she could stock up on some dodgy DVDs. I had a good idea of the bits to see and the bits to avoid, and that would come in useful later in the day.

As the days counted down before the game, more and more first-choice players pulled out. The Manchester United trio of Ferdinand, Rooney and Wes Brown were already declared injured before the squad was announced but it came as no shock when firstly Steven Gerrard and then Frank Lampard withdrew after playing a full match for their clubs a few hours before (the latter would also play a full ninety minutes less than seventy hours later as well). Paul Robinson, who must have thought, along with ninety-nine per cent of Blackburn Rovers fans, that his international career was over, was called up and with no place still for Michael Owen, there was a lot of speculation as to who would start up front from the quartet of Defoe, Crouch, Bent and Agbonlahor, while the central midfield pairing of Gareth Barry and Michael Carrick would start together for the first time.

I had managed to snare flights on a rumour, twenty-four hours before the fixture was officially announced. The flight was at 7 a.m. on the day of the match, direct to Tegel, returning twenty-four hours later. Dagenham Dan and Shents Bull were flying with me and Dan gave me a lift, although the pick-up from Embankment at 4.30 a.m. meant another chance to say hello to the milkman on leaving the house.

This was going to be my first visit to Heathrow's Terminal Five, and first impressions were very positive although you could see why it took so long to build.

The airport had a heavy police presence since this was a game too tempting for a number of 'old faces' to resist. In general the police at the airports are very personable and will try and have a joke – especially in Dan's case when he was recognised straight away for the heinous crime of being a Dagenham and Redbridge fan. After security we passed through the terminal very quickly, including a Full English pit stop. We had turned down a Wagamama's Full English early on, not exactly relishing the thought of sausage, bacon and wasabi, as well as Gordon Ramsay's Plane Food offering that at £20 was a tad overpriced, settling for the Express Full with a guarantee of fifteen-minutes service.

Fast forward ninety minutes and we were boarding a bus at Tegel for the city centre. Tegel airport is so small that from taxi to the jetty, which connects to the plane, is less than thirty steps. There are firm plans to demolish it in 2012 when the new Brandenburg airport opens in the south-east of the city.

The bus stopped outside Zoo Station, made famous by U2 in 1991 as the title of the opening track of the *Achtung Baby* album, and we headed around the corner so the boys could drop off their bags at their hotel. It was time for sightseeing. Acting as tour guide, I took them on a circular route from Potsdamer Platz along the original Wall route to the Brandenburg Gate and down to Checkpoint Charlie. We had also picked up a few more visitors on the way including Young Joe, who, when he discovered I wrote a blog, insisted he be referred to as Gypsy Joe. I cannot possibly comment on why he liked to be called this, although we did lose him a couple of times as we passed building sites that needed a driveway completed.

After a brief souvenir stall stop at Checkpoint Charlie (where we filled our passports with genuine East German and Soviet border stamps) we went for lunch at one of my favourite spots, the Play Off Bar and Diner, located in the Arkaden shopping centre at Potsdamer Platz.

You may ask what is so special about an American diner in a shopping centre. There are four main factors. First they are one of the few bars in the city to serve Schwarzbier, or 'black beer', which is addictive once tried; second, they serve huge portions of every type of meat known to man; third, TVs are dotted around the bar showing sport from all over the world; and finally there are the waitresses. We are not talking about Hooters (google if you must) league here, but they are above average for German women. Our waitress, Steffi, took a shine to Dan and me straight away and flirted like mad. She kept 'squeezing' past us to get to other tables and taking the opportunity for a quick feel as she passed. She was certainly not backward in coming forward and I think things could have got a bit messy had we stayed for a few more Schwarzbiers.

Berlin was gearing up for its annual Christmas market, with stalls being set up around Potsdamer Platz. Most were not yet open but some sweet stalls were, including the infamous 'let's dip all the fruit we can find in chocolate and put it on a stick' stall. One was a Milka stand, selling a variety of purple cow products. Being brave after the black beers, I went with Shents to the pretty maidens behind the desk and asked, hopefully with a dollop of irony: 'Do you know anywhere that sells chocolate?'

The reply was succinct: 'Are you English people so stupid you cannot see? We sell chocolate here – now do you want some or are you going to sod off?' In one of the biggest climbdowns known to man, and with my support crew in hiding around the corner, I handed over €2 for a bar of Milka with chilli. I could have at least got something I liked.

In preparation for the change in temperature that was due to kick in at the weekend, the local authorities had installed a real snow slope where for €1.50 you could speed down in a tyre. Only Gypsy Joe and Shents were brave enough, and their girly screams were enough to have the rest of us heading into the U-Bahn in fits of laughter.

We went back to Zoo as the boys were fascinated by the Erotik superstore and museum located across the road from the station. It was here in April 2006 that I nearly walked into a scene from a porno movie – although not the kind either CMF or I would want to watch.

It was the trip with Football Jo and she wanted to try and 'outporn' her brother. She wanted to look in the 'special' section of DVDs. Now, as Germany is the most liberal country in Europe, where hardcore porn is shown regularly on state TV before the watershed and they have monthly magazines such as *Golden Shower Monthly* and *Bukkake Bonanza*, the special section caters for a minority of the market, and Jo was in her element. I was desperate for the bathroom and noticed a gents in the corner. As I was about to push the door open, three young men with leather pants and very tight T-shirts emerged, swiftly followed by a middle-aged man in a suit who looked a little flustered. On seeing the potential for a new 'trick' they smiled at me and I rushed back to Jo in the Stacheldraht und Vanillepudding section (use Babel Fish if you want to know!), much to her amusement.

This time, after a thirty-minute giggle, we felt the need for more culture and travelled east to Alexanderplatz, once the centre of the East German universe. Slap bang in the middle of the square is the Fernsehturm (TV Tower), built in the late 1960s and one of the tallest free-standing structures in Europe at three-hundred and sixty-eight metres. The viewing platform at two hundred and four metres is a great place to see the city and Shents and I were the only ones of our party brave enough to take the thirty metres a second lift and see the magnificent panoramic views.

One day is nowhere near enough time to take in all the history and grandeur Berlin has to offer. There is always a balance to be struck on these trips between culture and behaving like a football fan. So, after seeing most of the city's important sites, we did what the vast majority of English football fans would do and headed for a bar and a beer. In moderation, though, as the danger abroad is to be caught in the wrong place at the wrong time. Alcohol magnifies this problem considerably and it is always prudent to try to avoid the main gathering of fans. One was enough for now as time was getting on, and we walked down Unter den Linden, the triumphal avenue that was the centre of Hitler's plans for his empire, for a final slice of culture before going to the stadium.

The train was packed with fans from both countries. The Germans were quiet, drinking their litre bottles of beer, while the English were full of tuneless songs which started off fine, such as 'God Save The Queen' and 'Rule Britannia' but then progressed to 'Ten German Bombers' and other great songs taken from the Xenophobes' greatest hits CD.

We pulled into the station next to the stadium and within a few minutes passed through the security cordons, collected our free programmes and stocked up on warming food and drink as the temperature started to fall.

What more is there to say about the stadium? It is truly magnificent and history seems to seep from every brick. The venue for the infamous 1936 Olympics, it was taken apart block by block in the 1990s, completely cleaned and reconstructed. A huge roof was put in place and it was ready to host the 2006 World Cup Final.

England had been given the upper and lower tiers either side of the Olympic torch platform, and the view from my seat in the upper tier was very impressive. The teams emerged to a 'raise the flag' that was inspiring, although we couldn't actually see what the message was. Christians entering the Coliseum perhaps? Well, ninety minutes would decide whether we would exit battered and bruised or carried on the shields of the vanquished.

Germany 1 England 2 – Olympic Stadium – 19th November 2008

The major surprise in the team was the inclusion of Agbonlahor in attack and in the early exchanges it was England who played the ball around with confidence. While Germany had made some interesting selections, including René Adler in goal for just the second time, and Hoffenheim full back Marvin Compper for his debut, they started with the experienced pair of Miroslav Klose and Mario Gómez in attack. They had scored fifty goals at this level between them, which gave us travelling fans some cause for concern.

The opening goal came after twenty-four minutes when Adler dropped a corner and the Hammers' own Matthew Upson prodded the ball home for his first international goal, and importantly the first goal scored for England by a West Ham player this century. Everything seemed to be going England's way as Carrick and Barry stopped any threat from the young German team, although it is impossible to know what would have happened had Michael Ballack been in the middle of the park.

Towards the end of the first half there was a flare-up in the German fans' section closest to the England fans. It appeared that a group of away fans had bought tickets on the black market, and the locals objected to them joining in with the theme to the *Dambusters*, which was being sung by many of the travelling fans. A stand-off occurred for a few minutes, then beer was thrown and all hell broke lose for twenty seconds before the English bid a hasty retreat into the arms of the German riot police and a banning order from travelling to watch England play abroad again.

Capello brought on Scott Carson at half-time and he had little to do until the sixty-third minute when a huge punt by the substitute German keeper Wiese cleared Matthew Upson. John Terry appeared to have the ball under control and waited for Carson to come and collect it. Both took their eyes off it, which allowed Patrick Helmes to nip in and give the Germans an undeserved equaliser. In the past the England fans would have reacted by booing Carson, but this wasn't Wembley with its plastic fans. Sure, there were ironic cheers the next time he handled the ball, but that was it. Terry must also take some of the blame as he had taken his eye off the German player, but he responded with the type of performance a captain should give, and with just seven minutes left he rose to head in a Stuart Downing free kick to win the game.

Full marks again to Fabio Capello, who had won the tactical battle with Joachim Löw and was earning more respect by the day from fans and media for his team selection and tactics.

Leaving for the station, we were initially impressed by the way the fans had been segregated. The idea was that the rival fans were at either end of the platforms and boarded alternately, so that there were no trains containing both sets. Good idea in theory, but in practice it failed. The stream of trains soon slowed to a trickle and we were sent from platform to platform with no one really knowing what was going on. A train had been sitting on the platform for ten minutes when all of a sudden the doors of one carriage were pushed open and a fight broke out on the platform. Riot police arrived within seconds although they were slow to work out who had started it. They infiltrated the crowd, setting all of us on edge thinking they might simply take us as token arrests.

Eventually we got back into the centre and headed to the boys' hotel for a couple of beers. I was screwed either way as I had to be up at 4 a.m. for the return flight. As it doesn't make much difference if you get two or three hours' sleep, I enjoyed a drink and walked back from the hotel to the accompaniment of police sirens.

Wind forward five hours and it is the departure lounge at Tegel. To my left is Alan Smith, the ex-Arsenal striker, now a well-known TV pundit, and to the right is Teddy Sheringham with his latest companion. Straight ahead is the wettest, whiniest, pathetic England fan I have ever seen. After seeing a fight in a bar in the city centre, he decided against going to the game, watching it in his hotel room instead. He tried to argue his case as to why his moisturiser should not be confiscated by security because 'it was expensive' and 'it was unfair on him'. Yet he still wanted to tell everyone that he planned on going on a day trip to Kazakhstan, completely unaware of the nine-hour flight each way.

A crazy twenty-four hours in Berlin was just what the doctor ordered as a break from work. It was never going to be quiet and relaxing but the surprising result had at least made it worthwhile. We had certainly seen the best of what Germany has to offer, and some of the worst of what the England fans could do, although the German fans were notably absent from most bars after the game.

IL BELLO GIOCO HA GIOCATO IN UNA PUNTA DEI RIFIUTI . . .

or The Beautiful Game played in a rubbish tip

I'd always planned to end my travels for this book with England's visit to virgin lands in June 2009 when they visited Kazakhstan but a better opportunity arose. I decided to take a different view and looked at the largest capacity stadiums in Europe to see which ones I had not yet visited. Of the top twenty-five I was able to tick off all the way down to number twelve: the Stadio San Paolo in Naples, with a capacity of just over seventy-eight thousand. This figure was not strictly accurate as a number of 'accidents' at the stadium over the past few years have reduced the actual capacity to around the sixty thousand mark, which ejected it from the top twenty-five elite. However, a trip to watch Italian football was long overdue. I hadn't set foot in a Serie A stadium since West Ham's miserable failure in Palermo in 2006.

Naples has an appalling reputation in the outside world, as a city dogged by corruption and violence. Unsavoury characters have blighted the area for decades. What makes the region so unusual is that it is surrounded by some of Italy's most exclusive tourist areas. The Amalfi Coast, world-famous resorts such as Sorrento, the islands of Capri and Ischia, which attract the wealthy during the long, hot summers, and the historic Roman towns of Pompeii and Herculaneum have seduced tourists from around the world for decades. Yet visitors are still scared of venturing into the city centre of Naples for fear of robbery and violence.

I have a clear picture of places in Europe I try to avoid at all costs, which, dear reader, you will know includes Barcelona, Amsterdam and Paris, and so a trip to Naples held no real fear. However, my companion was to be Football Jo, so I was assured of paranoia from the moment the easyJet plane landed on the tarmac.

Tickets for the football had been sorted through Seatwave because watching the game in Italy is not what it was. Gone are the days of pitching up at an almost empty stadium a few minutes before kick-off and buying a seat. Now, because of a number of high-profile violent episodes, all games are classed as 'all ticket'. In most instances no tickets can be sold on the day of the game, and spectators' names have to be printed on them and their identification verified on entry into the stadium. All very noble gestures, but all of the violent episodes had taken place outside the stadiums and in some instances away from the grounds.

It meant the tickets had to be sorted in advance, and the privilege paid for of course. The €18 ticket cost more than €55 once commissions for middlemen and delivery were included (I now see how football agents make their money.) But at least the tickets were in my hand before we travelled, albeit in the name of Joenne Richards Joenne and Stuar Fulle.

Fortunately the match was moved from Sunday afternoon to 6 p.m. on Saturday night, meaning we would have a full day's sightseeing after the football. Our easyJet flight first thing on the Saturday morning was on time and for once sitting at the front had some advantages as, after experiencing more than two hundred and fifty easyJet flights, I realised that there was actually a stewardess worthy of more than a passing look. She brightened up the two-and-a-half-hour flight, and even Football Jo had to admit that she was 'cute'. We took off into the most stunning sunrise, full of oranges and purples that mesmerised most passengers. Red sky in the morning, and all that – it would come back to haunt us in less than forty-eight hours.

Landing in Naples just before 11 a.m., we waited for a bus to take us to the terminal building. That would be the terminal building no more than fifty yards away? Surely not? Ah, but this was Italy, home of the hearts of darkness and a bureaucracy that put the Brown government to shame. We boarded the bus, drove around the plane and got off on the other side. However, again this being Italy, they failed to realise that two planes had landed at the same time and there was only one man on passport control. Of course, this was not an issue for the Italians among the waiting passengers. They just pushed their way to the front. The rest of us queued for nearly thirty minutes until the border guard was joined not by one or two, but three colleagues, who processed us within a few minutes.

Fifteen minutes later we were disembarking from the airport bus in the first place most visitors see of Naples, Piazza Garibaldi. This traffic-filled rectangle is the heart of the transportation network with buses, taxis, cars and scooters competing for any space and trying to avoid the wandering pedestrians.

The area is also home to the railway station, which means it is home to most of the undesirables the city can muster, as we would see over the next twenty-four hours. We decided to go straight to the hotel and drop off the bags before starting on sightseeing. But we were simply not prepared for Naples and what it was going to throw at us.

Rubbish was piled up on every street corner, overflowing onto pavements and even into cars. Dubious characters lurked in doorways, selling a variety of pirated (or stolen) goods such as PSPs, iPods and iPhones.

We came across a welcoming sight on one corner of a woman, resplendent in a short skirt and slippers (think of a cross between Nora Batty and Bella Emberg (google the Benny Hill show) wearing one of Cheryl Cole's outfits and a pair of your gran's slippers), burning a suitcase full of rubbish on the street.

I had given Jo a brief lesson in how to cross a road like an Italian but she couldn't get it. Instead of walking confidently diagonally across the road, she acted as if in a real-life 'Frogger' game, hopping backwards and forwards with yelps and squeals. Finally reaching the hotel side, we walked past one of the least-interested-looking working girls you will see in a long time. Wearing purple tights and matching boots, she was leaning against a lamp post and smoking in an unalluring way. It might have looked very fetching on a twenty-something who kept herself in shape but this one appeared to be the daughter of the bonfire woman. It was no surprise that on the two other occasions we returned in the next five hours she was still in the same uninterested position, sans customers.

Carrying the smallest possible amount of personal belongings, we set off into the city, avoiding gaping holes in the pavement, scooter riders mounting the same and, of course, beggars. We wandered for a good hour, trying to find something classed as 'interesting', but failed, apart that is from a decent restaurant for lunch. Jo then gave an update on the

219

sex lives of her friends, including the fascinating tale of one young lady with a phobia of midgets. As a hen night surprise they hired a troop of 'performing' short men to entertain her.

After lunch we walked around the 'Royal' parts of the city, with the Castel Nuovo, Palazzo Reale and Teatro San Carlo further proving the lack of pride the citizens have in their city. They were covered in graffiti and rubbish bags. What I do not understand about Italian society is that they are so passionately patriotic yet feel no shame at throwing rubbish on the floor or scrawling on a centuries-old building. We had still not experienced any threatening atmosphere, though, and during the long trek back to the hotel we were approached only once by a beggar.

After a short snooze it was time for football, and so we went into the bowels of the Stazione Garibaldi opposite the hotel for another slice of Italian-organised mayhem. The police were holding back fans at the top of the stairs to stop overcrowding on the platforms. So the younger fans just walked to the next entrance, down the stairs and crossed the railway lines. Did the police do anything? Of course not. They were too busy standing chatting and smoking beneath a no-smoking sign. The train arrived, and now I understood what had happened to England's 1970 Football Special trains. They had been taken to Naples and were being used as their prime underground rolling stock.

The Stadio San Paolo is in the historic area of Fuorigrotta, one of the city's more upmarket areas and just twenty minutes away from the bedlam of the central station.

Napoli 2 Udinese 2 – San Paolo Stadium – 31st January 2009

When we got off the train there was no one around. We could see promising signs that a game was about to take place, but there was a distinct lack of fans. They'd been there at the station but where were they now? There were police in numbers, street vendors and merchandise stands but it was as if the fans had gone on strike. I checked the ticket to see if the kick-off time was correct, and sure enough it was. When we reached the stadium we could hear where the fans had gone. They were inside already. With thirty minutes to kick-off they were trying to raise the roof.

We now had to get in. We headed round to Curva B and started to queue with some rough-looking *tifosi*. There was a police helicopter flying overhead. Again queuing went out of the window as some fans simply jumped over the barriers. We were supposed to have our ID checked against the tickets but the stewards weren't interested. At the second check point another steward took the tickets, putting them into a barcode reader. This was irrelevant for the *tifosi*, who just pushed past the turnstiles.

Once inside, we went to the top of Curva B for the fantastic view. We sat with the chain-smokers, including one guy who through the course of the game smoked forty-two cigarettes (I counted the butts at the end), which means his match-day habit would probably cost him around £1,000 a year – three times as expensive as the seat.

It appeared that the kick-off had been delayed because traffic problems had prevented the Udinese team getting to the stadium in time. When they finally made it and strode onto the pitch for the customary warm-up they ignored the abuse being aimed at them by the home fans and it took a stern word from the referee for them to leave the pitch. They returned five minutes later to kick off amid a crescendo of noise and smoke.

The game started at a cracking pace as Napoli needed to make up for a surprise 3-0 home defeat to Roma the week before. Although Udinese had most of the possession, Napoli pressed them hard and took the lead in the twenty-fourth minute after a very fast break through the middle. It was a move of which the greats who once played for Napoli, such as Maradona, Zola and Di Canio would have been proud. The new-look Napoli were one of the few teams in Serie A who believed attack was the best form of defence. They'd had a great first half of the season, spendinging Christmas in the top five, but their form since had been poor.

Three minutes later it was two as Hamšík headed home completely unmarked. The few hundred travelling fans could not believe what they were seeing. Udinese had played some good football but somehow found themselves two goals down. Udinese's start to the season had been electrifying but they had fallen away in the run-up to Christmas.

But they refused to capitulate. Within five minutes a silly push on Asamoah resulted in the referee pointing to the spot, ignoring the deafening abuse raining down on him. Italian international Antonio Di Natale stepped up and sent Napoli keeper Nicolás Navarro the wrong way.

With time running out in the first half, a wild cross from the left was met on the volley by Udinese's Fabio Quagliarella and the ball flew into the corner for the equaliser. As the Italian international ran to the corner to celebrate it was interesting that there was as much applause for a stunning goal as there were boos and abuse. It proved that quality does rise to the surface and deserve respect.

The second half didn't hit the heights of the first. Napoli shaded it and would have wrapped up the game with time running out had Lavezzi taken one of two chances. One surprise, though, was the lack of histrionics on the pitch, which led to an overall impression of two teams playing the game in the right spirit.

On the final whistle the fans evacuated the stadium swiftly but we lingered to take photographs and savour the surroundings. With only a few hundred spectators left the arena lost a lot of its magic and felt soulless, exposing the poor facilities for fans.

The visit, however, meant I had ticked off the empty box in the top twenty-five list and we could return to the hotel for a few beers and look forward to a day of culture.

I am not going to dwell too much on the events of the Sunday in Naples. The rain fell from first light and we took the thirty-minute journey through the drab suburbs to Pompeii for a few hours. It really is an amazing place, and the restoration work enables you to picture life in the Roman era. The site is huge and it takes hours to do it justice. One of the highlights was the amphitheatre where gladiators, treated like present-day Premier League footballers, did battle. It was here that a riot broke out in the stands and the city's governor banned any events in the stadium for ten years.

We went to the brothel, where frescos on the wall served as a menu for the offerings in each room, and the Roman equivalent of McDonald's, complete with phallic stools for women to sit on. We also looked at the theatre, where Jo asked (she claimed as a joke) whether the Romans watched plays written by Shakespeare.

With a few hours to kill we continued on the Circumvesuviana line to Sorrento for lunch. I expected big things of the small town perched on the cliffs of the Bay of Naples. It was certainly clean and tidy and much more upmarket than Naples, but everywhere was closed. We had hoped to find a bar showing the Tyne–Wear derby but were lucky to find a small restaurant serving excellent home cooking which justified this out-of-the-way trip. Filled up with pasta, meat and enough tiramisù to feed a small army the journey back on the train was a very snoozy affair.

Getting regular updates on the worsening weather in London, I had concerns about the flight but it arrived on time in Naples and set off on time as well. All seemed to be going well until on our final approach into Stansted we flew right over the airport. Based on the position of the moon we appeared to be heading north. And sure enough, a few minutes later our captain told us poor runway conditions meant we were being diverted.

Not to anywhere convenient like Luton, Cambridge (yes, there is an airport there and it can take a 747) or Gatwick – thirty minutes later we landed at a snowy East Midlands, some one hundred and twenty miles from Stansted. Later it was announced that Stansted was closed for the night, and with more diverted planes landing all the time a fleet of coaches was ordered to ferry us back.

Chaos reigned as people fought to get on them, worried they would be stuck in the Midlands for the night. We got on one and while sitting on it saw people take other people's bags from the luggage compartments and put theirs in – actions which would not have been a surprise in Naples but were completely alien to British society.

After we finally left the airport at midnight conditions got steadily worse the further south we went. The M1 around Luton and the M25 in Hertfordshire were almost impassable and we crawled along at 20mph. CMF was sending regular updates of conditions in SE9 and it didn't sound good. She was starting a new job in the morning, and Lolly was due to go on a school trip so I was determined to get home. I felt like Steve Martin from *Planes, Trains and Automobiles*, always thinking one step ahead.

We arrived at Stansted at 4 a.m., to an airport humming with people turning up from all four corners of the UK. Driving carefully, I eventually limped into the drive at 6.15 a.m., fifteen minutes after CMF had got up. Fortunately the following day was saved by South Eastern trains, who couldn't be bothered to clear any of the railway tracks which meant that I could not get into work.

So the final adventure for this book had come to a close. A marathon journey that took in twenty countries in two-and-a-half years, seeing some of the strangest people in the world of football as well as some excellent matches. I calculated that the thirty trips had involved more than two hundred pints of beer, thirty-seven sausages, nine travelling companions and countless incidents that have made it all worthwhile.

THE STADIUMS

Information and exchange rates valid at April 2009. Club websites are usually in the local language, although many have English versions available via the homepage.

Chapter 1 – Moscow

Dinamo Stadion – Dinamo and CSKA Moscow
Capacity: 34,650 all-seater

The Russian ground merry-go-round continues. The Dinamo Stadium is now home to Dinamo Moscow and tenants CSKA Moscow. However, it is showing signs of age, having opened in 1928. Amazingly, considering the harsh climate in eastern Russia, the stadium is completely uncovered, offering no protection. One of its most notable characteristics is the huge floodlights that seem to have enough bulbs to light up the whole city. Seats are bolted on to the terrace, meaning that they have little legroom and the rake of the steps is poor. The stadium looks smart in the sunshine, but very miserable when the autumn rains start. It has a small athletics track, which pushes the end stands back, adding further issues for those fans behind the goal. Very little has changed in terms of stadium feel and design since the ground was chosen to host the 1980 Olympics football tournament.

How to get there
By far the easiest way is Metro Line 2 (the green line). It runs straight through the centre of the city to the Dinamo metro stop. The ground is just behind the station. Obviously, on a busy match day the station can be crowded so it may be wise to use the next stop at Aeroport and walk back down Leningradsky Prospect. Dinamo station is five stops from Red Square and the trip takes no longer than ten minutes.

Getting a ticket
Ticket prices vary depending on whether CSKA (http://www.cska.ru; website in Russian) or Dinamo (http://www.fcdynamo.ru) are at home. Tickets behind the Dinamo goal start from just 300 Roubles (£6) and range to 4,000 Roubles (around £80) for a VIP seat (still uncovered!) which comes with all of the trappings of Russian luxury. For CSKA games (excluding the Champions League), tickets start from 200 Roubles behind the goal (£4) to 2,000 Roubles for a VIP seat (£40). Neither team

is very well supported. Despite being top of the table for most of the season, CSKA averaged just 12,000, while Dinamo's crowds have dropped to below 8,500. A few games do sell out though, such as the derbies against Spartak and Lokomotiv.

Luzhniki Stadion
Spartak and Torpedo Moscow – Capacity: 84,745 all-seater

While many see the National Stadium as a relic of the past, UEFA decided it was important enough, and more relevantly suitable, to host big games, and awarded it the honour of staging the 2008 Champions League Final. The stadium was built in 1956 and redeveloped as the showpiece for the 1980 Summer Olympics, being used for the opening and closing ceremonies and the track and field competition. It is still the biggest stadium in Russia. It is also one of the few major stadiums with an artificial grass pitch. The stadium originally had a capacity of 103,000 and has hosted events as varied as showjumping, speedway and ice hockey. In 1982 during a UEFA Cup game between Spartak and HFC Haarlem more than sixty people were killed in a stampede caused by a last-minute goal. Initially the Soviet media was instructed to cover this with no more than a paragraph in the local press, which stated there had been only a few minor injuries, but there is now a small plaque at the stadium commemorating those who died. There is also a magnificent statue of Lenin on the main North Boulevard. The stadium is very smart from the inside, with seats in three bands of yellow, orange and red. The athletics track hinders the atmosphere, although the roof added since the Olympics means the noise generated by the home fans at the west end can be intimidating.

For most league matches, only the north and south stands are open. When Torpedo are at home, the fans are placed in the south stand, with any away fans opposite. When Spartak are at home, the home fans use the west curve as well.

How to get there

The stadium forms the focal point of a sports complex, and sits on a bend in the Moskva River in the south-west of the city. The closest metro stop is Sportivnaya, just to the north, almost under the central ring road. From the city centre, it is just four stops or seven minutes by metro on the Red Line 1. To the east of the stadium, and built on a bridge over the river, is the Universitet station, one stop further down the line from Sportivnaya.

Getting a ticket

With more than 65,000 spare seats for most league games, turning up a few minutes before kick-off is never a problem at the Luzhniki. The ticket windows are located to the left-hand side of the main entrance, at the stadium's northern end. As with most public places in Moscow, terrorism is a threat and an airport-style metal detector is used, plus bags are inspected. For a run-of-the-mill 'B' grade league game, a seat watching Torpedo in the south stand costs less than 2,000 roubles (£5), while prices are almost doubled for Spartak matches (http://eng-spartak.com).

Lokomotiv Stadion – Lokomotiv Moscow
Capacity: 28,800 all-seater

This is an oasis of calm in the middle of muddle in terms of Russian football grounds. It was built in 2002 on the site of the former stadium and is a shining beacon of modern design that would not look out of place in the Premier League. It has four

225

almost identical two-tier stands, linked by a pillar at each corner which hold up the roof. All seats are covered, offering protection from the harsh Russian elements as well as giving unobstructed views. Each stand has seats of a different colour, which helps indicate your position if you can't understand the Cyrillic alphabet. The low roof also helps generate an excellent atmosphere, especially when the visitors are CSKA or Spartak Moscow.

How to get there

It is located in the north-east quadrant of Moscow, just outside the second ring road. The area around the stadium isn't plush – there's a market and a few 'budget' supermarkets. The stadium has its own metro stop on the Red Line 1 at Cherkizovskaya, one stop from the north end of the line. From Red Square (Okhotny Ryad) it is eight stops and around twenty minutes. There is also an overland railway station above the Metro – trains here run on the outer Moscow Loop line. There is an alternative route that involves using the Dark Blue Line 3 to Partizanskaya (five stops from Ploshchad Revolutsii in Red Square), and then a fifteen-minute walk northwards from the station, passing Izmaylovo market. The final option is a taxi. You can hail almost any car in Moscow, and if the driver feels like stopping you can commandeer his car as an unofficial or 'gypsy' taxi. Agree a fee beforehand but you should not pay more than 200 roubles from the city centre to the stadium.

Getting a ticket

Despite having the best-looking stadium in Moscow, the *Field of Dreams* adage that you should 'build it and they will come' hasn't quite held true for Lokomotiv (http://www.eng.fclm.ru). Average attendances at the old ground were always low, reaching at best 6,000 and while these have increased to around the 12,000 mark since the new stadium was built, it still means lots of empty seats each week. Tickets for a Lokomotiv match go on sale online via the website from ten days before a game, or can be bought from the ticket booths on the main road to the south of the stadium. Tickets range in price from 1,400 Roubles (approx. £4.50) behind the goals to 6,000 Roubles for a seat in the VIP section of the West Stand. Tickets for CSKA's Champions League games start from 3,000 Roubles (£9).

Chapter 2 – Skopje

The Philip II National Arena (Gradski Stadium) – FK Vardar and FK Rabotnički
Capacity: 18,104 all-seater

The stadium is dominated by a very steep main stand containing more than 12,000 seats. This offers protection from the elements, although the wind blowing across the river can bite during cold nights. The remaining three stands are open and consist of eight to ten rows of plastic seats bolted direct to the old terraces. There is a small perimeter fence around the pitch as well as a six-lane running track. Views are not bad from most stands, although from the first few rows it is not the best. The seats at the back of the stand are also quite steep and if you do have a ticket for this area try not to drink too much before the game in order to prevent a nasty fall on the way up (or down!). The stadium is currently undergoing a major redevelopment programme which is intended to see it almost completely rebuilt by 2011.

How to get there

The stadium is north-west of the city centre, close to the River Vardar, in the City Park area. The area close by the stadium is certainly where all the action is. The major nightclubs (Colosseum, Cabrio and Havana) are located across the road and the Zoo and Natural History Museum are within a two-minute walk. From north of the Vardar, and in the region of the Swan English Pub, go north up Stiv Naumov away from the river and then turn left onto BD Goce Del ev. Follow this past the Kale and across the river, where you can then turn right onto the riverside path to the stadium. The walk should take fifteen minutes at the most. If you are south of the river, in the region of the Holiday Inn, Irish Pub or the main square, just follow the river westwards, past the Stone Bridge and you will reach the ground in about ten minutes. Allow an extra fifteen minutes if you are coming from the main station (follow BD Jane Sandanski towards the river, where you will see the riverside walk).

Getting a ticket

The stadium has sold out only twice in Macedonia's history – both times when England were the visitors. Crowds rarely break the four-figure barrier for domestic matches so buying advance tickets is not necessary. Tickets for the main stand are a good bet as from the top the views both over the pitch and to the city to the east are excellent. For national matches, tickets can be reserved in advance (depending on the opponents) from the Macedonian Football Association (http://www.macedonianfootball.com).

Chapter 3 – Tallinn

The Le Coq Arena – FC Flora Tallinn
Capacity: 9,300 all-seater

Fans of Scunthorpe United and Walsall will feel really at home in the Le Coq Arena in Tallinn. Just to underline the importance of football to the Estonians it was felt that such a small stadium was more than adequate for the national team's purposes. FC Flora Tallinn, who play here, struggle to get over 1,000, while the national team average just over 3,000. The stadium is a fine venue from which to watch football on a long summer's night, as the sight lines and legroom are excellent; each stand has a large bar and refreshments area and the roof offers protection from the occasional Estonian shower. The two side stands are identical – resplendent with green seats. Both have two tiers with the lower tier much larger than the upper. The concertina-style roof is also unusual as it sits quite a way above the final row of seats. The end stands are set above the action on the pitch by eight feet, which allows an additional 1,000 seats to be installed when demand exists. The hardcore Estonian fans, if you can call them that, tend to inhabit the lower tier of the south stand.

How to get there

The stadium is in the south-west of the city, just outside the main ring road. On a sunny day it is easily walkable from the city centre in around thirty minutes. The main railway line causes a small logistical problem. You have two options. The shortest way is to go south along the Pärnu Mnt main road until you reach the elevated bridge over the railway line. At this point go down the steps on either side of the road and turn right into a residential road. You will then see the unmanned crossing over the railway line. The other option is to use Tram number 3 which runs down Pärnu Mnt from the town to the stadium entrance road every twenty minutes, and takes less than ten minutes. A taxi should cost £5.

Getting a ticket

Assuming you are in town for a league match, just go to the stadium and buy a ticket from the table in the corner of the south-east stand. For a mere 30EEK (£1.75) you will get a ticket for the main stand and a programme. If you want to sit with the dozen or so hardcore fans in the south stand a ticket costs 5EEK less. Or contact http://www.fcflora.ee.

Chapter 4 – Palermo

The Stadio Renzo Barbera – USC Palermo
Capacity: 36,980 all-seater

Named after one of Palermo's presidents. It is hardly an impressive or classic ground but it is similar to a number of those in Italy. It has one covered and three uncovered stands, framed by the huge hill behind the north end. The stands are two-tiered, with both end stands curving away from the pitch. The Curva Nord is where you'll see the flares as it is home to the *tifosi*. Away fans are located in the stadium's south-east corner in a fully enclosed cage, where facilities are basic at best.

How to get there

The stadium is around two miles north of the city centre, close to the A29 Autostrada in the San Lorenzo area. To get there from the Stazione Centrale, catch bus number 101 or 107. The nearest suburban station is the Imperatore Federico Stadio, on the road of the same name just south of the stadium and a ten-minute walk away.

Getting a ticket

Tickets range in price from €27.50 (£25) for a Curva Sud ticket to €72 (£62) for a top of the range Tribuna Laterale ticket. They can be bought from a number of SNAI outlets in Palermo and from the stadium ticket office located in the main stand. Tickets may not be on sale on the day of the game due to changes in regulations made by the Italian authorities after a number of serious crowd incidents. All ticket holders have to prove their identity, so if you do book tickets online (http://www.ilpalermocalcio.it) you will need to show your passport when you pick up them up.

Chapter 5 – Zagreb

The Maksimir Stadium – Dinamo Zagreb – Capacity: 38,923 all-seater

Classed as the national stadium despite not being the country's biggest – that is the redeveloped Poljud stadium of Hajduk Split. However, the Maksimir is very atmospheric. Dinamo have played there since their inception in 1945. The first real redevelopment didn't take place until the mid-1980s when the stadium was chosen to host the 1987 World Student Games. It is an odd affair. All four stands are uncovered. There are two large two-tier stands, one smaller single-tier stand and finally a curved bank behind the goal. It is another stadium that suffers from having a running track, meaning fans behind the goal are quite a way from the action. The home fans – the Blue Boys – congregate in the north stand. There are plans to redevelop the stadium, with a new south stand, the corners filled in, and one of the largest retractable roofs ever built. There is no definite timescale, and it is expected that Dinamo will continue to play at the Maksimir while the work is carried out.

How to get there

The easiest way is to jump on a tram on line 4 from the central station, alighting at Bukovačka, seven stops and fifteen minutes. If you are coming from the bus station then catch tram line 7 which takes ten minutes. The stadium's main (west) stand is just beside the tram stop.

Getting a ticket

Only the big national team games and the Croatian derby between Dinamo and Hajduk raise the average attendance above 10,000. Tickets can therefore be purchased on the day from the booths to the right of the stadium as you approach it from the tram stop. It might be worth avoiding the Blue Boys stand if you want to watch the football, and not your back. Website: http://www.nk-dinamo.hr.

Chapter 6 – Orlando

The Florida Citrus Bowl
Capacity: 65,438 all-seater

Used by the University of Florida for their home matches in the American Football College league. Despite this being a purely amateur sport, crowds regularly exceed 60,000. It was opened in 1936 with a 10,000 capacity, and has been expanded over the years – specifically for the 1994 World Cup finals when it held more than 70,000. The stadium is being redeveloped as part of a $1bn programme which will see the capacity raised again to more than 70,000. The two side stands are triple-tier with floodlights sitting on top. The seats are of the cheap bench variety. Behind the goal (one end is open) the stand is single-tier. All three stands are open-air and the views are good from everywhere.

How to get there

The stadium is around a mile or so west of downtown Orlando, which is twenty miles north of the tourist area referred to as Kissimmee/Lake Buena Vista or Disney World Resort. The only real option is driving. You can exit the I-4 Interstate at junction 82A, B or C and just follow Church Street westwards, or you can take the East-West Expressway and exit at Lake Lorna. Parking is plentiful around the stadium and costs $8.

Getting a ticket

These are sold from the box office at the T.G. Waterhouse Center, located just off junction 82A of the I-4 Interstate and well signposted. The other alternative is using Ticketmaster, which sell seats for most events from sixty days before the event. Ticket prices depend on the importance of the event and tickets can also be purchased pre-match from a small ticket office on the east side of the stadium. Website: http://www.fcsports.com.

Chapter 7 – Amsterdam

The Amsterdam ArenA – Ajax
Capacity: 51,100 all-seater

Opened to a great fanfare with a friendly against AC Milan in 1996, after taking two years to build – the cost of €98 million being met by the local authorities. The plan was that the stadium would be the centrepiece of a 1992 Olympic bid, but this was lost to Barcelona. The stadium was the first in Europe to have a retractable roof, allowing it to be used as a multi-purpose arena. However, this brought problems as the grass failed to grow because of the shadow of the roof, and the pitch was replaced four times in the first year. Fans enter at ground level, but the pitch is three levels up, with the lower two levels taken up by a car park and a road which links the east and west of the stadium area. The lowest levels of seating are located around six feet above the pitch level, so views are excellent, as is the legroom. The stadium was also one of the first in the world to be cash free, using the ArenA card, similar to those used by Schalke and Vitesse Arnhem. There are a number of points around the stadium to buy these cards, which come in €10, €20 and €50 denominations. Once you have one it can be topped up on any further visits. If you have any credit left at the end of the day you can exchange the card for cash at the same kiosks.

How to get there

The stadium is within walking distance of two railway stations – Duivendrecht and Biljmer. The latter is the nearest, being less than a five-minute walk, but consequently is the most crowded. Services run to these stations from the Central station on platforms 2 and 7b and take less than fifteen minutes. The stadium has its own metro stop, Strandvliet/ArenA, close to the north and east stands. The station is on line 54 in the direction of Gein. A taxi from the city centre will cost around €20, and they wait outside the main entrance to the stadium after the game.

Getting a ticket

The club reserves a number of tickets for foreign fans. It also offers packages that combine lunch at the training ground (the Toekomst), entry to the museum, an official picture taken on the pitch and a ticket for the game. These packages start from around €95 (£87) per person and can be booked direct from the club. The average attendance at the ground for league games is close to 48,000 so expect tickets to be available on a match day. The ticket office is on the west side of the stadium, close to gate B. Ticket prices for a seat in the east or west stand start from €35 (£32). Website: http://www.amsterdamarena.nl.

Chapter 8 – Tel Aviv

The Ramat Gan Stadium – Israel National Team
Capacity: 41,583 all-seater

Israel's national stadium is the biggest in the country and was completed in 1951. It is a strange mixture of styles: one large two-tier stand with the remainder single-tier. All are open-air, which in that area of the world is not that much of an issue. The stadium does suffer from having an athletics track. In recent years it has hosted Champions League games featuring Maccabi Tel Aviv as their ground is not up to UEFA's standard. There are plans to demolish the Ramat Gan and build a new 70,000 all-seater in its place, although no firm dates are in place. There are a few bars around the stadium although visiting fans will find the port area the best place to go for pre-match food and drink, then get a taxi to the Ramat area for the match.

How to get there

The area of Ramat Gan is not technically part of Tel Aviv, being a city in itself. It is noted for being the home of the Bar-llan University as well as the Diamond Exchange and is distinguishable by a number of skyscrapers including the Moshe Aviv Tower, Israel's tallest building. The nearest railway station is Bnei Brak, a five-minute walk to the east of the stadium. Across the park to the west is the University bus terminal and railway station. A taxi from the port area will take around fifteen minutes, depending on traffic, and cost no more than £20.

Getting a ticket

Most national team games are sold out, or close to it. Tickets can be purchased in advance from a number of outlets in the city centre as well as from http://www.leaan. co.il, although the website is in Hebrew and may take a bit of help to translate.

Chapter 9 – Barcelona

Estadi Olímpic Lluís Companys – RCD Espanyol
Capacity: 54,000 all-seater

The Olímpic Lluís Companys stadium was built in 1929 but it wasn't until 1987, when the city won the bid for the 1992 summer Olympic Games, that a major redevelopment programme began. The refurbished stadium opened in 1991 with a capacity of 55,000. In 2000 RCD Espanyol moved in after the closure of their Sarriá ground. The stadium is a UEFA five-star venue even though it hasn't hosted a major game. It was also the home to the Barcelona Dragons American Football team for a number of seasons in the 1990s. The stadium is far from ideal for football, with the stands set quite a long way back from the pitch. Also the lack of a roof on three of the four sides means the atmosphere is easily lost. For normal league games the Lateral and Tribuna stands are the only ones in which the upper tiers are used. This means that if bad weather is forecast, demand for the seats in the covered Tribuna rises significantly. The views from all stands are unobstructed. If the weather is good, go for the upper tier in the Lateral which offers a fantastic backdrop over the west of the city.

How to get there

The stadium sits on the Montjuïc hill, overlooking the city and the Mediterranean. While there are a number of options available, one of the best ways to get there is by cable car from the port area (Torre de Sant Sebastia) which offers magnificent views. The stadium is a five-minute walk down the hill from the cable car stop. There is also a funicular railway running from Paral-lel metro station which operates until 8 p.m. daily. Bus numbers 9, 27, 30, 37, 50, 55 and 56 all run from Plaça Espanya if your legs can't manage the walk up past the national museum (although there are escalators to take out much of the hard work). The nearest metro is Plaça Espanya which is on Red line 1 and Green line 3.

Getting a ticket

Tickets for most games are on sale up until kick-off from the two ticket offices on either side of the stadium. If you want to book tickets before you arrive for an Espanyol game, you can do so via the official website http://www.rcdespanyol.com which has an impressive online booking facility. For a normal league game (i.e. not Barcelona or Real Madrid), tickets for the Lateral Superior (upper tier) are €30 (£28), Tribuna Superior (upper tier under cover) €40 (£37) and for a place among the hardcore Espanyol fans then head for the Gol section where tickets are €25 (£23).

Chapter 10 – Basle and Berne

St Jakob Park – FC Basle
Capacity: 42,000 all-seater

When it was announced that the joint bid to host Euro 2008 from Austria and Switzerland had been successful, the Basle city council wasted no time in drawing up plans to provide a stadium that could stage European matches in the future. Similar to those in Berne and Geneva, the outer shell of the stadium is hidden on one side by a shopping centre, but inside it is very much as you would expect from the Swiss: compact, neat and efficient. It is very British in design with four stands close to the pitch and excellent sight lines. Behind each goal there are identical two-tier stands, with a screen perched on the roof. The south stand's upper tier is smaller as the stand holds a double layer of executive boxes. The north stand is a three-tier affair, with the roof sloping up in the corners.

How to get there
Located in the east of the city, it is hemmed in by the train line to Zurich and a motorway. It is almost the demarcation point between the city centre and the suburbs. The stadium is walkable from the main station in no more than thirty minutes. On a match day, special shuttle trains run every fifteen minutes from the central station to a stop behind the north stand. Alternatively you can catch tram number 14, which runs through the centre of the old town. From Markplatz, the stadium stop at St Jakob is eight stops or around eleven minutes and tickets cost 3CHF each way. If you are driving from out of town, it may be easier to drive to the areas to the east of the stadium close to the tram line and use the frequent service direct to the stadium.

Getting a ticket
Domestic football in Switzerland is not the most passionate. Attendances tend to be quite low, and the big four of Young Boys, FC Basle and the two Zurich clubs fail to attract an average of more than half of their capacity, meaning tickets are always available on the day. They can be purchased from the kiosks around the stadium on a match day, or if your German is good via the official website (http://www.fcb.ch). Prices range from 25CHF (£15) to 60CHF (£36). The 'hardcore' fans are located in the east lower tier. A good seat for the neutral is in the north stand upper tier.

The Stade de Suisse – Young Boys Berne
Capacity: 31,000 all-seater

The Stade de Suisse, or to give it its proper name, the Wankdorf Stadium, is one of the elite ten in Europe to have hosted a World Cup Final. In 1954 it staged the game between West Germany and Hungary, forever known as the 'Miracle of Berne'. In 2008 the stadium hosted European Championship group matches featuring the Netherlands, France and Italy. The original stadium, the Wankdorf, which opened in 1925, was built as a home for the Young Boys Berne club. Its original capacity was 20,000, but that was soon expanded during the next decade or so as the team progressed. When Switzerland was chosen to hold the 1954 World Cup, the stadium was further extended to 64,000. Facilities were pretty basic – one covered main stand and three open terraces – and it remained that way until July 2003. Then they started work on the new stadium. It is certainly smart. A complete two-tier 'box' ground, with stands that are almost identical, the views are standard from wherever you sit.

The concourses are very wide, and there are plenty of concession stalls. There are also two large screens on the roofs of the stands behind the goals, which allows everyone a view of them.

How to get there

The stadium is located in the north of the city, close to the main railway line and the Autobahn, A6. On a match day special buses run from the railway station (Bahnhof) direct, which complement the route number 20 which runs every five minutes. A special shuttle train also runs from the Bahnhof to the Wankdorf station, taking less than five minutes. Other bus routes that run close to the stadium are 28, 40 and 41.

Getting a ticket

Young Boys Berne average around 17,000, meaning there are around 14,000 spare seats on match day. The hardcore fans, as much as they get hardcore in Switzerland, are based in the east lower tier. Tickets can be purchased online from the website http://www.stadedesuisse.ch. Ticket prices range from 20CHF (£12) in the lower tier behind the goal to 50CHF in the upper tiers along the side of the pitch. A good bet for the neutral is the lower side tiers which are 34CHF (£20). Tickets go on sale on the day of the game from the windows on the corners of all stands.

Chapter 11 – Copenhagen

Brøndby Stadion – IF Brøndby
Capacity: 29,000 all-seater

Opened in 1965, although at the time it was no more than a field with raised embankments. It is astonishing to think that until 1980 the ground featured just one single stand holding 1,200 and a couple of rudimentary floodlights. A new 5,000-seat stand was built in 1982, and as the team became more successful further stands were added, taking the capacity to just under 20,000 in 1990. The latest redevelopment work started in 1999 and was completed in October 2000, when 28,000 crammed into it to watch the Copenhagen derby. The stadium is almost identical in look and feel to Derby's Pride Park, Southampton's St Mary's Stadium and the new Ricoh Arena in Coventry. All four stands are two-tiered, with a complete wraparound roof. The hardcore fans tend to congregate in the Faxe Tribunen. Views from all stands are excellent, although if you are going to a match in the late summer when the sun is setting it is worth avoiding the east stand.

How to get there

The easiest way is to catch a Line B S-Tog train to Glostrup or a Line A S-Tog train to Brøndby Strand Station and then catch a bus, either a 131 or 500S. Extra buses run on a match day. A return ticket for the train from any of the six city centre stations is 60 Danish Kroner (£5.50). Press the 3 Zone button on the ticket machines. The journey to Glostrup should take twenty minutes from central station. A taxi from the centre will take fifteen minutes and cost around 200 Danish Kroner (£24).

Getting a ticket

It is almost unheard of for domestic games to sell out, except those against FC Copenhagen, which means you can turn up on the day. Tickets are sold in the club shop on the west side of the stadium. They can also be bought from most post offices in the city centre, or from the club's website (http://www.brondby.com). For normal matches, tickets cost between 110 Danish Kroner (£14) and 130 Danish Kroner (£16). For the derby matches they rise to 170 Danish Kroner (£21) and 190 Danish Kroner (£23).

Chapter 12 – Vienna

Gerhard Hanappi Stadion – Rapid Vienna
Capacity: 18,456 all-seater

This is the second biggest ground in Vienna, and is in the western part of the historic city centre. For visitors interested in the more famous sites, the stadium is close to the Tiergarten (zoo) and the impressive Schloss Schönbrunn complex. The stadium is similar in design to the Stade Gerland in Lyon, even down to the curved roof design. It has four separate stands, the side ones being two-tiered, while the ones behind the goals are simple single-tiers with around twenty rows. Views are very good from all seats, although if you are in the Süd Tribune be prepared for the fact that the seats are metal and very uncomfortable. Further development work was put on hold after the decision in 2003 not to use the venue for the 2008 European Championships. The stadium is named after the great Austrian and Rapid Vienna player of the 1940s to 1960s.

How to get there
It's almost opposite the Hütteldorf S-Bahn and U-Bahn stations. From the city centre you need a U-Bahn to Westbahnhof before changing onto S-Bahn line 45. If you are travelling from the old town, U-Bahn Line 4 terminates at Hütteldorf, although this is not the most direct route. Allow twenty-five minutes if using the U4. If you arrive at the Südbahnhof catch U-Bahn 1 from the nearby Südtiroler Platz station north two stops to Karlsplatz, where it intersects with U-Bahn Line 4, and then head westwards. A one-day travel pass for all public transport in Vienna costs €6.20 and can be purchased from the red machines at any station.

Getting a ticket
Attendances in Austria are not great, and if it wasn't for the recent Red-Bull-fuelled marketing activity in Salzburg, Rapid Vienna would be the best-supported team in the league. Attendances average over 13,000, which is quite impressive considering the ground's modest capacity. Tickets are therefore quite easy to pick up on the day from the windows along Keisslergasse. Alternatively you can buy them online from the club's website at http://www.skrapid.at or by phone on +43 1 544 5440. Tickets for the most expensive seats in the Süd Tribune start from €22 (£20). For a more neutral view then get a seat in the upper tier of the Nord Tribune for €18 (£16).

Chapter 13 – Malmö

The Malmö Stadion – Malmö FF
Capacity: 27,500

Until the old stadium was replaced in 2009, it was possible to confuse it with IFK Gothenburg's Ullevi Stadium. They were both designed by the same architect for the 1958 World Cup finals. During that tournament, the stadium hosted four games including the opening Group A game between West Germany and Argentina that attracted the (still) record attendance of 32,000. The new stadium, next to the old one, was a host venue for the 2009 UEFA Under-21 Championship.

How to get there

The stadium is south of the city centre, in a very green residential area. It is a twenty-minute walk from the central station, or around ten minutes from the bus station. Bus number 2 runs close to the stadium, although this gets very busy before the game. A single ticket costs 60SEK and buses wait outside the stadium after the game, leaving when they are full. A taxi from the central station will cost around 75SEK.

Getting a ticket

While attendances are on the up, there will be plenty of spaces for those turning up to pay on the gate at the new stadium. The average attendance over the last few seasons in the old ground was around 14,000, making Malmö the second best supported team in the Allsvenskan behind AIK Solna. Tickets can be bought in advance from the website http://www.ticnet.se. They range in price from 180SEK (£15) in the upper tier of the main stand to 105SEK (£9) behind the goal on the terraces. At the gate these prices are increased to 200SEK (£17) and 110SEK (£9.50) respectively.

Chapter 14 – Groningen

Euroborg – FC Groningen
Capacity: 20,055 all-seater

When plans were initially published for a brand new multi-purpose stadium in Groningen for the then Second Division club, many people wondered what could be the point. The old Oosterpark stadium, which stood on the same spot as the Euroborg, was small and intimate, with a capacity of just over 11,000, and was known for the closeness of the crowd to the action. However, it was showing signs of ageing in the early part of this century – having been constructed in 1933. The 19,980 capacity may have at first seemed ambitious, but the stadium is full for almost every match. It is an impressive venue both inside and out. Around the perimeter there is a health spa, supermarket, Chinese restaurant, cinema and a casino. Inside it is a simple two-tier arena, with a double row of executive boxes in the upper tier of the main stand. Views are very good from all parts, although the presence of a perimeter fence does hinder the first few rows of the lower tier. The stadium lives up to its green tag as all the seats are a bright green colour.

How to get there

The Euroborg is to the south-east of the city centre, next to the A7/E22 motorway. From the old town and railway station it is a pleasant twenty-minute walk. Simply follow Trompsingel eastwards until you reach the bridge over the canal, then turn right and follow Winschoterdiep southwards along the canal. Once you pass under the E22 ring road, the stadium is in front of you – although you need to walk around an office block. Alternatively, use bus number 20, which runs from the bus station next to the central station and drops you right outside the stadium. Journey time is around five minutes.

Getting a ticket

FC Groningen's attendances have risen dramatically over the past few seasons. In 2005–6 the rise was more than 30 per cent to 15,500 and included three sell-outs, and then it rose to 19,180, meaning tickets for most games were in short supply. Tickets range in price from €20 (£18) in the Eerste Ring to €40 (£36) in the main stand. Website: http://www.fcgroningen.nl.

Chapter 15 – Monaco

The Stade Louis II – AS Monaco
Capacity: 18,500 all-seater

One of the most surreal venues in Europe. It is in the middle of the world's richest playground, where space is at an absolute premium. The club started playing in the principality in 1919, although they had to wait until 1939 for their first stadium to be constructed on land reclaimed from the sea. In the early 1980s, when Prince Rainier III came to power, he funded the building of a new stadium a few hundred yards away from the existing ground in Fontvieille, overlooking the cliffs of the Côte d'Azur. The new stadium was built with a car park, offices, swimming pool and a gymnasium all underground, such is the demand for space in the principality. It was named after Prince Rainier's grandfather, who officially opened the complex in 1985. Despite its small capacity, it was chosen to host the 1986 Cup Winners' Cup final between Dynamo Kiev and Atlético Madrid. Since 1998 the stadium has also hosted the annual UEFA Super Cup match, played in late August between the Champions League and the UEFA Cup winners.

How to get there
The stadium is located close to the centre, just south of the Royal Palace. It is a five-minute walk from the main railway station, or a three-minute walk from the heliport from where you can fly direct to Nice airport in less than ten minutes. Just to the south, past the heliport, you can see how close the stadium is to the Mediterranean Sea.

Getting a ticket
Despite it having one of the most affluent supporter bases in the world, crowds don't flock to the Stade Louis II on a regular basis. Even at the height of AS Monaco's 2004 Champions League run, there were tickets available on the day for the semi-final against Chelsea. Tickets can be bought online at http://www.asm-fc.com, by emailing the ticket office at billeterie@asm-fc.com, by phone on +377 92 053754 or from a number of shops around the region, including FNAC in Monaco, Cannes and Nice. Prices start from just €8 (£7), with a ticket in the Tribune d'Honneur costing €40 (£36), making it one of the cheapest clubs in Europe to watch. Tickets for the annual Super Cup are sold via the UEFA.com website from mid July onwards.

Chapter 16 – Salzburg

The Red Bull Arena – Red Bull Salzburg
Capacity: 30,085 all-seater

The Red Bull Arena is completely unrecognisable from 2006 when it was known as the Wals-Siezenheim Stadion and was home to SV Austria Salzburg. However, with the investment from the local government and Red Bull, the stadium now has a much expanded capacity and is used by the new Red Bull Salzburg club. In fact it is hard to escape from Red Bull on visiting for a domestic match. The new-look stadium was completed in 2007 as a venue for Euro 2008 and was officially opened with a friendly against Arsenal in July 2007. It is one of a select few using the FIFA-approved artificial Ligaturf. The previous 18,200-capacity stadium has had an additional tier added, bringing the capacity to around the 30,000 required for it to qualify as a tournament host. This was achieved by raising the 1,900-tonne roof by ten metres and slotting in the extra tier. Views are excellent from everywhere. Like the stadium in Klagenfurt, only three sides have two tiers, with the main West Stand having a row of executive seating instead.

How to get there

Located almost at the end of the airport's runway, less than a kilometre from the terminal building alongside the A1 West Autobahn, and opposite the casino. It is around three kilometres (two miles) from the city centre. Bus lines 1, 10 and 18 run from the central bus and railway station to the stadium stop in Stadionstrasse on the east side of the ground. Close to the stadium is the Europark commercial centre, which includes an IKEA and the new Taxham railway station, which is on the railway line to Munich. Trains run regularly from Salzburg Hauptbahnhof and take less than five minutes.

Getting a ticket

Tickets can be bought from the Bulls shop at the stadium from 9 a.m. to 6 p.m. Monday to Friday or until 2 p.m. on a non-match day Saturday. You can also call +43 662 43 33 32 and arrange to collect and pay for tickets on a match day. The website http://www.redbulls.com has an online ticketing function which you need to register to use.

Chapter 17 – Fürth

The Playmobil Stadion – Greuther Fürth
Capacity: 15,500

A typical German affair, with one single terrace, the north stand, and three separate seated stands. The main stand is a tall affair, similar to that at Lincoln City's Sincil Bank, which runs only a third of the length of the pitch. Opposite it is a covered single-tier structure raised six feet above the pitch, meaning views are very good. Behind the south stand (opposite the main stand) there is a narrow but tall temporary stand that is home for the away fans, next to an open seated area that wraps around and almost joins the main stand. The stadium looks and feels like one from a lower division, with the impression that stands have been added on a piecemeal basis. There are plenty of refreshment bars outside, as well as a covered area behind the main stand which doubles up as a stage for after-match partying. There is a big screen above the south stand that replays goals scored by the home team, although not the visitors.

How to get there

Located less than a mile from the town centre of Fürth and around five miles from Nuremberg. The nearest station is Rathaus on U-Bahn line 1, some ten stops from Nuremberg Hauptbahnhof. There is either a fifteen-minute walk from the station or a regular, free shuttle bus that waits outside and takes five minutes to the west of the stadium. If you want to walk, turn left out of the station and follow the road downhill. When reaching the river, turn right across the bridge and follow the main road for five hundred yards. At this junction turn left and go up the hill. The stadium is around four hundred yards on the right.

Getting a ticket

There are no problems in buying tickets on the day. The main ticket office is outside the main stand on the west side of the stadium. Tickets range in price from €14 (£13) for a place on the north terrace to €21 (£19) in the covered main stand. During the winter months when temperatures plummet, watching a game on either the open terrace or the open seating in the south stand is very uncomfortable. A good bet for neutrals is the covered seats in blocks G or H which cost €19 (£16). The official website (http://www.greuther-fuerth.de) does have an online facility, but you will have to pick up tickets on the day of the game from the ticket office.

Chapter 18 – Vienna 2

Ernst Happel Stadion
Capacity: 49,844 all-seater

This UEFA five-star stadium in central Vienna hosted a number of games in the 2008 European Championships, including all Austria's group games and the final between Russia and Spain. The stadium is a favourite with UEFA although it is the only stadium with a capacity of less than 50,000 to be given five-star status. The capacity was temporarily expanded to 53,008 for the Euro 2008 final. It has been used on four occasions as the venue for European Champions League finals, the last in 1995 when Ajax beat AC Milan. It has been on its present site since 1931, when it was built for the Workers' Olympiad. Originally the capacity was more than 70,000 and it was expanded soon after the war to a massive 90,000. The record attendance of 91,000 came in 1960 for a match with Spain. The capacity has been slowly reduced since, both for reasons of practicality (nobody likes playing in front of a half-empty stadium) and safety. It is elliptical, with an athletics track separating fans from the pitch. The roof was added in 1986 and is similar in design to the AWD Arena in Hannover, or the Mercedes-Benz Arena (formerly the Gottlieb-Daimler-Stadion) in Stuttgart. It appears to float above the stands. The stadium was used as a transit camp for Viennese Jews during the Second World War and there is a memorial to them.

How to get there
Located on a large island separating the River Danube and the Danube Canal from the old town of Vienna, it is an integral part of Prater Park. The iconic Ferris wheel can be seen from a number of seats. The nearest station is on U-Bahn line U2. Alternatively, fans should use the U-Bahn station Wien Praterstern on line 1. This is only six stops from Südbahnhof (Südtiroler Platz). Bus line 80a also runs to the stadium from the old town.

Getting a ticket
For the national team games, tickets are readily available via the official site http://www.oefb.at. Tickets for club games are available via the official club websites.

Chapter 19 – Bremen

Weserstadion – Werder Bremen
Capacity: 42,500

The home of Werder Bremen for nearly one hundred years, although it has gone through a number of major changes. It is now one of the most distinctive looking grounds in Germany because of its unique floodlights and oval shape. It was originally used as a general sports field in the early part of the twentieth century before being developed for political rallies in the early 1930s when the Nazi party was on the rise. The stadium was extensively remodelled in the 1970s, with a new roof added, as well as another 9,500 seats. During the 2001–2 season the pitch was lowered to allow the addition of a further 8,000 seats. The stadium has a dual capacity depending on the nature of the match being played – for normal Bundesliga games it is 42,500, but this falls to around 35,000 for internationals as terracing has to be converted to seating. In September 2005 the German national team played a friendly against South Africa, the first played there for a number of years. The stadium also houses a museum, and the club holds regular tours costing €5 for adults and €2.50 for concessions. Plans have been drawn up for a new 50,000 all-seated stadium a few hundred yards away but no work had started as of January 2009.

How to get there
Located to the south-east of the city centre on reclaimed land next to the River Weser. The stadium is reached easily by public transport, as well as being close to the A1 Autobahn. From the Hauptbahnhof take tram line 10 in the direction of Sebaldsbrücke and alight at Juergen Strasse, or take line 3 in the direction of Weser. The journey should take less than ten minutes and is free for match ticket holders.

Getting a ticket
Werder do sell out a number of matches, but the average attendance hovers around 39,500, meaning that for matches against the majority of opposition tickets are available up until kick-off. They can be purchased from the stadium on match days, from the ticket offices on the east side of the stadium, as well as online at http://www. werder.de. Prices range from €11 (£10) behind the goals to €29 (£26) in the upper tiers close to the halfway line. Prices tend to be ten per cent higher for Champions League matches.

Chapter 20 – Istanbul

Atatürk Olimpiyat Stadi – Istanbul BBS
Capacity: 75,486 all-seater
Constructed between 1999 and 2002 as the centrepiece of Istanbul's bid for the 2012 Olympic Games. While Istanbul has three big club teams in Besiktas, Fenerbahçe and Galatasaray, the stadium was constructed as a neutral venue in the hope of being granted some of Europe's biggest games. It did not have to wait long as UEFA granted the stadium five-star status in 2003, and two years later it hosted one of the most memorable Champions League finals of all time when Liverpool overturned a 3-0 half-time deficit to beat AC Milan on penalties. The stadium is unique in design – a two-tier stand opposite a three-tier stand (both covered) towers above uncovered end stands.

How to get there
The stadium is on the European side of Istanbul in the Olympic Park district called Ikitelli, to the west of the city centre, although there is nothing in the area close to it. It is easily accessible from the main roads running between the centre and the airport. When the stadium is hosting a big match, free shuttle buses run from the airport and from Taksim Square in the city centre. The only other way to get there is by taxi – the fare from the city centre should not cost more than 50YTL (£20). If you are there to see one of the two club sides who use the stadium do not expect an easy journey. In

fact, the main reason why the crowds are so low at these games may be due to these extreme difficulties. Bus route 149T runs from the main road that passes underneath the railway station at Yenikapi which is reached from the main Sirkeci railway station on the Golden Horn. Tickets cost YTL1.30 for the train and YTL1.50 for the bus. The bus journey takes around forty-five minutes, and you will be dropped off at the bottom of the access road. The walk from here is around fifteen minutes through a landscape best described as lunar. On the way back, wait on the opposite side of the road for a return bus – but be warned that you are standing on the hard shoulder of a main road and cars and lorries pass close by!

Getting a ticket
For club matches tickets can be purchased from the small booth at the south end of the stadium for 10YTL (£4). One window will sell home tickets – located in the main stand lower tier – and the other will be for the open away stand. Entry to the main stand is gained by walking clockwise round the stadium to Gate E. In 2006–7 when Galatasaray held their Champions League matches there, tickets were available from the Ali Sami Yen Stadium in the city centre. Or from http://www. ataturkolimpiyatstadi.net.

Ali Sami Yen Stadi – Galatasaray SK
Capacity: 25,500 all-seater

The Ali Sami Yen will always be associated with the awful memories of the abuse given to Manchester United's fans and players during their matches in the Champions League in the 1990s when they were 'Welcomed to Hell'. The stadium is very basic. It has two large stands – both with small lower tiers and shallow roofs, with the two ends behind the goals being set back in a curve and open. The view from behind the goals is not good, and nor are facilities. The view from the upper tiers of the side stands is much better, although the stadium does lack atmosphere due to the distance from the pitch. It is certainly a lot less atmospheric in real life than you would have thought from TV. However, there is some good news on the horizon for the club as work is due to commence soon on a new 50,000 arena, inspired by the Amsterdam ArenA – which was planned to be ready for the start of the 2009–10 season. It is located across the main road from the existing stadium.

How to get there
Relatively easy to get to, as it is in the city centre. From Taksim Square catch any bus in the direction of Mecidiyeköy. The stadium is a five-minute walk from the bus station. Alternatively, use the metro system to the stop at Şişli which is two stops from Taksim. Leave the station in the direction of travel and follow the crowds. If you are on the far side of the stadium, it is a good idea to cross the road to avoid the crush, pickpockets and potential risk of being run over.

Getting a ticket
Galatasaray have some of the most fanatical supporters in Europe although, despite the small capacity, sell-outs are rare, especially if the visitors are local. The club has around 10,000 season ticket holders, leaving around 14,000 seats available for purchase on a game by game basis. Tickets for the main covered stands start from YTL40 (£16), with a place in the curved ends YTL30 (£12). Tickets for most games can be purchased via Biletix (http://www.biletix.com), a Ticketmaster company,

from three weeks before the game. Tickets can be posted to the UK should time permit, otherwise you will need to pick them up from the ticket office at the stadium: you just need to remember to take ID with you – or buy from any Biletix outlet in the city centre, including the one in the shopping centre next to the metro exit. In the past few seasons, due to the poor condition of the stadium and pitch, Champions League games have been played at the Atatürk Olympic Stadium. Website: http://www.galatasaray.org/en/futbol.

The Şükrü Saracoğlu Stadium – Fenerbahçe
Capacity: 50,500 all-seater

In 1929 Fenerbahçe moved into a small, basic stadium on the site of the current ground and immediately began the task of renovating it. Further expansion to 40,000 took place over the next few decades, although a decision to make it an all-seater in 1995 reduced this to 25,000. Funding was secured in 1999 to increase the capacity to more than 50,000 and the stadium was renamed the Şükrü Saracoğlu. In 2002, as part of the failed bid by Greece and Turkey to host Euro 2008, the stadium was granted a five-star status by UEFA, thus enabling it to host major finals – a feat it fulfiled by hosting the 2009 UEFA Cup final. It is very impressive – a two-tier bowl, with yellow and blue seats throughout. It has a British style – like a bigger version of St Mary's in Southampton. Sight lines are excellent, and in keeping with the fanatical support of the Turks, the intimate surroundings make the match-day experience awesome. The stadium is the preferred choice for the national team, and all bar one of the qualifying games for the 2006 World Cup were played there, as too was the infamous play-off game with Switzerland.

How to get there
Located on the Asian side of the Bosphorus, so a trip across the strait is necessary. You can cross via a bridge or take a boat from landing number 2 at Eminönü to Kadiköy harbour (tickets cost YTL1.30 and journey time is thirty-five minutes if it stops at Hyderpasa or twenty-five direct and ferries run every twenty minutes or so until midnight), then take Bus 4 to the Dere Ağzi stop on the canal or alternatively walk up the main shopping street and bear around to the right when the road forks. The nearest railway station is Söğütlüçeşme, around a five-minute walk from the stadium, but this only links to stations on the Asian side.

Getting a ticket
Tickets for most games can be purchased via Biletix (http://www.biletix.com) from three weeks before the game. They range in price from YTL45 (£18) in the Tribunes, to YTL180 (£72) in the main stand upper tier. A good seat for the neutral is the Fenerium stand, which start from YTL60 (£24). The club averages less than 40,000 – some 10,000 less than capacity. The derby games against Besiktas and Galatasaray normally attract close to capacity – although tickets can still be purchased in advance using the same method. On a match day tickets are sold from kiosks on each corner of the stadium. Gates open up to seven hours before derby matches to allow the fans to come in and set up. Website: http://www.fenerbahce.org/eng.

Chapter 21 – Copenhagen 2

Hvidovre Stadion – Hvidovre IF
Capacity: 15,000

This basic stadium is one of the ten biggest in the country. It was opened in 1941 as a municipal athletics stadium and through a redevelopment in the 1950s became the biggest athletics stadium in the city. Today it has a park feel with big hedges surrounding three sides, and a huge single stand that holds more than 8,000 fans. The remaining spectators are accommodated around the edge of the track on wooden terraces. Views from the steps are not bad, but as the rake of the terraces is not particularly good, and the track separates the pitch from the fans, it is better to sit in the stand for a decent view.

How to get there
Located in the south of the suburb of Copenhagen named after the stadium. It is a short walk from Friheden S-tog station, on Line A from Central Station, approximately ten minutes and five stops away in the direction of Hundige. A single ticket will cost 20 Danish Kroner. The stadium is visible when you arrive.

Getting a ticket
Unless the visitors are either of the big teams from across the city, tickets can be bought at the turnstiles. Attendances rarely reach the four-figure mark so there is no need to rush to make sure you get in. Entrance is 60 Danish Kroner (£7.50) and includes a free programme. Website: http://www.hif.dk.

Chapter 22 – Paris

Stade de France
Capacity: 79,959 all-seater

In 1992 FIFA announced that France would host the 1998 World Cup finals. One of the conditions was the provision of a stadium that could hold more than 70,000. With only Marseille's Stade Vélodrome anywhere near this, and the fact that it was almost unheard of for a capital city not to host a World Cup final (only Washington DC in modern times has not staged the final), it was decided to start work almost immediately on finding a site. Once it had been located in the north of the city, and funding put in place, construction started in 1995. Paris Saint-Germain were given the opportunity to move there, but decided to stay in the south-west of the city. For a few games in 1999, it was home to Red Star Paris, who attracted a crowd of more than 45,000 for a league game against St Etienne. The stadium also hosts the French rugby team's Six Nations matches and the annual game between Stade Francais and Toulouse, which is normally sold out. It has also hosted two Champions League finals – firstly in 2000 when Real Madrid beat Valencia, and again in 2006 when Barcelona beat Arsenal.

How to get there
Well served by public transport with access points at either end of the stadium. RER station, Stade de France-St Denis, is on the Green Line that passes through the city from Créteil in the south, while RER station, Le Plaine-Stade de France, links Paris Charles De Gaulle airport in the north with Orly airport in the south on the Blue Line B. Both stations are one stop from Gare du Nord and the journey time is about seven

minutes. Metro line 13 also serves the stadium through the stop at St Denis-Porte de Paris.

Getting a ticket
The ease of getting a ticket depends on the event. Most French rugby internationals are sold out and tickets never go on general sale. Tickets for the French League and Cup finals go on sale around four weeks before the events via http://www.ticketnet.fr. They also sell tickets for the French Football team internationals and it can be possible to get these within a day or so of the game.

Chapter 23 – Budapest
Stadion Hidegkuti Nándor – MTK Hungária
Capacity: 12,700

The Hidegkuti Nándor stadium opened its doors in 1912 as home to MTK Budapest. Today it is a pleasant place from which to watch football, although a little rundown. The stadium is named after one of Hungary's most famous footballers, who helped beat England 6-3 and 7-1 in 1953. Since 1995 the stadium has been undergoing renovation, although there is no date for the work's finish, and no real clue as to what they have already done! On a match day only the two side stands are open and the main covered stand offers a more comfortable viewing position.

How to get there
Fifteen minutes' walk south of the national stadium on Hungarian Utca. The nearest tram stop is opposite the main stand and is called Köbánya Utca on lines 287 and 185. The journey time from the city centre is less than ten minutes.

Getting a ticket
With crowds struggling to top 1,000, it is not difficult to get a ticket for a game to see MTK. The ticket windows are by the main stand (and seem to double up as the women's toilets!) and tickets cost either 1,800Ft (£6) for a seat in the upper (covered) part of the main stand, 1,200Ft (£4) for the lower part or 600Ft (£2) for the uncovered side stand opposite. Website: http://www.mtkhungaria.hu.

Chapter 24 – Kraków
Stadion Wisły – Wisła Kraków
Capacity: 25,500

Home to Wisła Kraków since May 1953 when the stadium, then with a capacity of 35,000, opened its doors, replacing the smaller Oleandy stadium just to the north. The new stadium was a converted speedway track, with mud mounds placed behind the goals and two simple stands along the side of the pitch. Very few changes took place until the arrival of Polish millionaire Bogusław Cupiał in the late 1990s. He started a slow but thorough redevelopment which will eventually see each side rebuilt to form the smart stadium you can see in part today. However, plans have been drawn up for a more ambitious redevelopment for a new 35,500-seater stadium. It was first thought that the new stadium could hold 40,000 and host both clubs from Kraków, but opposition from both sets of fans saw this idea soon dropped. The pitch was turned through ninety degrees and new side stands complete with roofs added. The traditional main stand is still being used but the crumbling open-air terrace has now been condemned, although on occasion away fans are housed here.

How to get there

Located on the north side of the Błonia open grounds, and about a kilometre away from the home of rivals Cracovia which is visible from the south side of the stadium. It is no more than a fifteen-minute walk from the old town. Head westwards down Szewska from Rynek and then turn left into Krupnicza. This road will then become ul Reymonta and the stadium is on the right-hand side immediately after the park. Tram lines 15 and 18 terminate just to the south of the stadium.

Getting a ticket

Tickets can be bought in advance but only from the ticket windows on the northern or southern sides of the stadium. On match day, queues for tickets can be long and so unless you arrive an hour or so early it is prudent to get them beforehand. Tickets start from 30 Zloty (£6) in the open stands to 120 Zloty (£24) in the covered main stand. Website: http://www.wisla.krakow.pl.

Chapter 25 – Geneva

Stade de Genève – FC Servette
Capacity: 30,030 all-seater

Located quite a distance to the south of the city in the suburb of Lancy, the Stade de Genève is shoehorned between the La Praille shopping and entertainment complex, the main railway line and an industrial estate. It was opened in March 2003 for FC Servette, being built because their previous ground in Les Charmilles was too small (9,250) to be considered as a venue for the Swiss bid to host Euro 2008 with Austria. When the two countries were awarded the championships in 2002, a suitable site was found for the stadium and work commenced quickly. There are excellent unobstructed views from all sections, although there are perimeter fences behind the goals. Legroom is also generous. Hanging down from the roof at the back of the south stand is a huge TV screen which can be seen by everyone, even if it means craning your neck if seated underneath it. The concourse areas are wide and spacious, meaning crowding is kept to a minimum. Concession stands also have multiple serving points and queues move quickly. The stadium has a feel of some of the new English grounds such as Southampton's St Mary's and Coventry's Ricoh Arena. It has one stand that is noticeably bigger than the others, with the roof curving down to meet the end stands, but little has been done or incorporated to make it have a unique feel.

How to get there

The stadium wasn't built with public access in mind. On match days public transport is free for ticket holders. Trams 12 and 13 run from the centre of Geneva to close to the stadium. The trams terminate at Bachet de Pesay, a five-minute walk to the south of the stadium. The journey from the city centre should take twenty minutes. From Cornavin station tram number 15 runs in the direction of Lancy-Pont-Rouge. From here it is a ten-minute walk, following the pathway alongside the dual carriageway. There is a direct bus from Cornavin station on match days. Route D runs about every ten minutes and takes twenty minutes, dropping off opposite the stadium's east stands.

Getting a ticket

If you are planning on going to a Servette match you don't have to worry about buying tickets in advance. With average crowds of less than 2,000 and a capacity of 30,000, you have a choice of quite a few seats! Website: http://www.stade.ch.

The Letzigrund – FC Zurich
Capacity: 16,100

The stadium in the western suburbs of Zurich represents the ambition of the Swiss football authorities to create a real legacy from the 2008 European Championships. Zurich has always had a fierce rivalry between FC Zurich and Grasshoppers, and so the authorities had a difficult job to decide whether to develop either of their stadiums or build a new one. In the end they chose to completely rebuild the Letzigrund, home of FCZ since 1925. It opened with the Zurich derby in September 2007 after being primarily designed as a multi-purpose venue and so there is an athletics track (the Letzigrund has been home to the world's most prestigious track and field meeting, the Weltklasse, since 1928), but the stands were designed to support football as well. Spectators enter the stadium from wide concourses at the top of the stands as the pitch is some way below ground level. All of the views are unobstructed and there are two large TV screens on the north and south stands. The unique feature of the stadium, however, is the floodlights. There are thirty-two floodlight spikes which pierce the roof and act as supports as well as lighting.

How to get there

Located in the western fringes of the city centre, near to the main railway line. The new stadium has enhanced public transport access, although for some of the big games during Euro 2008 it was quicker to walk by following Badenerstrasse all the way from Werdsstrasse in the old town. The walk should take around twenty minutes. Tram lines 2 and 3 also run at regular intervals down Badenerstrasse. The nearest train station is Hardbrücke, one stop from the central station. Go southwards across the railway bridge and take third right into Bullingerstrasse and the stadium is 400 yards away.

Getting a ticket

There are no problems getting tickets on the day of the game. FC Zurich have an average attendance of 10,000 and even the Zurich derby does not sell out. Tickets can be purchased in advance from http://www.ticketcorner.com or by calling 0848 800 800 (from Switzerland only) and cost 20CHF (£12) for the Kurves behind the goal, to 50CHF (£30) for a seat in the main stand.

Chapter 26 – Stockholm
Söderstadion – Hammarby IF
Capacity: 16,100

The stadium has two almost identical covered stands that run the length of the pitch and offer protection from the elements. At the east end of the stadium there is a large open terrace, where the hardcore fans gather. However, the most dominant feature of the stadium is the west stand. This stand is a small covered terrace but on top of this is a four-storey structure, which includes offices and residential apartments that overlook the pitch. The stadium was opened in 1966, and has recently been upgraded with the removal of a covered stand, which curved away from the pitch, at the east end of the stadium. The grey seats give the ground a bland feel but Hammarby's fans are among the most passionate in Sweden and so match days are very rarely as dull as the seats.

How to get there

A fifteen-minute train ride on the green T-line from the central station. Leave the train at Globen, turn right over the bridge and then left when you reach the T-junction in the pedestrian area.

Getting a ticket

In terms of capacity, Hammarby fares better than most, regularly filling about seventy-five per cent. However, they average just over 12,000 so you will not struggle to get a ticket on the day from any of the ticket booths around the ground. However, after crowd trouble at a Stockholm derby with Djurgården caused the match to be abandoned tickets for high-profile games must be bought in advance. Tickets can be purchased from the club shop at the ground and at the Globen shopping centre. They may be reserved by emailing the club at biljett@hammarbyfotboll.se, or from the Swedish equivalent of ticketmaster at http://www.ticnet.se. Tickets for all matches (except Malmö, Djurgården and AIK) start from 60SEK (£5) for a place on the terrace, to 265SEK (£23) for a covered seat. For the 'A' list games the ticket prices start from 240SEK (£20) and rise to 500SEK (£43).

Chapter 27 – Minsk

Dinamo Stadion – Dinamo Minsk
Capacity: 41,040

The national stadium of Belarus is a typical Soviet affair. Big, imposing floodlights tower over the open-air bowl of a multi-purpose stadium. What that basically translates to is a visitor experience that is unpleasant to say the least. It means that for ten months of the year it is either too wet, too cold or too hot to really enjoy a game in the open-air seats. Come springtime it's a wonderful venue! The presence of the athletics track is an irritation – especially if you are in the stands behind the goals where the height of the converted terracing means views are poor. The two-tier main stand offers the best views, and if available is worth the extra few roubles. During the qualifying tournament for European Championships in 2008 the national team averaged 21,000 for the games played in Minsk, almost ten times the average attendance for Dinamo home games, meaning that you should have no problems at all getting a ticket. The stadium opened in 1934 with a capacity of more than 50,000. It was badly damaged during the Second World War and was completely reconstructed before opening again in 1954. It went through another major redevelopment programme in the late 1970s in time for it to be a major venue in the 1980 summer Olympics football tournament. While the stadium did not host the most attractive matches, it provided enough interest to sell out the quarter-final match between Yugoslavia and Algeria.

How to get there

No more than a five-minute walk north-east of the main station. Exit the station and follow Ульяновская to the ground. From the Palast de Republik simply head south down Ул ленина – approximately a ten-minute walk.

Getting a ticket

It has been a long time since a game at the Dinamo Stadium sold out. During qualifying for Euro 2008 they averaged just over 20,000. Any empty seats in the stadium tend to be filled by the Belarusian army. Tickets for home internationals are sold via the Belarusian football website at http://www.bff.by. Tickets for Dinamo Minsk games are sold from the small cabins around the stadium – with an average attendance of under 2,000 you will have no problems getting a ticket. Tickets for the upper tier of the main stand cost 5000BYB (£4).

Chapter 28 – Sofia

Georgi Asparuhov Stadion – Levksi Sofia
Capacity: 29,880

The wide open spaces of the Georgi Asparuhov Stadium are rarely filled these days. Since it opened in the 1960s very little modernising has taken place and it's showing its age. It used to have a running track but this is now just a vast expanse of concrete. There is a small terraced area to the north which is home to any away supporters who bother to turn up. The home fans are located in the open seated area to the south. The stadium's colourful seating makes it look more modern than it really is. It has held more than 60,000 several times although high-profile games are now played at the National Stadium in the Borisova Gardens. It is named after a former player who was killed in a car crash in 1971.

How to get there

Located in the east of the city, close to the main railway line, it is well served by bus lines 78 and 70 which run from the main railway station along Boulevard Slivnica as well as tram line 22 that runs from Avenue Aleksandâr Dondukov past the Nevsky cathedral.

Getting a ticket

There are very few games which require an advanced ticket purchase. Website: http://www.levski.com. On a match day tickets are sold from the small ticket windows either side of the entrances on the east and west sides of the stadium. Tickets for the covered seats cost 4Lv (£1.60) and for behind the goal they are 2.5Lv (£1).

Chapter 29 – Berlin

Olympiastadion – Hertha Berlin
Capacity: 74,400 all-seater

One of the world's most impressive and historic stadiums. It appears almost monumental from the outside – a perfect elliptical structure of finest German limestone. In fact some of the original inspiration of the design was taken from Rome's Coliseum. The architect, Werner March, designed it with input from both Adolf Hitler and his chief architect Albert Speer. It was meant to be a showpiece arena, where Hitler could show the world the power of the German state during the 1936 Olympic Games. In 1998 the state government decided on modernisation. The work, which took more than four years, saw the inside demolished and replaced, piece by piece, as well as a much-needed roof being added. All this took place with events continuing to take place, albeit with a reduced capacity. The stadium went on to host five games in the 2006 World Cup including the classic quarter-final between Argentina and the host nation and the final itself.

How to get there

The easiest way to reach the stadium is by either U-Bahn on line U2, or by S-Bahn on lines S5/S75. Both stations are called Olympiastadion. The U-Bahn station is located to the east of the stadium on Rominter Allee – which will bring fans out on to the huge Olympischer Platz and the view of the famous Olympic towers. A journey from Zoo Station in the west of Berlin takes around fifteen minutes. The S-Bahn station is located to the south of the stadium, and is around two hundred yards from the Sudtor entrance. Trains run from Zoo Station, Alexanderplatz and the newly constructed Hauptbahnhof. The journey from Zoo should take ten minutes.

Getting a ticket

Tickets can be booked in advance via the website http://www.olympiastadion-berlin. de. Hertha also have their own ticket website at http://www.hertha.de. Tickets range in price from €13 (£12) behind the goal to €45 (£37) for one of the best seats in the house in the Süd Tribune.

Chapter 30 – Naples

Stadio San Paolo – S.S.C Napoli
Capacity: 78,210 all-seater

One of Italy's great stadiums, the third largest behind Milan and Rome. It was constructed in the late 1950s, with a huge renovation carried out in the late 1980s in time to host some of the most dramatic matches of the 1990 World Cup finals, including the semi-final between Argentina, led by local hero Diego Maradona, and the host nation, a game which the South Americans won on penalties, and England's dramatic victory over Cameroon. The stadium is a huge bowl, with a small lower tier, almost completely shaded by the upper tier that alone can hold over 65,000. The stadium has an athletics track which means views are poor from some seats. Between 2000 and 2001 the stadium was closed three times. It lost most of its roof during some huge storms, forcing the team to play its games in smaller stadiums in the region. Then in 2001 local flooding caused the stadium to be closed once again. It was also used in the 1980 European Championships for three matches including the third and fourth play-off between Italy and Czechoslovakia. The stadium also welcomes the national team on a regular basis.

How to get there

Located in the western part of the city, not too far from the bayside. The view across the Bay of Naples to Mount Vesuvius is very impressive. The nearest station is Campi Flegrei, seven stops from the centre of the city on the FS Metropolitana line (Line 2) towards Bagnoli. Allow fifteen minutes. As you leave the station, the stadium will be easily visible up the hill through the trees.

Getting a ticket

The stadium rarely sells out, although crowds are definitely on the up from the dark days of Serie C and bankruptcy in 2002. Tickets can be bought for most games on the day from the ticket offices on the road from the station or from any Listicket office in the city centre. Away fans are located in the Distinti Curve A, while the Napoli Ultras are in the Curve B, although it is safe to sit there as well. Tickets are also sold in the city centre from newsagents and in a number of sports shops from fourteen days before home games. Prices start from €18 (£17) for a place in the Curve to over €100 (£92) for a Tribuna seat. Website: http://www.sscnapoli.it.

More football books from SportsBooks

Finn McCool's Football Club

Stephen Rea

After jetting around the world, Stephen Rea left his hometown of Belfast with his American wife to settle in New Orleans in 2004. Not surprisingly, life in the Deep South proved to be startlingly different from that in Northern Ireland, and Rea struggled to find an outlet for his love of football. But before long the Ulsterman stumbled upon Finn McCool's pub and the wonderfully eccentric, international crowd that gathers there to watch European football games. Soon Rea and this idiosyncratic mix of locals and ex-pat regulars formed a pub soccer team, joined a league, and began dreaming of victory.

On August 27, 2005 members of the team sat in the pub discussing their upcoming match. The next day, Hurricane Katrina enveloped the Gulf Coast, scattering Rea and his teammates around the world in seek of shelter and stability.

This luminous, gripping work follows the author and Finn regulars as they rebuild their lives and their team. With a masterful combination of dry humour and astute profundity, Rea reflects on his adopted city, providing powerful insights into the lives of the foreign-born and minority groups that stayed behind during Katrina because they had little to lose. 'Finn McCool's Football Club' stands out as a haunting and powerful memoir filled with laughter, loss, astonishment, and, of course, football.

ISBN 9781899807 86 4
Price £8.99
Paperback

Tales from the Gwladys Street

David Cregeen and Jonathan Mumford

Fans have been having a rough time of it in recent years. Clubs have hiked their admission prices while TV demands have resulted in odd kick-off times which often mean long and difficult journeys. But still they flock to football matches. Tales from the Gwladys Street tells the story of one club, Everton, through the mouths of their fans and players. Gwladys Street is the legendary 'end' behind the goal at Goodison Park that contains the biggest concentration of the club's supporters.

The resulting stories show how obsessive football fans can be and how they seek humour in every situation. The stories are from Evertonians but the type of experiences recalled are not unique to one club. All fans will be able to relate to the stories collected by authors David Cregeen and Jonathan

Mumford. You don't have to know what Nil Satis Nisi Optimum* means or get goose-bumps when you hear the Z Cars theme to enjoy it.
* nothing but the best is good enough (Everton's motto)

ISBN 9781899807 89 5
Price £7.99
Paperback

William Garbutt – the Father of Italian Football
Paul Edgerton
Born in Stockport, William Garbutt was a successful winger with Blackburn Rovers in the First Division, having first played for Woolwich Arsenal, when injury finished his career at the age of 29. He was good enough to have played for the Football League against the Scottish League in 1910. The usual route for ex-professionals was to become a publican but in 1912 Garbutt moved to Italy and took charge of Genoa Cricket and Football Club. In doing so he became the first professional football manager in Italian football. His professionalism and revolutionary ideas had a great impact on the club and under his guidance Genoa won the Italian League Championship three times – in 1915, 1923 and 1924. Garbutt is still considered an icon in Genoese football circles and is the reason why, to this day, Italian players call their manager 'Mister'.

In 1927 he joined the newly formed AS Roma and guided them to a cup win in his first season. He then moved to Napoli for six seasons, taking them to third position in the league - the highest spot they had ever enjoyed and which they only bettered many years later. Garbutt repeated his remarkable success on moving to Spain in 1935, where he guided Athletic Bilbao to the championship of the Spanish League before returning to his first love, Genoa, shortly afterwards. As a British citizen he was an exile under Mussolini's fascists and was interned during World War II, with the cruel irony that his wife, Anna, was killed by Allied bombing. He returned to England in the late 1940s and died in 1964 in Warwick.

Author Paul Edgerton traced his adopted daughter Maria, who sadly passed away in August 2009, for a unique insight into an extraordinary man.

ISBN 9781899807 82 6
Price £7.99
Paperback